Compass

FIFTH EDITION

KAPLAN
BAR REVIEW

Special thanks to: Brian Carlidge, Adam Feren, Esq., Elizabeth Horowitz, Esq., Adam Maze, Esq., Shalom Sands, Esq., Amit Schlesinger, Esq., Ryan Williams, Esq., Lauren Yost, Esq., Jacob Zampier

Published by Kaplan North America, LLC.
1515 W. Cypress Creek Road
Fort Lauderdale, FL 33309

Printed in the United States of America

October 2024

10 9 8 7 6 5 4 3 2

ISBN: 978-1-5062-9465-0

MASTER TABLE OF CONTENTS

KAPLAN BAR REVIEW

Constitutional Law

Exercise Set 1

Question 1a

What is the state action doctrine?

Question 1b

Identify the two doctrinal exceptions to the state action doctrine.

Question 2a

Identify the three ways a party making an equal protection challenge can meet its initial burden of proving that the government acted with discriminatory intent.

Question 2b

Identify the three factors courts will use to determine what process is "due" once they have established that government action has deprived someone of life, liberty, or property.

Question 2c

Identify some of the privacy rights currently protected under the application of the substantive due process doctrine.

For the following exercises, you are given a question prompt. After reading the question prompt, consider the applicable rules. Then, brainstorm possible issues that could be raised or tested based on the given question prompt.

Question 3

Is the legislation constitutional?

Question 4

Will the plaintiff's equal protection challenge be successful?

Question 5

If the plaintiff makes a substantive due process challenge, will the plaintiff be successful?

Question 6

For this equal protection issue, which of the following most accurately states the applicable burden of persuasion?

Question 7

Which provision of the U.S. Constitution is most likely to support the plaintiff's claim?

For each of the following fact patterns and question prompts, write out the relevant issues and their corresponding rule statements.

Question 8

An owner of a plumbing company employs 19 plumbers, all of whom are male. State law requires that there be a shower for every 10 employees. The owner installed two showers in the men's room in compliance with state law. Recently, a woman applied for a plumber's apprentice position with the plumbing company. Before hiring the woman, the owner filed a building permit with the building and safety department to install a new shower in the women's bathroom. The building inspector rejected the permit because it failed to conform to the city's building code. As a result, the owner refused to hire the woman.

If the woman sues the city alleging a violation of her equal protection rights, how should the court rule?

Question 9

A city zoning ordinance provides that, in order to prevent dangerous overcrowding, an upscale neighborhood would be limited to single-family homes that may be occupied by only one "family unit." The ordinance defines a "family unit" as one or two parents plus their unmarried children. An aunt has lived in this neighborhood for 52 years. Because her health was slowly deteriorating, her unmarried nephew left his residence in a neighboring state and moved into his aunt's house. Shortly thereafter, the aunt received a notice from the city that she was in violation of the new zoning ordinance.

Which of the following is the strongest constitutional argument the aunt can make against the application of the ordinance?

Question 10

A federal statute expressly provides for the different treatment of people based upon their occupational status. A plaintiff believes that this statute subjects her to unfavorable treatment in violation of her constitutional rights.

If the court upholds the plaintiff's challenge, which provision will be most important to its ruling?

Exercise Set 2

Question 1a

Complete the following chart. For each level of scrutiny, identify the party with the burden of persuasion as well as the key components of the standard the court will apply to the challenged government action.

LEVEL OF SCRUTINY	THE BURDEN IS ON...	TO SHOW THAT THE GOVERNMENT ACTION IS...	TO FURTHER OR PROMOTE A GOVERNMENT INTEREST THAT IS...
Strict			
Intermediate			
Rational basis			

Question 1b

Complete the following chart. For each level of scrutiny, identify the type of classification scheme to be reviewed by the court, as well as examples of each type of scheme.

LEVEL OF SCRUTINY	TYPE OF CLASSIFICATION SCHEME CHALLENGED	EXAMPLES
Strict		
Intermediate		
Rational basis		

Question 2

Complete the following chart. For each right or set of rights listed, identify the provision that is its constitutional source.

CONSTITUTIONAL PROVISION	INDIVIDUAL RIGHT(S) PROTECTED
	• The right of a citizen of one state not to be discriminated against by the laws of any other state in matters that are fundamental to the promotion of interstate harmony. • The right not to be discriminated against on the basis of one's out-of-state residency.
	• The right of a citizen of one state to enter and to leave any other state. • The right of a citizen of one state to be treated as a welcome visitor rather than an unfriendly nonresident when temporarily present in any other state. • The right to choose to become a permanent resident of any state and be treated like other citizens of that state.
	• The right not to be prosecuted under a criminal statute that purports to criminalize acts that were legal when committed. • The right not to be subject to criminal punishment that is greater than that which existed at the time the crime was committed. • The right not to be prosecuted pursuant to a statute that purports to decrease the prosecutor's evidentiary burden as compared to what had existed at the time the alleged crime was committed. • The right not to be subject to prosecution because a statute purports to extend the limitations period beyond the expiration of a prior statute of limitations that had existed at the time the alleged crime was committed.
	• The right of contracting parties not to have contractual obligations modified by government regulation (unless such modification is reasonably related to an important public interest).
	• The right of any individual or ascertainable group not to be punished legislatively without there being provision made for a judicial trial.

For the following fact patterns, complete the chart with the relevant facts that correspond to the rule(s) provided.

Question 3

A man recently moved his family from a rural community to an urbanized metropolitan area in the same state. When the man informed his insurance carrier of the change of residence, he was notified that his auto and home insurance rates would increase by 300% due to the large number of traffic accidents and theft claims occurring in the city. The man's insurance carrier is licensed by the state.

If the man unsuccessfully brings an equal protection challenge against his insurance carrier, which is the most likely reason?

RULE	RELEVANT FACTS
State action doctrine	

Question 4

A man was a resident noncitizen living in State A. The man applied for a landscaping position with the State Department of Parks and Recreation (DPR). The hiring manager at the DPR returned the man's application with a brief letter indicating that he would not be considered for a position per State A regulation, because he was not a U.S. citizen. The man, believing that he was denied employment based on alienage, brought a suit against the DPR.

What is the likely outcome of the man's suit?

RULES	RELEVANT FACTS
State action doctrine	
Equal protection (plaintiff's initial burden)	
Strict scrutiny (Equal Protection Clause)	

Question 5

State A's legislature enacted a statute which provided that "any person engaging in the business of electrolysis in State A is required to first obtain a duly issued license from State A's Bureau of Commercial Affairs." The statute further required, among other things, that "the license applicant must show proof of residency within the state for a period of not less than twelve (12) months and proof of U.S. citizenship." The plaintiff is a U.S. citizen who moved to State A eight months before she applied for a license to operate an electrolysis business in State A. The state's bureau denied her application.

Is the state statutory provision requiring a one-year residency before applying for a license a violation of the Article IV Privileges and Immunities Clause?

RULES	RELEVANT FACTS
State action doctrine	
Article IV Privileges and Immunities Clause	

Question 6

A couple of years ago, a state passed legislation that required a contraceptive procedure to be performed only in a facility that had obtained a state-issued license authorizing it to perform such a procedure. The legislature's express purpose for providing this legislation was the protection of the health and welfare of its citizens. Although there were 25 major hospitals operating within the state, each also operating several satellite facilities providing medical services to otherwise under-serviced localities, only one facility has been able to obtain the license necessary to legally provide contraceptive procedures.

A woman, a U.S. citizen and state resident who lived on the other side of the state from where the lone licensed facility was located, claimed that the state has unduly infringed upon her rights.

Will the woman prevail?

RULES	RELEVANT FACTS
State action doctrine	
Substantive due process (right to privacy)	

Question 7

In August of last year, the defendant was arrested on misdemeanor charges. At the time of the alleged crime, the maximum punishment prescribed by statute for this class of misdemeanor was a month in jail and a $1,000 fine. At the time of sentencing, a new criminal statute had gone into effect. Pursuant to this new statute, the class of misdemeanors that included the defendant's crime were now subject to a maximum penalty of a month in jail and a $2,000 fine. The prosecutor now seeks a sentence that includes no jail time, but a fine of $1,500.

In sentencing the defendant, should the court be guided by the prosecutor's recommendation?

RULE	RELEVANT FACTS
Article I Ex Post Facto Clauses	

For each of the following fact patterns and question prompts, identify the applicable rules and complete the chart with the relevant facts.

Question 8

State A's long seacoast is a prime location for harvesting sea cucumbers, an industry that has recently experienced a boom in demand. Concerned that its sea cucumber population would be overharvested like other fish populations in the recent past, State A's legislature enacted a statute requiring the licensing of any individual harvesting sea cucumbers within the state's coastal waters. The licensing fee was set at $500 for state residents and $2,000 for nonresidents. A fisherman lived nearby on the State B coast. His state's coastal waters did not contain enough colonies of sea cucumbers to support an industry or even several independent fishermen.

If the fisherman, a U.S. citizen, challenges the nonresident licensing fee on grounds other than the Fourteenth Amendment Equal Protection Clause, will the court uphold the State A licensing statute?

RULES	RELEVANT FACTS

Question 9

For certain job-related injuries, a federal statute provided benefits, including survivors' benefits, to workers and their families. A train engineer sustained on-the-job injuries that ultimately proved fatal and triggered the protections of this federal statute. His wife applied for survivors' benefits for herself and the worker's children, including his oldest natural child, who had been born before the engineer had ever married. However, the survivors' benefits regulation provides that only legitimate children of a deceased worker may claim benefits.

Will the older child prevail if she challenges the regulation as discriminatory?

RULES	RELEVANT FACTS

Question 10

A state legislature recently passed a provision that identified members of a particular religious sect as "traitors" and prohibited them from participating on juries or holding local elective office. The plaintiff, a U.S. citizen and resident of the state, was also a member of this particular religious sect. In an upcoming election, she hoped to run for a position on the county's Board of Education.

In challenging the state legislation, what constitutional provision should the plaintiff rely upon?

RULE	RELEVANT FACTS

KAPLAN BAR REVIEW

Quiz 1

Question 1

The state legislature enacted a statute requiring permanent removal from parental custody of any child born to a mother currently receiving state welfare payments. A young mother recently lost her job and had been receiving state welfare assistance. She now has given birth to her second child and the state brought an action under the statute to terminate her custody rights solely because she was receiving the state welfare payments. Her defense is based on the ground that the statute is unconstitutional as applied.

Which is the most probable burden of persuasion on this constitutional issue?

(A) The state has the burden of persuading the court that the application of the statute to the mother is necessary to vindicate a compelling government interest.

(B) The state has the burden to persuade the court that the application of the statute to the mother is rationally related to a legitimate government interest.

(C) The mother has the burden of persuading the court that the application of the statute to her conduct is not necessary to vindicate an important state interest.

(D) The mother has the burden of persuading the court that the application of the statute to her conduct is not rationally related to a legitimate state interest.

Question 2

A state held an election in which there were many charges of voter fraud and vote manipulation. Concerned about voting fraud, the state legislature passed a bill providing that any resident of the state who wished to vote in a state election could not vote until he or she had lived within the state for at least one year. The governor of the state signed the bill into law. A group of new residents who wished to vote in a state election but were prohibited under the new law brought suit to enjoin the enforcement of the statute.

How should the court rule?

(A) In favor of the plaintiffs, because under the strict scrutiny analysis, a one-year residency requirement is unconstitutional.

(B) In favor of the plaintiffs, because under the rational basis analysis, a one-year residency requirement is unconstitutional.

(C) In favor of the state, because under a strict scrutiny analysis, the statute is necessary to further a compelling state interest, namely to prevent voter fraud.

(D) In favor of the state, because under a rational basis analysis, the statute is rationally related to a legitimate state interest, namely to prevent voter fraud.

Question 3

A statute regulating the practice of midwives in a state was passed at midnight at the end of the regular legislative session. There were few legislators in attendance at the time of the vote, because most of the work of the legislature had been done and most members had gone home for the holidays, although a quorum existed. The sponsor of the legislation finally succeeded in persuading a core group to vote for the bill, which included a provision that the founder of the midwives' lobbying group would no longer be licensed under the state's laws. The group's founder was a practicing midwife who had lobbied successfully against health maintenance organizations and on behalf of a number of state laws guaranteeing patients the right to treatment in the area of pregnancy and childbirth. The bill's sponsor saw the midwives' successes as having driven up the cost of health care treatment throughout the state.

If the group challenges the revocation of the founder's license in federal court, what is the most likely outcome?

(A) The state will prevail, because regulation of the group does not implicate interstate commerce.

(B) The state will prevail, because a license is a privilege that can be revoked without procedural due process.

(C) The lobbying group will prevail, because the revocation constitutes a bill of attainder.

(D) The lobbying group will prevail, because the revocation violates members' right to work under the Privileges and Immunities Clause.

Question 4

A county decided to revamp its voting procedures in order to streamline the process. The county ordered new touch-screen voting machines, solicited more volunteers for election days, lengthened voting hours, made vote-by-mail available to all residents, and enacted various other rules to help make sure that election days ran more smoothly. One new rule required people to check in at the polls at the table labeled with their party affiliation: Republican, Democrat, or Other. A voter in that county objected to this particular rule. She was a Democrat who sent her child to a school in her neighborhood that was very heavily populated with Republicans. She served on the board of the parent-teacher organization at the school. The voter did not wish for her party affiliation to be public in case it might cause controversy for herself or her child.

Assuming proper standing, if the voter challenges the constitutionality of the rule requiring voters to line up according to party affiliation at the polls, what is the likely outcome?

(A) The rule will be invalidated, because it violates her right to privacy.

(B) The rule will be invalidated, because it violates her procedural due process rights.

(C) The rule will be upheld, because it passes strict scrutiny.

(D) The rule will be upheld, because it passes the rational basis test.

Question 5

A woman was employed as a state trooper. Although the state provides both sexes with equal pay and benefits, the state has adopted a policy that prohibits the assignment of female officers to its special undercover narcotics division. This is a moderate risk position that sometimes involves violent encounters with drug dealers. Since the special narcotics division was first established, five undercover agents have been killed in the line of duty. It is because of the state's concern with the safety and well-being of its female officers that it has adopted such a policy. The woman, who desired to be a member of the narcotics division, filed an application for assignment as a special drug agent. After she was rejected for the position, the woman sued the state in federal court to enjoin enforcement of its stated policy on the grounds that it is unconstitutional.

As a matter of constitutional law, which of the following results in this suit is most appropriate?

(A) Judgment for the woman, because the facts asserted do not demonstrate that the particular classification contained in this policy is substantially related to the advancement of an important state interest.

(B) Judgment for the woman, because the terms and conditions of state government employment are privileges or immunities of state citizenship that may not be abridged by the state on the basis of gender.

(C) Judgment for the state, because it is within a state's police power to insulate the terms and conditions of governmental employment.

(D) Judgment for the state, because the state has articulated a rational basis for this classification and, therefore, a court may not substitute its judgment for that of responsible state officials.

Question 6

In a 2010 lawsuit, a state university was held to have unlawfully refused applicants into the engineering masters program on account of their race in the past. The university agreed to hold 20 places in each class for black students, pursuant to a consent decree entered that same year. In 2012, a white male student applied to the engineering masters program at a state university and was rejected. The student's engineering aptitude test score and grade point average was above 15 of the 20 black students admitted.

If the student brings suit to require that he be admitted because the university has unlawfully discriminated against him because of his race, what would the court do?

(A) Grant relief, because a state may not use race as a criterion in making admissions decisions.

(B) Grant relief, because a classification solely by race, even to achieve a worthy purpose, is not necessary to satisfy a compelling state need, and therefore violates the Equal Protection Clause.

(C) Deny relief, because a state may consider race as a factor in admissions when it is attempting to aid disadvantaged minorities and penalizes no particular group.

(D) Deny relief, because the racial classification is designed to remedy past unlawful discrimination.

Question 7

A 68-year-old man drove his car into a restaurant while attempting to leave the parking lot. A police investigation showed that the man confused the accelerator for the brake pedal, causing his car to jump the curb and break through a large window. No one was hurt in the accident. However, the man's license was revoked pursuant to a state law requiring all drivers involved in three serious accidents in the previous five years to have their licenses automatically suspended or revoked for the safety of other persons. The law provided for a full administrative hearing to be held after the suspension or revocation if requested by the licensee, and allowed for a licensee who could establish hardship to obtain a restricted driving permit.

The man is a retired doctor who now volunteers by driving to the homes of patients who are otherwise unable to receive medical treatment. The man was now unable to attend to these patients due to the revocation of his license. He brought suit against the state challenging the automatic revocation of his license without his first having an opportunity to present evidence on the accident at the restaurant.

How should the court rule?

(A) For the man, because a pre-termination hearing is required.

(B) For the man, because his Fourteenth Amendment rights have been violated.

(C) Against the man, because he is now retired.

(D) Against the man, because he received adequate due process.

Question 8

A state resident could purchase a license solely for hunting elk for $9.00. A nonresident, in order to hunt elk, was required to purchase a combination license at a cost of $225.00; this entitled him to take one elk, one deer, and one black bear. A nonresident, however, could obtain a license restricted to deer for $51.00. A resident was not required to buy any combination of licenses, but if he did, the cost to him of all the privileges granted by the nonresident combination license was $30.00.

Due to its successful management program for elk, the state has not been compelled to limit the overall number of hunters by means of drawings or lotteries, as have other states. Elk are not hunted commercially in the state. Nonresident hunters seek the animal for its trophy value; the trophy is the distinctive set of antlers. Whereas the interest of resident hunters more often may be in the meat, among nonresident hunters, big-game hunting is clearly a sport in the state.

Two residents of another state bring suit against the state. They assert in their complaint that the disparities between residents and nonresidents in the state hunting license system is unconstitutional.

How should the court rule on the state's hunting license system?

(A) The license system is constitutional, because it is within the police power of a state to regulate a recreational, noncommercial activity.

(B) The license system is constitutional, because there is a compelling state interest.

(C) The license system is unconstitutional, because it violates the Privileges and Immunities Clause of Article IV, Section 2.

(D) The license system is unconstitutional, because it violates the Equal Protection Clause of the Fourteenth Amendment.

Question 9

A state requires aspiring applicants who wish to become officers in the state National Guard to take a "leadership exam" that consists of 100 multiple-choice questions. The questions measure literacy, knowledge of National Guard procedures, and judgment of possible courses of action in hypothetical combat and noncombat situations. The racial composition of the applicant pool for officer candidates is 54% white and 46% racial minorities. Historically, 60% of white applicants pass the exam, while only 25% of racial minority applicants do so. As a result of the exam requirement, the officer corps of the state National Guard is disproportionately composed of white officers compared to both the proportion of minority applicants and the proportion of racial minorities in the population of the state as a whole.

Is the state's leadership exam requirement constitutional?

(A) Yes, because a state's police powers includes the absolute right to prescribe qualifications for state officers, including members of its National Guard.

(B) Yes, because there is no evidence of intentional race discrimination in the administration of the test.

(C) No, because the test has a disparate impact on the success of racial minority candidates.

(D) No, because tests that disadvantage racial minorities receive strict scrutiny and are presumptively unconstitutional.

Question 10

A state enacted a statute that required, for any business with more than five employees, that at least half of its employees be residents of the state. A man worked for a department store in the state as a shoe salesman and commuted the five miles to his job from a neighboring state. The department store had 10 employees, eight of whom lived outside of the state. The man was informed by his supervisor that he was one of the three nonresident employees who would be fired pursuant to the new statute. The man properly filed an action challenging the statute on constitutional grounds.

Is the state statute constitutional?

(A) No, because it unfairly discriminates in favor of residents of the state against nonresidents.

(B) No, because it authorizes employers to arbitrarily dismiss some nonresidents while retaining others.

(C) Yes, because a state is permitted to treat nonresidents differently from residents whenever it sees fit.

(D) Yes, because the man was discharged in compliance with the statute and was not otherwise discriminated against by his employer.

Question 11

A man who was legally blind applied for admission to a state medical school. The medical school is a state institution and receives financial grants from the state government. After receiving notice of his rejection, the man contacted the director of admissions, who admitted that the man was denied admission solely due to the fact that he was blind. The man has since initiated an appropriate action against the medical school asserting that his equal protection rights have been violated.

Which of the following correctly states the applicable burden of persuasion?

(A) The man bears the burden to show the medical school's actions are not rationally related to a legitimate state interest.

(B) The man bears the burden to show the medical school's actions do not further a compelling state interest.

(C) The medical school has the burden to show that the man's denial of admission furthers an important state interest.

(D) The medical school has the burden to show that the man's denial of admission is rationally related to a legitimate state interest.

Question 12

A city police department needs to hire an undercover agent to infiltrate a racist militant group whose members are all white. An African American officer applied for the assignment but was rejected even though he had extensive undercover experience. A much less experienced white officer was chosen for the position.

The department admitted that race was the determinative criteria in filling the position. If the officer who did not receive the position sued, what would be the most likely result?

(A) The department's decision will be upheld as necessary to achieve a compelling interest.

(B) The department's decision will be upheld as rationally related to a legitimate state interest.

(C) The department's decision will be overturned because race cannot be used as a criterion in government job assignments.

(D) The department's decision will be overturned as a violation of the Equal Protection Clause of the Fourteenth Amendment.

Question 13

A fast-food ethnic restaurant chain wanted to construct a restaurant on Route 44, a business-zoned, secondary road running through the town. It purchased a buildable lot with sufficient frontage and submitted engineering and architectural plans to the appropriate town authorities. The building inspector, backed by the town planning board, denied the restaurant chain's application for a building permit, stating the following reasons in a written decision: (1) Route 44 cannot sustain any further traffic entering and exiting businesses on the road; (2) Route 44 currently has 17 fast-food restaurants, five of which are in the immediate vicinity of the chain's planned location; and (3) the location of the entrance to the planned chain eatery is too close to a dangerous intersection. In a letter to the town planning board members and building inspector, the fast-food chain requested an opportunity to address each of the stated reasons for the denial of the building permit, but the town authorities responded that the decision was final. The chain then sought a declaratory judgment of its right to address the permit denial.

If the chain obtains declaratory relief, what provision would provide the strongest argument?

(A) Substantive due process.

(B) Equal protection.

(C) The Takings Clause.

(D) The Fourteenth Amendment.

Question 14

A man entered into a franchise contract with a company to operate a fast-food restaurant in a city. The company's national headquarters is located in another state. After the contract was executed, the man leased a store in a shopping mall where he planned to open his restaurant. City public officials, however, refused to grant the man the necessary food vendor's license despite the fact that he could prove his restaurant complied with all provisions of the municipal licensing ordinance. The city ordinance provided, in part, that "a food vendor's license shall be issued to any applicant who properly complies with all of the health requirements of this ordinance." After the man's application for a food vendor's license was rejected, he requested a hearing to establish his qualifications. City officials refused this request and also declined to give any reason for his license denial.

Which of the following is the strongest constitutional argument that the man may use to challenge the refusal of city officials to grant him a food vendor's license?

(A) The city action denied him procedural due process.

(B) The city action denied him substantive due process by arbitrarily regulating economic activity.

(C) The city action constituted an undue burden on the potential interstate commerce between the man and his out-of-state franchisor.

(D) The city action impaired the obligation of the man's contract with the franchising company and his rental agreement with the shopping mall.

Question 15

A state has a policy of hiring new state attorneys on a probationary basis for a two-year period. Prior to the end of those two years, the lawyer can be let go for any reason. After those two years, the lawyer receives the added job security of only being able to be fired "for cause". The state has followed no consistent pattern with respect to the termination of probationary employees. Some were fired with no explanation or warning. Others were given hearings after notice, during which their job performance as probationary employees was discussed.

If a probationary employee who was terminated without a hearing challenged the constitutionality of the state's action, how should the court rule?

(A) The employee would succeed, because she was denied a notice and hearing.

(B) The employee would succeed, because the state's action is an act of attainder.

(C) The employee would not succeed, because a state's procedure with respect to state employees is a matter reserved to the state under the Tenth Amendment.

(D) The employee would not succeed, because she does not have a right to notice and a hearing protected by the Due Process Clause of the Fourteenth Amendment.

Question 16

Until 1954, a state required segregation in all public and private schools, but all public schools are now desegregated. Other state laws, enacted before 1954 and continuing to the present, provide for the free distribution of textbooks to students in all public and private schools. In addition, the state accredits schools and certifies teachers. One private school that offers elementary and secondary education in the state denies admission to all non-Caucasians.

Which of the following is the strongest argument against the constitutionality of the free distribution of textbooks to the students at the private school?

(A) No legitimate educational function is served by the free distribution of textbooks.

(B) The state may not aid private schools.

(C) The Constitution forbids private, as well as public, bias in education.

(D) Segregation is furthered by the distribution of textbooks to these students.

Question 17

A state university offers a merit scholarship to those high school students who scored above a certain score on their SATs. Resident noncitizens are not eligible for this scholarship. A student is a legal resident of the state, but is not a citizen of the United States. He has been denied this scholarship solely because of his citizenship status.

If the student should challenge the constitutionality of his exclusion from the program, will he win?

(A) Yes, because the action of the state violates the Privileges and Immunities Clause of Article IV of the Constitution.

(B) Yes, because there is not sufficient justification to discriminate against noncitizens as a class.

(C) No, because noncitizens are not per se a discreet and insular minority; therefore, a classification excluding them is valid.

(D) No, because the exclusion is rationally related to legitimate state purposes.

Question 18

A staff assistant for a state agency was convicted in federal court of taking bribes from a foreign government for the purpose of influencing an upcoming vote on a waterworks bill. He was sentenced to probation. The staff assistant had served in the agency long enough to become fully qualified for his pension upon retirement under the terms of an agreement between the pensions board and the union. The staff assistant retired and immediately started receiving monthly pension checks. Subsequently, the governor signed into law an act which provided in part:

"Section 8. Any member of a state agency's staff who is convicted of bribery shall not be entitled to receive any retirement or other benefit or payment of any kind from the state. Such conviction shall be considered a breach of the staff member's employment contract."

The staff assistant received a letter from the state which stated that pursuant to this new act, the state was immediately discontinuing pension benefit payments to him on account of his bribery conviction. The staff assistant then contacted an attorney, who challenged the discontinuance of benefits on the grounds that the new law was unconstitutional.

To counter one of the attorney's possible arguments regarding the unconstitutionality of Section 8 of the act, which of the following arguments would serve as the state's best rebuttal?

(A) The staff assistant was afforded an opportunity to express his views about the new legislation at public hearings prior to the enactment of the statute.

(B) Deprivation of pension benefits is not cruel and unusual punishment.

(C) A letter sent through ordinary mail is sufficient notice to satisfy due process for the discontinuation of pension benefits.

(D) It is implicit that one of the conditions of the state's contract of employment with a state agency staff member is that he shall not engage in bribery.

Question 19

Concerned by the number of large commercial properties being purchased by foreign nationals, the legislature of State Red enacted a statute prohibiting the sale of commercial properties in excess of 10,000 square feet to noncitizens. A resident noncitizen who has lived in the State Red for several years enters into a contract with an investor to buy a commercial printing business in the industrial zone of State Red's capital city. The square footage of the physical plant is 23,000. The resident and the investor decide to test the constitutionality of the State statute, and to that end they seek a declaratory judgment in federal court.

Which of the following statements regarding the declaratory judgment action is most accurate?

(A) The state has the burden of showing a compelling state interest in carrying out the statute's purposes regarding large commercial properties.

(B) The resident has the burden of showing that the state has no compelling interest in carrying out the statute's purposes regarding large commercial properties.

(C) The investor has the burden of showing that there is no rational basis for the statute's purposes regarding large commercial properties.

(D) The court will find that the resident, but not the investor, has standing.

Question 20

An animal rights activist group always fought developers when construction projects threatened wildlife in the area. Some members of the group became involved in a battle with a corporation that owned the largest ski resort in town. The corporation obtained permits to expand its operations by adding additional trails on the mountain and increasing the square footage of its ski lodge. Members of the group resisted all expansion efforts in the proper public forums, but when the corporation's permits were approved, some of the more extreme members decided to take desperate action.

Fringe members flooded the unoccupied ski lodge by opening the gates of a local dam during the off-season. The dam water flooded the lodge, rendering it a total loss and causing millions of dollars in damages. Thereafter, the state legislature enacted a law restricting the rights of members of the group in several ways, one of which was excluding members of the group from holding elected office in the state. A senator justified the legislation on grounds that "terrorists have no place in our placid state." A member of the group was in the middle of his campaign for mayor. The member did not participate in the flooding of the ski lodge.

If the member challenges the constitutionality of the exclusionary legislation in court, what is the likely outcome?

(A) The state will prevail, because the group is a subversive organization.

(B) The state will prevail, because it acted within its police power.

(C) The member will prevail, because the law is a bill of attainder.

(D) The member will prevail, because he did not engage in violence as a member of the group.

KAPLAN BAR REVIEW

Quiz 2

Question 1

A state legislature, in an attempt to curb teen pregnancies, recently enacted a statute denying welfare assistance to parents for illegitimate children. A young woman was receiving welfare assistance after being awarded sole custody of her two children following her divorce several years earlier. She recently gave birth to a third child and applied for an increase in her welfare assistance as a result. However, her request was denied pursuant to the state law. The woman sued the state, claiming that the law was unconstitutional and violated the Equal Protection Clause.

Which of the following correctly states the burden of persuasion in this case?

(A) The woman has the burden of persuading the court that the statute is not necessary to further a compelling interest.

(B) The woman has the burden of persuading the court that the statute is not substantially related to achieve an important government interest.

(C) The state has the burden of persuading the court that the statute is substantially related to achieving an important government interest.

(D) The state has the burden of persuading the court that the statute is rationally related to a legitimate government interest.

Question 2

A man recently moved to a new town and fell in love with its charm. A month later, deciding to get as involved as possible, the man submitted his name for an upcoming election for city council. However, the city refused to put his name on the ballot, citing a statute requiring residents to have lived within the town boundaries for at least 60 days prior to being considered for candidacy. The man sued the city, claiming that the statute violated the Due Process Clause.

How should the court rule?

(A) In favor of the city, because under a rational basis analysis, the statute is rationally related to a legitimate state interest.

(B) In favor of the city, because under a strict scrutiny analysis, the statute is necessary to further a compelling state interest.

(C) In favor of the man, because under a rational basis analysis, the 60-day residency requirement is unconstitutional.

(D) In favor of the man, because under a strict scrutiny analysis, the 60-day residency requirement is unconstitutional.

Question 3

The plaintiff has held various public offices for many years, and is currently a state representative. After a recent scandal broke involving inappropriate text messaging with a minor, the plaintiff was convicted of felony obscenity charges, and was sentenced to time served and placed on probation. A week after the conviction was announced, the plaintiff was informed that, pursuant to a state statute, he was being immediately suspended from office without pay until such time as he had exhausted his appeals. Should his conviction become final, another statute authorized the attorney general to file suit to permanently remove the plaintiff from office, following a hearing on the matter and appellate review of the hearing decision. The plaintiff filed suit to prevent his suspension, claiming that the state statute was an unconstitutional bill of attainder and a violation of his due process rights.

How should the court rule?

(A) The plaintiff will prevail, because the statute violated his procedural due process rights.

(B) The plaintiff will prevail, because the statute was an unconstitutional bill of attainder.

(C) The state will prevail, because the statute provided for a judicial hearing.

(D) The state will prevail, because the statute was not a bill of attainder.

Question 4

In the wake of a recent presidential election mishap that garnered national media coverage, a state revamped its voting procedures in an attempt to streamline the process. Among the many changes the state instituted were vote-by-mail, same-day voter registration, and the requirement that voters check in (or register) at the table labeled with their party affiliation. One couple in the state, who were very active within their local community, were registered Republicans in a heavily Democratic district. The couple did not wish for their party affiliation to be made public, fearing repercussions. The couple challenged the constitutionality of the rule requiring voters to check in or register according to party affiliation.

Assuming proper standing, should the court invalidate the rule?

(A) No, because it passes strict scrutiny.

(B) No, because it passes the rational basis test.

(C) Yes, because it violates their procedural due process rights.

(D) Yes, because it violates their right to privacy.

Question 5

In order to combat a rise in organized crime within the state, an anti-organized crime task force was created. After reviewing the previous attempts by various state and local agencies to infiltrate the criminal organizations, the state also adopted a policy that prohibited the assignment of female agents to the undercover infiltration division of the task force. Over the course of 10 separate attempts, seven agents were killed attempting to go undercover, including all five women that were sent in, none of whom managed to make even an initial penetration into the crime families. While undercover assignments were a very successful way to advance to a higher position, it was because of the state's concern with the safety and well-being of its female officers and agents and the demonstrated misogyny of the crime families under investigation that it adopted such a policy. One female agent, desiring to be a member of the undercover division in order to help her achieve her next promotion, submitted an application for the undercover division. After her application was rejected, the agent sued the state in federal court to enjoin enforcement of its stated policy on the grounds that it was unconstitutional.

As a matter of constitutional law, which of the following results in this suit is most appropriate?

(A) Judgment for the agent, because the particular classification contained in this policy is not necessary to further a compelling interest.

(B) Judgment for the agent, because the terms and conditions of state government employment are privileges or immunities of state citizenship that may not be abridged by the state on the basis of gender.

(C) Judgment for the state, because the policy is substantially related to the advancement of an important state interest.

(D) Judgment for the state, because the state has articulated a rational basis for this classification and, therefore, a court may not substitute its judgment for that of responsible state officials.

Question 6

A fitness instructor wanted to open a new gym in a city neighborhood known locally as "Fitnessville," because of its many gyms, fitness studios, and juice bars. The man purchased an empty lot and submitted the appropriate plans to the city authorities for a building permit. The building inspector, backed by the city zoning and planning commission, denied the instructor's application for a building permit, stating the following reasons in a written decision: (1) the local neighborhood could not sustain any further traffic entering and exiting the area; (2) the neighborhood already had 12 gyms of a similar nature, four of which would be on the same street and block as the proposed gym location; and (3) the location of the entrance to the planned gym was too close to a dangerous intersection. The fitness instructor requested an opportunity before the city zoning and planning commission to address each of these reasons for denying his building permit, but the city authorities replied that the decision was final. The fitness instructor then brought an appropriate action challenging the constitutionality of the city's decision.

Which of the following provides the fitness instructor with the strongest argument?

(A) Procedural due process.

(B) The Contract Clause.

(C) The Privileges and Immunities Clause of the Fourteenth Amendment.

(D) The Takings Clause.

Question 7

A resident noncitizen was recently certified to be a teacher by a state regulatory agency. She applied to several schools that were hiring in her district, but all of them refused to hire her, citing a state law prohibiting non-citizens from teaching in a public school. The woman contacted the schools and was told that, if not for the state law, they would have hired her. The woman sued the state to challenge the constitutionality of the law prohibiting non-citizens from public school teaching.

What is the most likely outcome?

(A) The statute is constitutional, because the woman will not meet her burden under rational basis review.

(B) The statute is constitutional, because the challenged statute concerns the qualifications of public school teachers.

(C) The statute is unconstitutional, because the action of the state violates the Privileges and Immunities Clause of Article IV of the Constitution.

(D) The statute is unconstitutional, because there is not sufficient justification to discriminate against noncitizens as a class.

Question 8

A state owned vast tracts of woodlands containing highly desirable lumber, and provided licenses to businesses to exploit these resources, with various regulations in place to ensure that a certain percentage of them would be preserved and the woodlands would not be completely depleted. State building codes required that a minimum of 10% of the lumber used by construction companies be the highly desirable, locally sourced lumber, and in-state commercial enterprises could obtain a license from the state to cut timber up to a set amount for an annual fee of $7,500. Out-of-state commercial enterprises, which made up only about small fraction of the lumber industry in the state, could obtain a license for an annual fee of $20,000, but were permitted to remove 10% more lumber than in-state businesses, a difference which enabled those nonresident enterprises to make a profit greater than the difference in license costs. The schemes were adopted after research showed that they would keep the level of exploitation at or below the rate of regrowth without requiring the state to resort to a lottery system for available licenses, which would have been administratively costly and burdensome.

A nonresident commercial enterprise sued the state claiming that the disparities in the licensing and regulatory scheme were unconstitutional.

How should the court rule on the state's resource management system?

(A) The license system is constitutional, because it is within the police power of a state to regulate and preserve state-owned natural resources.

(B) The license system is constitutional, because there is a compelling state interest.

(C) The license system is unconstitutional, because it violates the Equal Protection Clause of the Fourteenth Amendment.

(D) The license system is unconstitutional, because it violates the Privileges and Immunities Clause of Article IV, Section 2.

Question 9

A state provided for the free distribution of textbooks to all public and private school students, certified teachers, and offered vouchers and tuition grants for families wishing to send their children to private schools. One private school that offers elementary and secondary education in the state denies admission to all children of Canadian descent.

Two children whose family originated from Toronto, and who had lived in the state for several generations, were denied admission to the private school. The parents subsequently filed an action against the state challenging the distribution of vouchers and tuition grants to the school was unconstitutional.

What of the following is the strongest argument in favor of finding the challenged public aid unconstitutional?

(A) Issuing tuition grants to this private school furthers segregation.

(B) It is unconstitutional for a state to provide aid to private schools.

(C) The Constitution forbids private, as well as public, bias in education.

(D) Tuition grants for private schools do not serve any legitimate educational function.

Question 10

Following a judicial determination that it had engaged in past discrimination, a state university agreed to hold 15% of the admissions spots in each department for minority students. A couple years later, a white female student applied to the state university's comparative poetry program and was rejected. The student's aptitude test scores and grade point average were above more than half of the minority students admitted into the program. The student subsequently brought suit against the university claiming that she was unlawfully discriminated against because of her race.

Should the rule in favor of the student?

(A) No, because a state may consider race as a factor in admissions when it is attempting to aid disadvantaged minorities and penalizes no particular group.

(B) No, because the racial classification is designed to remedy past unlawful discrimination.

(C) Yes, because a classification solely by race, even to achieve a worthy purpose, is not necessary to satisfy a compelling state need, and therefore violates the Equal Protection Clause.

(D) Yes, because a state university may not use race as a criterion in making admissions decisions.

Question 11

An environmental activist group vehemently opposed the planned expansion of an oil pipeline that would take it through a wildlife preserve. Despite long periods of protests and media coverage, the oil company was nevertheless granted all of the necessary state and federal permits and permissions to go ahead. Deciding that nonviolent protests were not enough, a splinter faction of the environmentalist group decided to take a more hands-on approach. Late one night when nobody was present, the faction detonated blasting caps on a nearby mountain that caused a small avalanche above the oil company's supply cache. The falling rocks destroyed material and machinery and blocked necessary roads into and out of the wildlife preserve, costing the oil company millions of dollars and months of delay while it had to clear and rebuild many roads.

Thereafter, the state legislature enacted a law restricting the rights of members of the environmentalist group in several ways, one of which was excluding members of the group from holding elected office in the state or working for a government agency or contractor. A representative justified the legislation on the grounds that "ours is a peaceful state, and these verminous scum clearly have no place here." Several members of the group who did not participate in the blasting were soon informed that they would no longer be allowed to remain in elected positions, including a city council member and a county school board official.

If the members challenges the constitutionality of the legislation in court, what is the likely outcome?

(A) The members will prevail, because the law is a bill of attainder.

(B) The members will prevail, because they did not engage in violence as a member of the group.

(C) The state will prevail, because it acted within its police power.

(D) The state will prevail, because the group is a subversive organization.

Question 12

A state enacted a statute which required that at least 60% of an in-state business's employees be residents of the state if that business employed more than 10 people. A woman, a U.S. citizen, worked at a telemarketing firm close to the state's border, commuting from the neighboring state where she resided. The telemarketing firm had 20 employees, 14 of whom lived outside of the state and either commuted into the office or worked remotely. The woman was informed by her manager that she would be one of 10 nonresident citizens whose employment was being terminated pursuant to the new state statute. The woman properly filed an action challenging the state statute on constitutional grounds.

Is the state statute constitutional?

(A) No, because it authorizes employers to arbitrarily dismiss some nonresidents while retaining others.

(B) No, because it unfairly discriminates in favor of in-state citizens against out-of-state citizens.

(C) Yes, because a state is permitted to treat nonresidents differently from residents whenever it sees fit.

(D) Yes, because the woman was discharged in compliance with the ordinance and was not otherwise discriminated against by her employer.

Question 13

Concerned by the number of large commercial properties being purchased by foreign nationals, a state legislature enacted a statute prohibiting the sale of commercial properties in excess of 20,000 square feet to noncitizens. A resident noncitizen who has lived in the state for several years entered into a contract with his business partner to buy a commercial manufacturing business in the state. The factory was 30,000 square feet in size. The resident and the business partner decide to test the constitutionality of the state statute, and so sought a declaratory judgment in federal court.

Which of the following statements regarding the declaratory judgment action is most accurate?

(A) The business partner has the burden of showing that there is no rational basis for the statute's purposes regarding large commercial properties.

(B) The court will find that the resident, but not the business partner, has standing.

(C) The resident has the burden of showing that the state has no compelling interest in carrying out the statute's purposes regarding large commercial properties.

(D) The state has the burden of showing a compelling state interest in carrying out the statute's purposes regarding large commercial properties.

Question 14

A woman who was missing one of her legs applied to be a city firefighter, but was rejected. The woman then contacted the station chief, who admitted that the woman was denied admission solely due to the fact that she was missing one leg. The woman then filed an appropriate action against the city asserting that her equal protection rights had been violated.

Which of the following correctly states the applicable burden of persuasion?

(A) The city has the burden to show that the woman's rejection furthers an important state interest.

(B) The city has the burden to show that the woman's rejection is rationally related to a legitimate state interest.

(C) The woman bears the burden to show the city's actions are not rationally related to a legitimate state interest.

(D) The woman bears the burden to show the city's actions do not further a compelling state interest.

Question 15

A city with a majority nonwhite population has historically had a nonwhite police commissioner. After a recent election, the new city mayor appointed the first white police commissioner in decades. Two months into the job, the new commissioner instated a "qualification exam" requirement for all current police officers and those seeking to become officers. The stated purpose of this exam was to "ensure that only the most qualified people are upholding the laws of this city and state." Current officers who failed the exam would have their employment terminated, and new applicants would need to pass the exam before being considered to join the police academy. For those who failed the exam, an appeals process was also put in place, allowing the applicant to argue that they were qualified for the position despite failing the written exam.

In the wake of the new requirements, 80% of the nonwhite police officers failed the exam and were fired, while only 20% of the white officers failed. Of those who appealed, over 75% of white officers had their appeals granted, while only 10% of nonwhite officers had theirs granted. After six months, it was found that white applicants passed the test 68% of the time, while only 12% of nonwhite applicants passed. Half of the white applicants who appealed were admitted to the police academy, while no nonwhite applicant's appeal was granted.

Is the city's qualification exam requirement constitutional?

(A) No, because tests that disadvantage racial minorities receive strict scrutiny and are presumptively unconstitutional.

(B) No, because the test has a disparate impact on the success of racial minority candidates.

(C) Yes, because a state's police powers includes the absolute right to prescribe qualifications for city police officers.

(D) Yes, because there is no evidence of intentional race discrimination in the administration of the test.

Question 16

A man was recently hired as a professor at a state university. The university had a policy of offering tenure to its professors after three years. Prior to that, the professor could be let go for any reason, though the university typically offered notice and conducted a hearing prior to terminating any professor's employment.

Two and a half years after he was hired, the university administration underwent a change of personnel, and during this period, the professor was told that he was being let go. The professor was never given notice or a hearing prior to his termination.

If the professor sued challenging the constitutionality of the state's action, will the professor succeed?

(A) No, because a state's procedure with respect to state employees is a matter reserved to the state under the Tenth Amendment.

(B) No, because he does not have a right to notice and a hearing protected by the Due Process Clause of the Fourteenth Amendment.

(C) Yes, because he was denied a notice and hearing.

(D) Yes, because the state's action is an act of attainder.

Question 17

In the wake of the federal government suspending welfare benefits and subsidized medical care, states began to see a significant influx in citizens claiming such benefits under state programs. One state in particular, which provided better coverage than most others, soon found that many people were moving into the state for the sole purpose of claiming these benefits. In response to the suddenly increased drain on the state budget, the legislature passed a bill requiring that anyone filing a claim for welfare or state-subsidized medical care show proof of having resided within the state for at least one year prior in order to be eligible for such benefits.

A woman moved to the state six months ago for a job, but was currently unemployed after being fired due to downsizing. The woman applied for state welfare benefits, but her application was denied because she had not been in the state for a full year. The woman filed a proper suit challenging the constitutionality of the statute.

Is the statute constitutional?

(A) No, because it discriminates against the poor in violation of the Equal Protection Clause.

(B) No, because it violates the Privileges and Immunities Clause of Article IV, Section 2.

(C) Yes, because it is rationally related to a legitimate government interest.

(D) Yes, because it violates the Due Process Clause of the Fourteenth Amendment.

Question 18

After driving his car up a curb and hitting a streetlight, an accident for which he was found to have been at fault after a trial, a 70-year-old retiree had his driver's license automatically revoked pursuant to a state law requiring all drivers over the age of 65 who are involved in a serious accident to have their licenses revoked until they complete a safety course and pass another driving test. The retiree was a handyman who now volunteered by going to the homes of people who could not afford to hire someone to make various repairs. The man was now unable to help these indigent people due to the revocation of his license. He brought suit against the state challenging the automatic revocation of his license without his first having an opportunity to present evidence on the accident to the state's department of motor vehicles.

How should the court rule?

(A) Against the retiree, because he is now retired.

(B) Against the retiree, because he received adequate due process.

(C) For the retiree, because a pre-termination hearing was required before his license could be revoked.

(D) For the retiree, because his Fourteenth Amendment rights were violated.

Question 19

In the latest of a long series of government corruption scandals, a state employee was convicted in federal court of taking kickbacks in exchange for influencing government contract decisions. The employee was sentenced to time served plus probation, fined heavily, and given a significant amount of community service. The employee resigned from his position in the government and began to collect his pension, for which he had fully qualified after spending several decades in government service.

As a result of the new law, the state employee was notified that the state was immediately discontinuing pension benefit payments to him on account of his conviction. The state employee then properly filed a lawsuit challenging the termination of his retirement benefits on the grounds that the new law was unconstitutional.

Which of the following is the best argument the state could make in favor of the law's constitutionality?

(A) The notification that the state employee received was sufficient notice to satisfy due process for the discontinuation of pension benefits.

(B) Deprivation of pension benefits is not cruel and unusual punishment.

(C) It is implicit that one of the conditions of the state's contract of employment with a government official is that he shall not take kickbacks or otherwise engage in bribery.

(D) The state employee was afforded an opportunity to express his views about the new legislation at public hearings prior to the enactment of the statute.

Question 20

A state agency needed to select an officer to go undercover and infiltrate a white supremacist group whose members occupied a fortified compound within the state. A Hispanic officer with extensive undercover experience applied for the assignment but was rejected in favor of a much less experienced white officer. The agency admitted that race was the determinative criteria in filling the position.

If the Hispanic officer sued, should the court uphold the department's decision?

(A) No, because it was a violation of the Equal Protection Clause of the Fourteenth Amendment.

(B) No, because race cannot be used as a criterion in government job assignments.

(C) Yes, because it was necessary to achieve a compelling interest.

(D) Yes, because it was rationally related to a legitimate state interest.

Essays

Essay Question 1

IE13JUL050

ISSUE SPOTTING EXERCISE

Consider the fact pattern below and then answer the questions that follow:

In the State of Franklin, the number of female nurses has historically exceeded the number of male nurses by a 20:1 ratio. In an effort to remedy this disparity, the Franklin State Legislature passed the "Equal Opportunity in Nursing Act," which, among other things, provided that the state-operated nursing school would give extra weight to applications submitted by males.

During the debate over the Act, a number of legislators described the concerns of their constituents which prompted those legislators to support the Act, including the beliefs that: (1) nursing was an increasingly lucrative field of employment in the State of Franklin; (2) even qualified males seemed to have difficulty entering the profession; and (3) this was because female nurses were acting like "typical females" in trying to keep all the nursing jobs for themselves.

Judy, a prospective nursing student who was denied admission to the school, challenged the Act in federal district court, arguing that it violated the Fourteenth Amendment's Equal Protection Clause. The court ruled in favor of the State, concluding that the State's concern with the disparity between male and female nurses provided a rational basis for the law.

Did the court correctly rule in favor of the State? Explain.

1. **What sentence in the fact pattern provides you with the most information with regard to the issues being tested?**

2. **In order to determine whether the court's ruling was correct, which of the following issues do you need to resolve?**

   (A) Whether Judy has standing.

   (B) Whether the court properly applied rational basis review to Judy's equal protection claim.

   (C) Whether there was state action.

   (D) Whether the state can meet intermediate scrutiny.

Identify Issue 1:

Identify two key facts from the prompt that will help you resolve this issue:

1.

2.

Identify Issue 2:

Identify two key facts from the prompt that will help you resolve this issue:

1.

2.

Essay Question 1

IE13JUL050

RULE RECOLLECTION EXERCISE

A good rule statement will demonstrate your understanding of the law and provide the foundation for your analysis. This exercise is intended to help you practice: (1) recalling the relevant rules of law; (2) organizing rules of law; and (3) explaining legal concepts completely and concisely.

- PUT AWAY YOUR NOTES for this exercise and practice actively trying to recall the relevant rules.
- In FIFTEEN minutes, write out rule statements for the following issues.
- WRITE THESE RULES OUT IN FULL; do not merely jot down concepts, topics, or fragments.

STANDARD OF REVIEW

<u>Equal Protection</u>

<u>Rational Basis Test</u>

Strict Scrutiny

Intermediate Scrutiny

APPLICATION OF INTERMEDIATE SCRUTINY

Intermediate Scrutiny

Essay Question 1

IE13JUL050

ANALYSIS EXERCISE

Connect law (rules) to fact, and draft your analysis paragraph for each issue below.

STANDARD OF REVIEW

Equal Protection

Rational Basis Test

Strict Scrutiny

Intermediate Scrutiny

APPLICATION OF INTERMEDIATE SCRUTINY

Intermediate Scrutiny

Essay Question 2

IE13JUL088

Melissa, an instructor at a state public community college, often took extreme positions in order to stimulate class debates. Melissa initiated a debate in class by saying that she advocated not only taking terminally ill people off life support, but also withholding medical care from people with certain disabilities. The following day, an influential campus group, Religion for All (RFA), held a protest outside of Melissa's classroom. When the protesters began yelling "atheist scum!" loud enough to disrupt classes, Melissa cancelled her class and left for the day.

RFA petitioned the college for Melissa's removal as an instructor and suggested that RFA should have veto power over the hiring of any instructor. The college agreed to give RFA veto power.

Melissa wrote a guest editorial in the campus newspaper criticizing the college's inclusion of RFA in its hiring decisions. After the editorial was published, Melissa was fired on the grounds that she had left her class on the day of the protest and that her editorial violated the college's personnel policies by revealing internal hiring practices.

The college subsequently adopted a policy requiring the campus newspaper to submit all editorials to college administrators for approval before publication. Melissa sought a hearing on her termination, arguing that the termination was not "for cause" as required by her contract. The college refused to hold a hearing. The college hiring committee, which included an RFA member, hired a replacement instructor after receiving assurances from him that he was not an atheist and favored life support regardless of the extent of illness or disability.

In a lawsuit against the college, discuss the merits and likelihood of success of federal constitutional challenges that:

1. *Melissa could bring concerning her termination.*
2. *An unsuccessful applicant for Melissa's position could bring concerning the hiring of Melissa's replacement.*

Do not discuss First Amendment issues.

KAPLAN BAR REVIEW

Contracts

Exercise Set 1

Question 1a

Identify the three requirements to form an enforceable contract.

Question 1b

Identify the four ways to terminate the power of acceptance.

Question 2

Define the following forms of rejection.

1. Outright rejection:

2. Rejection via counteroffer:

3. Rejection via nonconforming acceptance:

For the following exercises, you are given a question prompt. After reading the question prompt, consider the applicable rules. Then, brainstorm possible issues that could be raised or tested based on the given question prompt.

Question 3

What is the legal significance of the letter?

Question 4

Did the parties form an enforceable contract?

Question 5

Is the owner required to pay the reward?

Question 6

Is the promise enforceable?

For each of the following fact patterns, write out the relevant issues and corresponding rule statements.

Question 7

Pursuant to a written agreement, a bakery promised to sell its entire output of baked goods at a specified unit price to a retailer for one year. The retailer promised not to sell any other supplier's baked goods. Shortly after making the contract, and before the bakery had tendered any goods, the retailer decided that the contract had become undesirable because of a sudden, sharp decline in its customers' demand for baked goods. The retailer renounced the agreement, and the bakery sued for breach of contract.

For whom should the court find?

Question 8

On July 18, a shovel manufacturer received an order for the purchase of 500 snow shovels from a wholesaler. The wholesaler had mailed the purchase order on July 15. The order required shipment of the shovels no earlier than September 15 and no later than October 15. Typed conspicuously across the front of the order form was the following: "The wholesaler reserves the right to cancel this order at any time before September 1." The manufacturer's mailed response accepting the order was received by the wholesaler on July 21.

As of July 22, has a valid contract been formed?

Question 9

Andy entered into a valid written contract to sell Blackacre, a large tract of land, to Bertha. At that time, Blackacre was owned by Andy's father, Frank; Andy had no title to Blackacre and was not the agent of Frank. After the contract was executed and before the scheduled closing date, Frank died intestate, leaving Andy as his sole heir. Shortly thereafter, Andy received an offer for Blackacre that was substantially higher than the purchase price of the contract with Bertha. Andy refused to close with Bertha even though she was ready, willing, and able to close pursuant to the contract. Bertha brought an appropriate action for specific performance against Andy.

What is the likely outcome of the action?

Question 10

On June 1, a gun retailer in State X received the following signed letter from a gun wholesaler in another state: "We have just obtained 100 of the assault rifles you inquired about and can supply them for $2,500 each. We can guarantee shipment no later than August 1." On June 10, the wholesaler sold and delivered the same rifles to another merchant for $3,000 each. Unaware of that transaction, on the morning of June 11, the retailer mailed the wholesaler a letter rejecting the latter's offer but, changing his mind an hour later, retrieved the letter of rejection from his local post office and immediately dispatched to the wholesaler a letter of acceptance, which the wholesaler received on June 14. On June 9, a valid federal statute making the interstate sale of assault rifles punishable as a crime had become effective, but neither party was aware until June 15 that the statute was already in effect.

As between the parties, has a valid contract been formed?

Exercise Set 2

Question 1

Complete the chart with the requirements needed to establish the following.

UNILATERAL CONTRACTS			
REJECTION VIA COUNTEROFFER			
INADEQUATE CONSIDERATION			

Question 2

Complete the following chart with the rule that corresponds to the given elements.

RULES	ELEMENTS
	• Agreeing to do something there is a legal right not to do. • Foregoing activity in which there is a legal right to engage.
	• Performance left to the discretion of the promising party.
	• Nothing promised in return. • Nothing given in return.

Question 3

Complete the chart explaining the distinction between the common law and the UCC.

RULES	COMMON LAW	UCC
Offer		
Acceptance		

For the following fact patterns, complete the following charts with the relevant facts that correspond to the rules provided.

Question 4

Sally owed Mona $1,000 plus interest at 8% until paid on a long-overdue promissory note, the collection of which would become barred by the statute of limitations on June 30. On the preceding April 1, Sally and Mona both signed a writing in which Sally promised to pay the note in full on the following December 31 plus any interest accrued up to that date, and Mona promised not to sue on the note in the meantime. Mona, having received some advice from her nonlawyer brother-in-law, became concerned about the legal effect of the April 1 agreement. On May 1, acting pro se as permitted by the rules of the local small claims court, she filed suit to collect the note.

Assuming that there is no controlling statute, is the April 1 agreement an effective defense for Sally?

RULES	RELEVANT FACTS
Offer	
Acceptance	
Consideration	

Question 5

A retailer ordered from a wholesaler 500 bushels of No. 1 peaches at a specified price "for prompt shipment." The wholesaler promptly shipped 500 bushels, but mistakenly shipped No. 2 peaches instead of No. 1. The error in shipment was caused by the negligence of the wholesaler's shipping clerk.

What are the retailer's rights and duties upon delivery of the peaches?

RULE	RELEVANT FACTS
Shipment of Nonconforming Goods	

Question 6

A nephew had a $1,000 contractual obligation to his aunt, which was due on July 1. On the preceding June 15, the aunt called her niece and said, "As my birthday gift to you, you may collect on July 1 the $1,000 your brother owes me." The aunt also called the nephew and told him to pay the $1,000 to his sister on July 1. On July 1, the nephew, saying that he did not like his sister and wouldn't pay anything to her, paid the $1,000 to his aunt, who accepted it without objection.

Will the niece succeed in an action for $1,000 against her brother?

RULE	RELEVANT FACTS
Offer	

Question 7

On March 1, an apartment complex received a letter from an air conditioner retailer offering to sell 1,200 window air conditioners suitable for the apartments in the complex. The offer stated that it would remain open until March 20, but that the apartment complex's acceptance must be received on or before that date. On March 16, the manager of the apartment complex posted a letter of acceptance. On March 17, the air conditioner retailer telephoned the apartment complex manager and left a voicemail advising that it was revoking the offer. The voicemail reached the apartment complex manager on March 17, but the apartment complex manager's letter did not arrive at the air conditioner retailer's address until March 21.

What is the nature of the relationship between the parties as of March 22?

RULES	RELEVANT FACTS
Firm Offer	
Mailbox Rule	

Question 8

On June 1, a widget manufacturer entered into a written agreement with a toolmaker whereby the toolmaker agreed to produce and sell to the widget manufacturer 12 sets of newly designed dies, to be delivered August 1, for the price of $50,000, payable 10 days after delivery. Encountering unexpected expenses in the purchase of the special steel alloy required for the dies, the toolmaker advised the widget manufacturer that production costs would exceed the contract price. On July 1, the manufacturer and the toolmaker signed a modification to the June 1 agreement increasing the contract price to $60,000. After the timely receipt of the 12 sets of dies conforming to the contract specifications, the widget manufacturer paid the toolmaker $50,000, but refused to pay any more.

What is the toolmaker's best argument in an action to recover the additional $10,000 for breach of the widget manufacturer's July 1 promise?

RULE	RELEVANT FACTS
Preexisting Duty Rule	

For the following rules, write a short fact pattern that could be used to analyze it.

Question 9

Acceptance by mail is effective upon dispatch so long as the acceptance is properly posted, with the correct address and postage.

Question 10

The mirror image rule requires that acceptance must mirror the terms of the offer, and any variation results in a counteroffer and rejection of the initial offer.

KAPLAN BAR REVIEW

Quiz 1

Question 1

An employee successfully negotiated a lucrative contract for her employer. As a result, her employer orally promised her a $10,000 bonus payable at the end of the year because of the employee's "good work." At the end of the year, the employer informed the employee that the company's profits were not as large as he expected, so the promised bonus would not be paid.

Which of the following is the legal effect of the employer's promise to pay the bonus to the employee?

(A) It is enforceable, because the employee conferred a material benefit on the employer by negotiating the lucrative contract.

(B) It is enforceable, because the employer was morally obligated to pay the bonus.

(C) It is unenforceable, because it was not supported by legally sufficient consideration.

(D) It is unenforceable, because it was not in writing.

Question 2

On Monday, a man told a gardener, "I am having a party on Sunday and I want my house to look good. If you will promise to mow my lawn by Saturday, I will pay you $50." On Friday, the gardener arrived at the man's home just as the man was leaving for work and began to mow the man's lawn. The man said nothing to the gardener, but drove off as he saw the gardener unloading his lawn mower. When the man arrived home from work that evening, he noticed that only half of his lawn had been mowed. He then found a note from the gardener slipped into his mailbox which read, "Sorry, but I ran out of gas to power the lawn mower and did not have time to buy more gas to finish the job. I'm taking the weekend off, but I will be back Monday morning to finish the work."

If the man brings suit against the gardener for breach of contract, who is likely to prevail?

(A) The gardener, because he never accepted the offer made by the man.

(B) The gardener, because he offered to cure the defective performance by finishing the job on Monday morning.

(C) The man, because the gardener's part performance necessarily implied an acceptance and a promise that he would render complete performance.

(D) The man, because under the doctrine of equitable estoppel, the gardener's part performance was evidence of his intent to honor the entire contract.

Question 3

A man offered to sell his barbecue to his neighbor for $100. After receiving the man's offer, the neighbor responded, "Let me think it over." The man then said, "If you say so." The next day, the man sold the barbecue to his brother for $100. Thereafter, the neighbor decided to accept the man's offer, but learned from a reliable source that the barbecue had been sold to the brother.

If the neighbor sues the man for breach of contract, judgment should be for whom?

(A) The man, because the offer to the neighbor terminated when the neighbor learned of the sale to the brother.

(B) The man, because there was no consideration to keep the offer open for an extended period of time.

(C) The neighbor, because the offer became irrevocable for a reasonable time when the man allowed the neighbor to "think it over."

(D) The neighbor, because he is a merchant.

Question 4

A homeowner said to a roofer, "My roof leaks. I think the old tiles are cracked. If you will replace them with all new tiles, I will pay you $5,000." The roofer replied, "Sure, if I can clear my busy schedule." The homeowner then remarked, "That's all right, but let me know soon." Three days later, the roofer drove his pickup truck to the homeowner's home and unloaded the materials and equipment needed to perform the roofing job. When the homeowner looked out his window and saw what was transpiring, he immediately ran outside and exclaimed, "Stop! The deal's off. I decided to repair the roof myself."

In an action by the roofer against the homeowner for breach of contract, which of the following would provide the roofer with his best theory of recovery?

(A) A bilateral contract was formed when the roofer purchased the materials and equipment needed to do the job.

(B) A bilateral contract was formed when the roofer said, "Sure, if I can clear my busy schedule."

(C) The homeowner made an offer that proposed a unilateral contract, and the offer became irrevocable when the roofer purchased the materials and equipment needed for the job.

(D) The homeowner made an offer that proposed a unilateral contract, and the roofer manifested an intent to accept the offer when he began performance by unloading the materials and equipment at the homeowner's house.

Question 5

A buyer ordered 1,000 widgets from a seller for immediate delivery. The seller responded by shipping 800 widgets, along with an accompanying notice to the buyer explaining that the seller did not have an adequate inventory to ship 1,000 widgets, and was therefore shipping 800 widgets as an accommodation to the buyer in light of the buyer's urgent need.

Which of the following is the most accurate statement?

(A) A contract was formed under the mailbox rule when the seller shipped the widgets.

(B) A contract will be formed once the widgets arrive at the buyer's address.

(C) No contract exists, because the notice of accommodation operates as a counteroffer.

(D) No contract exists, because the buyer's accommodation is not an acceptance.

Question 6

A seller sent the following terms in a writing to a buyer: "I will provide 100 units of furniture for a price of $50 per unit. This offer is good for 60 days from today." The seller dated the letter and signed it at the bottom. The buyer received the letter and immediately wrote a response accepting the seller's terms, but did not immediately send the letter.

A week after sending his letter to the buyer, the seller received an offer from a furniture wholesaler offering to buy as much furniture as the seller could make at $55 per unit. The seller wanted to accept the wholesaler's offer, but was concerned about the outstanding letter to the buyer.

Which of the following statements is most accurate?

(A) The seller can revoke his offer to the buyer as long as the buyer has neither accepted nor changed position in reliance on the offer.

(B) The seller can revoke his offer, because there was no consideration provided that would make the offer irrevocable.

(C) The buyer can accept the offer at any time within 60 days from the date of the letter, and the seller cannot revoke the offer.

(D) The buyer has three months from the date of the letter to accept, because firm offers are irrevocable for 90 days.

Question 7

A dog breeder lost her prized golden retriever puppy during a walk in a nature preserve. To enlist help in finding her dog, the breeder posted a notice on the internet and offered to pay $1,000 for the return of her puppy. A hiker saw the notice, equipped herself, drove to the nature preserve, and subsequently found the puppy. However, before the hiker could return the puppy, the breeder heard that the dog had been found and posted another notice on the internet withdrawing the reward offer. The hiker brought the breeder the dog and demanded the reward. The breeder refused.

Is the breeder liable to pay the hiker the reward?

(A) Yes, because the hiker had undertaken substantial steps toward acceptance of the breeder's offer before it was revoked.

(B) Yes, because the hiker did not actually see the breeder's purported revocation of her reward offer.

(C) No, because the hiker did not communicate her acceptance of the breeder's offer.

(D) No, because the breeder revoked the offer before completion of the hiker's performance.

Question 8

A dentist entered into an agreement with a supply company pursuant to which the dentist promised to purchase all of her supplies from the company for two years. However, when the dentist decided to move into a new office, she ordered three new dental chairs from a different company. The cost of the chairs was $9,000, payable 60 days after delivery. The agreement with the original supplier was primarily oral; the only document that could prove the agreement was a letter, signed by the dentist but not by the company, which outlined the general nature of the agreement. It contained no specific terms such as item or quantity.

Can the supply company enforce the agreement?

(A) Yes, under the doctrine of promissory estoppel.

(B) Yes, because the parties entered into a valid requirements contract.

(C) No, because neither party agreed to a quantity term.

(D) No, because the dentist's promise was illusory.

Question 9

The owner of a large social function hall hosts various banquets, meetings, and other types of community events in the social function hall. An entrepreneur is in the business of running bingo games sponsored by charities, a legal form of gambling in the state in which the social function hall is located. Without disclosing his intended use for the hall, on June 1, the entrepreneur entered into a one-year lease of the social function hall commencing on July 1. On June 15, a scandal erupted in the state in which the social function hall was located concerning corruption in bingo games sponsored by charities, and the state legislature passed legislation, effective June 30, outlawing bingo games. Upon passage of the legislation, the entrepreneur purported to cancel the lease.

In a suit by the owner against the entrepreneur, what is the likely outcome?

(A) The entrepreneur will prevail, because after the lease had been signed, the government made its subject matter illegal.

(B) The entrepreneur will prevail, because the contract is voidable under the doctrine of frustration of purpose.

(C) The owner will prevail, because the purpose of the contract was not illegal at the time that the contract was formed.

(D) The owner will prevail, because the parties formed a valid contract supported by consideration.

Question 10

On February 3, a florist left a note for one of his customers offering to pay $2,000 for his truck if the customer delivered the truck to the flower shop before 1:00 p.m. on February 13. The florist indicated that the customer needed to accept by delivering the truck because the florist had lots of deliveries for Valentine's Day. Two days later, the customer sent a letter to the florist indicating his acceptance of the offer to purchase. However, the letter was delayed by the post office and did not reach the flower shop until February 12. By then, having not heard back from his customer, the florist had purchased another used truck for $1,800. On February 13, the customer drove his truck to the florist, arriving at about 12:55 p.m., at which time the florist rejected the customer's truck. The customer then filed suit for breach of contract.

Which of the following most accurately describes the significance the court will attach to the customer's letter accepting the offer to purchase the truck?

(A) The customer's letter, upon its receipt by the florist, operated as an effective acceptance of the florist's offer to purchase.

(B) The letter from the customer, upon the customer's mailing of the letter, created a binding unilateral contract between the florist and the customer for the purchase of the customer's truck.

(C) The mailing of the customer's letter did not create a binding contract between the customer and the florist.

(D) The customer's letter bound the florist and the customer to a unilateral contract as of February 12, when the florist received the letter.

Question 11

A chef was a buyer for a gourmet grocery store. He contracted in writing with a seafood supplier for the purchase of 5,000 frozen swordfish steaks at $2 each, for a total contract price of $10,000. The manager of the gourmet grocery store was very pleased with the chef's purchase. The purchase price of the swordfish steaks was only half of the usual price. The gourmet grocery store would be able to sell each steak for $5 each, reaping a substantial profit. The manager approached the chef one afternoon and told him that, because of his good work, he would be receiving a raise in salary of $50 per week beginning the next pay period. Three days later, the manager of the seafood supplier called the chef and informed him that the price per swordfish steak was actually $4, for a total contract price of $20,000. Further, given the size of the error, the seafood supplier would not be able to deliver the swordfish unless the grocery store agreed to pay the additional $10,000. The chef advised the manager of the problem and the manager approved payment of the entire $20,000.

Which of the following accurately states the legal effect of the manager's promise to give the chef a raise in pay?

(A) The promise is unenforceable, because it was illusory.

(B) The promise is unenforceable, because it was not supported by consideration.

(C) The promise is enforceable, because the manager is morally obligated to perform.

(D) The promise is enforceable, assuming the chef conferred a benefit on the manager.

Question 12

A man makes the following statement to a woman: "I hereby offer to sell you Blackacre for $10,000. This offer expires in 30 days."

Which of the following is most accurate regarding the man's offer?

(A) It is a firm offer that is irrevocable before the 30-day period has passed.

(B) It is neither a firm offer nor an option contract, and is revocable at any time before acceptance has been made.

(C) Because the man is not a merchant, the woman has a reasonable time to accept.

(D) Regardless of the man's status, the woman must accept within 30 days and before receiving notice of the man's direct revocation.

Question 13

A baseball card dealer and a collector met at an auction. The baseball card dealer had in his inventory a mint condition rookie card of a famous baseball player that was valued at well over $50,000. The collector desperately wanted to buy the card, but knew that he could not make the purchase until he sold a few other cards that he currently owned. The two spoke for a while, and before leaving, the dealer wrote the collector the following note: "I, will hold the rookie card that we were talking about for sale to you alone for the next six months, in return for the $500 consideration I received from you today." The dealer signed and dated the note and handed it to the collector.

If the collector saw the dealer at another auction five months later and wanted to purchase the card, is the offer still in force?

(A) No, because the collector is not a merchant.

(B) No, because the UCC only makes a firm offer irrevocable for a maximum of three months.

(C) Yes, because there was consideration to support a common law option contract.

(D) Yes, because UCC firm offers are irrevocable for six months.

Question 14

Knowing that his niece was looking for a good used car, an uncle sent an email to his niece one Friday afternoon, promising to sell her his car for $1,000 if she accepted before the end of that weekend. After reading the email, the niece sent her uncle a reply email that stated, "The price is a little high. I'll give you $800." The uncle responded via email, "I will not accept $800; it is worth more than that." The next day, the niece emailed her uncle and said, "I changed my mind, I will pay $1,000." On Sunday, the uncle responded that he refused to sell the niece his car.

If the niece brings a cause of action against her uncle to enforce the agreement, will she prevail?

(A) Yes, because she accepted the uncle's terms.

(B) Yes, because she accepted the uncle's terms before the end of the weekend.

(C) No, because she made a counteroffer.

(D) No, because the uncle rejected her counteroffer.

Question 15

A six-year-old girl was kidnapped outside her home in a small town. Following the girl's abduction, her parents publicly announced a $50,000 reward to anyone responsible for the apprehension of the kidnapper. The girl's abductor was described as a Caucasian male between the ages of 25 and 30 with curly blond hair. He also was identified as having a pentagram tattoo on his left arm. One afternoon, while on duty, a police officer from a nearby town stopped at a local fast-food restaurant for lunch. Inside the restaurant, the police officer noticed a man fitting the description of the kidnapper. The police officer proceeded to arrest the individual, who, in fact, turned out to be the girl's abductor. After the girl was found unharmed, the police officer requested the $50,000 reward. However, the girl's parents have refused to pay the police officer the reward money.

If the police officer brings suit against the girl's parents to recover the $50,000 reward, for whom should the court enter judgment?

(A) The police officer, because he accepted the offer by apprehending the kidnapper.

(B) The police officer, if he knew of the existence of the reward offer when he apprehended the kidnapper.

(C) The girl's parents, if their intent was to make the offer open only to members of the general public.

(D) The girl's parents, because recovery by the police officer is against public policy.

Question 16

The owner of a seaside cottage had leased the cottage to a renter for the past three summers. Last year, on October 1, the owner sent the renter a letter stating, "Because you have been such a great tenant, I will rent you the seaside cottage on the same terms as last year. I need your answer by June 1." The renter, uncertain as to when he would be taking his annual seaside vacation, decided to put the letter aside for the time being, intending to respond to it by June 1.

On May 15, the owner received an offer from the renter's cousin to rent the seaside cottage at a higher price than the renter had paid the prior year. The owner accepted. On May 20, the renter telephoned the owner and said, "My cousin tells me that he has rented the seaside cottage from you. However, you said that I had until June 1 to decide, and even though your rents are too high, I have decided that I want the cottage for the summer." The owner replied that he had already rented the cottage to the cousin. The renter filed a lawsuit seeking to enforce the contract.

Will the renter succeed in his enforcement lawsuit?

(A) Yes, because the renter relied on the owner's statement that he needed an answer by June 1.

(B) Yes, because the renter contacted the cottage owner on May 20.

(C) No, because the renter's response was not the mirror image of the offer and constituted a counteroffer.

(D) No, because the owner had already rented the cottage to a different tenant.

Question 17

An owner planned to renovate her office building and requested several contractors to submit bids to perform the work. One of the contractors in turn sought bids from several subcontractors to determine the overall cost of the job. An electrician submitted a bid to the contractor that he used in computing the bid he sent to the owner. The contractor notified the electrician to the effect.

On November 1, the contractor submitted his bid to the owner in which he offered to perform the renovation work for $75,000. On November 4, the electrician notified the contractor that he was unable to perform the electrical work on the owner's project. On November 5, the owner sent the contractor a signed confirmation letter wherein she stated, "I hereby accept your offer to perform the renovation work for the quoted cost of $75,000." Thereafter, the contractor hired another electrician to complete the electrical work at a cost of $5,000 above the electrician's bid. The contractor explained the situation to the owner and informed her that the overall cost of the job would have to be increased to $80,000. The owner responded that she would hold contractor to his original bid of $75,000 and would not be responsible for any additional costs. The contractor then performed the renovation work, but the owner has not yet paid him anything.

Which of the following best supports a claim for $5,000 by the contractor against the electrician?

(A) The electrician made an offer that the contractor accepted by using the electrician's bid in computing the bid he submitted to the owner.

(B) The electrician's bid was a firm offer that was irrevocable, because both the electrician and the contractor were merchants.

(C) The contractor made an offer to the electrician that the electrician accepted when he submitted his bid.

(D) An option contract was created because the contractor used the electrician's bid in computing the bid he submitted to the owner and notified the electrician of that fact.

Question 18

An ice cream manufacturer and a small restaurant entered into a contract whereby the restaurant would buy all the ice cream it needed from the ice cream manufacturer, and the ice cream manufacturer would sell as much ice cream as it wanted to the restaurant at their current market price.

The restaurant sent its first order to the ice cream manufacturer. However, the ice cream manufacturer refused to deliver any ice cream to the restaurant, citing purchase orders it had just received from a large national chain of restaurants.

If the restaurant sued the ice cream manufacturer, which of the following is most accurate?

(A) A valid contract was formed, because there was valid consideration provided and the parties both acted in good faith.

(B) A valid contract was formed, because there was mutual assent to clearly defined terms understood within the industry.

(C) No contract exists, because the agreement was illusory.

(D) No contract exists, because the parties failed to include a quantity term.

Question 19

On October 1, a seller mailed a letter to a buyer offering to sell a specified quantity of shirts at list price. The buyer received the seller's offer on October 2. The next day, the buyer mailed the seller a letter of acceptance. The buyer then changed his mind and decided to reject the seller's offer. On October 5, the buyer mailed a letter of rejection to the seller. On October 4, the seller sent the buyer a letter revoking his original October 1 offer. On October 6, the seller received the buyer's acceptance. On October 7, the buyer received the seller's letter of revocation. The following day, the seller received the buyer's rejection. The buyer then demanded that the seller sell him the shirts at the specified price, and the seller refused. The buyer has sued for breach of contract.

Judgment should be for whom?

(A) The buyer, because he mailed his acceptance before mailing his rejection.

(B) The buyer, because the seller received the buyer's acceptance before receiving the buyer's rejection.

(C) The seller, because the buyer's dispatch of both a rejection and an acceptance evidences a lack of mutual assent.

(D) The seller, because he mailed his revocation before receiving notice of the buyer's acceptance.

Question 20

A publishing company offered to buy a manuscript for $100,000. The writer, as part of an ill-advised negotiating strategy, rejected the offer. The next day, the publishing company filed for bankruptcy. When the writer learned of the bankruptcy, she quickly realized that the original offer was the best she would receive and called the publishing company, telling the receptionist, "I accept your offer."

Will the writer be successful in her lawsuit to recover $100,000 from the publishing company's bankruptcy estate?

(A) No, because the publishing company's bankruptcy action negated its contractual liability.

(B) No, because the writer had already rejected the offer.

(C) Yes, because the bankruptcy action would not affect the valid offer.

(D) Yes, because $100,000 is sufficient consideration to support the contract.

KAPLAN BAR REVIEW

Quiz 2

Question 1

An emergency room doctor was camping with his family in a local state park. As the doctor was walking to get water, he heard a woman screaming that her husband was choking. The doctor rushed to help, but was unable to dislodge whatever was causing the man to choke, and the man died. The doctor now seeks your advice as to whether he can charge the man's estate for his services. This jurisdiction does not have a Good Samaritan statute, and the hospital that the doctor works at treats all doctors as independent contractors.

What advice would be most accurate?

(A) The doctor can recover, because he is not a full-time employee at the hospital.

(B) The doctor can recover, based on quasi-contract.

(C) The doctor cannot recover, because allowing a doctor to benefit in such a situation would be against public policy.

(D) The doctor cannot not recover, because the man died.

Question 2

On Monday, a man told a gardener, "I am having a party on Sunday and I want my house to look good. If you will agree to mow my lawn by Saturday, I will pay you $50. Think about it and let me know." The man did not hear from the gardener all week. Therefore, the man decided to mow the grass himself. On Saturday, the gardener arrived with his lawn mower, and saw that the grass had been freshly mowed. The man informed the gardener that he had just finished cutting the grass himself. The gardener then brought suit against the man for breach of contract, because he argued that he was within the window of time to accept and that he had given up another job in reliance on mowing the man's grass.

Who is likely to prevail?

(A) The man, because the gardener never accepted the offer.

(B) The man, because the offer to the gardener was indirectly revoked.

(C) The gardener, because the man did not specify that acceptance had to be by return promise.

(D) The gardener, because he gave up another job in order to accept the man's offer.

Question 3

On Monday, a man offered to sell his lawn mower to his neighbor for $100. After receiving the man's offer, the neighbor responded, "Let me think it over." The man then said, "If you say so, but I need to know in a day or two, tops." On Friday, the man sold the lawn mower to his brother. Thereafter, the neighbor decided to accept the man's offer and walked to his house, only to find the man's brother loading it onto his truck.

If the neighbor sued the man for breach of contract, judgment should be for whom?

(A) The man, because the offer to the neighbor terminated when the neighbor saw the brother loading the lawn mower onto his truck.

(B) The man, because the offer was terminated due to the lapse of time.

(C) The neighbor, because the offer became irrevocable for a reasonable time when the neighbor asked to "think it over."

(D) The neighbor, because the sale of a lawn mower is governed by the UCC.

Question 4

A homeowner said to a carpenter, "My porch is in need of repair. I think the boards are cracked. Can you do the job for $5,000?" The carpenter replied, "I'd be happy to, but $5,000 seems a little low. Make it $6,000 and you got a deal." The homeowner then remarked, "Deal." Three days later, the carpenter purchased the necessary materials, then drove his pickup truck to the homeowner's home and unloaded the materials and equipment needed to perform the job. When the homeowner looked out his window and saw what was transpiring, he immediately ran outside and exclaimed, "Stop! The deal's off. I decided to repair the porch myself."

In an action by the carpenter against the homeowner for breach of contract, which of the following is the most accurate?

(A) A bilateral contract was formed before the carpenter purchased the materials.

(B) A unilateral contract was formed when the carpenter started to perform.

(C) No contract was formed, because the carpenter did not start to perform.

(D) No contract was formed, because the carpenter rejected the homeowner's terms.

Question 5

A buyer ordered 1,000 widgets from a seller for immediate delivery. The seller responded by shipping 800 widgets rather than the full 1,000 ordered, because the seller did not have an adequate inventory and thought it better to ship something rather than nothing.

Which of the following is the most accurate statement?

(A) A contract was formed when the seller shipped the widgets.

(B) A contract will be formed once the widgets arrive at the buyer's address.

(C) No contract exists, because the seller shipped nonconforming goods.

(D) No contract exists, because the seller did not cure the nonconforming tender immediately.

Question 6

Knowing that his niece was looking at a red sedan on his used car lot, an uncle sent a signed email to his niece one Friday afternoon, promising to sell her the red sedan from his lot for $1,000, and stating that she could have the weekend to think about it and let him know. After reading the email, the niece sent her uncle a reply that stated, "The price is a little high. I'll give you $800." The uncle responded via email, "I will not accept $800; it is worth more than that." On Saturday, the niece emailed her uncle and said, "I changed my mind, I will pay $1,000." On Sunday, the uncle responded that he refused to sell the niece his car.

If the niece brings a cause of action against her uncle to enforce the agreement, will she prevail?

(A) No, because a firm offer is immediately revoked with a rejection.

(B) No, because the niece did not provide any consideration to create an option contract.

(C) Yes, because she accepted the uncle's terms before the uncle took any action contrary to the offer to the niece.

(D) Yes, because the uncle was a merchant.

Question 7

A man offered to buy a woman's farm for $100,000. The woman did not wish to sell her farm, but she jokingly accepted the offer because she did not believe that the man has the $100,000. The man and the woman worked out the terms of the contract and the woman, still joking, wrote out the contract on a sheet of paper which both parties signed. The man took the writing and subsequently tried to enforce it, arriving with a check for $100,000.

In a suit by the man against the woman, what is the likely outcome?

(A) The man will win, because they signed the agreement.

(B) The man will win, because the contract is binding even if the woman did not intend to sell her farm, as the man actually believed this to be a serious transaction and his belief was reasonable.

(C) The woman will win, because there was no good faith on her part to enter into a contract.

(D) The woman will win, because there was no true meeting of the minds.

Question 8

On Monday, a chicken farmer emailed a restaurant owner promising to sell him 500 chickens for $2,000. On Tuesday, the owner replied to the farmer that he was rejecting the offer because the price was too high. The farmer quickly replied, "Why don't you wait and think it over?" The following morning, the owner learned that due to a salmonella outbreak, there was a nationwide chicken shortage. He immediately telephoned the farmer to accept. The farmer knew it was the owner, and so he answered the phone by saying, "Good morning, I hereby revoke my offer." The owner replied, "You told me yesterday to think it over, and I have, I accept." The farmer then replied, "You had your chance and you blew it." After the farmer refused to sell the chickens to him, the owner sued for breach of contract.

Is there an enforceable contract between the parties?

(A) No, because the offer terminated due to lapse of time.

(B) No, because the farmer revoked the offer before the owner accepted it.

(C) Yes, because the farmer's statement, "Why don't you think it over until tomorrow," revived the offer, which the owner subsequently accepted in a timely fashion.

(D) Yes, because the farmer made the owner a firm offer, which was irrevocable.

Question 9

A rare coin dealer and a collector met at a stamp-and-coin fair that was held on a monthly basis. The dealer had a mint condition 1905 Silver Eagle in his inventory that was valued at well over $10,000. The collector desperately wanted to purchase the coin, but knew that he did not have enough money to make the purchase. The two spoke for a while, and before leaving, the following note was written from the dealer to the collector: "I will hold the 1905 Silver Eagle you were eyeing up at the fair today for sale to you alone until the next fair." The dealer signed and dated the note and handed it to the collector.

If the collector wanted to purchase the coin at the following fair, is the offer still in force?

(A) No, because there was no consideration provided to keep the offer open until the next fair.

(B) No, because "until the next fair" does not state a sufficient period of time.

(C) Yes, because it was a firm offer.

(D) Yes, because the offer concerned the sale of goods.

Question 10

A chef negotiated with a contractor to remodel his home kitchen to look like the kitchen in his restaurant. In order to do this, the contractor had to order top-of-the-line appliances. He also needed to remove some sections of a wall and install new electrical sockets to accommodate the appliances. The cost of the remodel was $50,000, with two-thirds of the price coming from the purchase of the appliances. A dispute arose and the parties both suspended their obligations. The contractor refused to further perform and the chef refused to pay the contractor.

What law should be used to analyze the dispute?

(A) The UCC applies to the purchase of the appliances and common law applies to the delivery, the wall removal, and the electrical socket installation.

(B) The UCC should be applied to the entire transaction, because the primary purpose of the contract was the appliances, which account for the overwhelming majority of the contract price.

(C) Common law should be applied to the entire transaction, because the primary purpose was to provide a service, regardless of the cost of the appliances.

(D) When a contract is for both goods and services, in the absence of a choice-of-law selection clause, common law is the default law to be applied.

Question 11

On October 1, a seller mailed a letter to a buyer offering to sell a specified quantity of shirts at list price. The buyer received the seller's offer on October 2. The next day, the buyer mailed the seller a letter of rejection. The buyer then changed his mind and decided to accept the seller's offer. On October 4, the seller sent the buyer a letter revoking his original October 1 offer. On October 5, the buyer emailed the seller indicating that he wished to accept the seller's offer. The seller read the email on October 6. On October 7, the buyer received the seller's letter of revocation. The following day, the seller received the buyer's rejection. The seller subsequently refused to sell the shirts to the buyer, and the buyer sued for breach of contract. Assume that the buyer's email complies with the Statute of Frauds.

Which of the following is most accurate?

(A) Judgment for the buyer, because he accepted in a reasonable manner and before receiving notice of the seller's revocation.

(B) Judgment for the buyer, because his acceptance was effective upon dispatch.

(C) Judgment for the seller, because he revoked his offer before receiving the buyer's acceptance.

(D) Judgment for the seller, because the buyer did not accept in a proper manner.

Question 12

A woman had known a hairstylist for many years. One day, the hairstylist was walking through the mall when he ran into the woman. The hairstylist said to the woman, "If you come by the shop tomorrow, I will straighten your hair for $20." The woman replied, "That's a great price." Thereupon the woman's husband approached and the three then started gossiping about a man who walked by wearing some out-of-fashion shoes.

The next day, the woman arrived at the hairstylist's shop and said, "I accept your offer." The hairstylist replied, "I can't straighten your hair because after we spoke yesterday, I contracted with several other people to do their hair, and now I'm all booked up."

If the woman sues the hairstylist for breach of contract, who will likely prevail?

(A) The woman, because she relied on the hairstylist's promise by coming to the shop.

(B) The woman, because she accepted the offer before the hairstylist revoked it.

(C) The hairstylist, because he contracted with other people to do their hair.

(D) The hairstylist, because the woman did not accept during their conversation.

Question 13

A six-year-old girl was kidnapped outside her home in a small town. Following the girl's abduction, her parents publicly announced a $50,000 reward to anyone responsible for the apprehension of the kidnapper. The girl's abductor was described as a Caucasian male between the ages of 25 and 30 with curly blond hair. He also was identified as having a pentagram tattoo on his left arm. One afternoon, an off-duty police officer from a nearby town stopped at a local fast-food restaurant for lunch. The officer was aware of the kidnapping, but was unaware of the reward. Once he entered the restaurant, the police officer noticed a man fitting the description of the kidnapper. The police officer proceeded to arrest the individual, who, in fact, turned out to be the girl's abductor. After the girl was found unharmed, the police officer learned of and requested the $50,000 reward. However, the girl's parents refused to pay the police officer the reward money.

If the police officer brings suit against the girl's parents to recover the $50,000 reward, for whom should the court enter judgment?

(A) The police officer, because he accepted the offer by apprehending the kidnapper.

(B) The police officer, because he was off duty when the apprehension occurred.

(C) The girl's parents, because the officer was unaware of the reward when he apprehended the kidnapper.

(D) The girl's parents, because recovery of a reward by a police officer is against public policy.

Question 14

A businessman lived in Japan. He sent a letter to a California car dealership stating that if the dealership would extend his son the credit, he would guarantee the purchase price of any car. The dealership received the letter on February 9, and on February 10, sold a car to the son for $11,500. On February 11, the businessman died suddenly. Unaware of his death, the agency sent him a letter indicating its acceptance of the offer and notifying him of the sale. The dealership also noted that the son had a good credit rating and that the dealership would have extended him credit even without his father's guarantee. Two months later, the son also died suddenly, leaving a bankrupt estate. The dealership then sought to recover the balance of the car's purchase price from the businessman's estate.

Would the dealership prevail in a suit against the businessman's estate for the balance owed on the car?

(A) No, because the dealership would have sold the car to the son even without the businessman's guarantee of the purchase price.

(B) No, because the businessman died before the dealership mailed the letter notifying him of its acceptance.

(C) Yes, because the dealership accepted the businessman's offer before his death.

(D) Yes, because the dealership foreseeably, justifiably, and reasonably relied on the businessman's promise.

Question 15

A carpet cleaner sent the following terms in a writing to a homeowner. "I will clean your carpets up to 1,000 square feet for a price of $100 per room. This offer is non-cancellable for 60 days from today." The carpet cleaner dated the letter and signed it at the bottom. The homeowner received the letter and immediately wrote a letter accepting the carpet cleaner's terms, but did not immediately send the letter.

A week after sending his letter to the homeowner, the carpet cleaner received an offer from a hotel owner requesting his services for the next month at several of his hotels. The carpet cleaner wanted to accept the hotel owner's offer, but was concerned about the outstanding letter to the homeowner.

Which of the following is most accurate?

(A) The carpet cleaner can revoke his offer to the homeowner, because the mailbox rule does not apply to option contracts.

(B) The carpet cleaner can revoke his offer to the homeowner, because there was no consideration provided that would make the offer irrevocable.

(C) The homeowner has manifested his intent to accept, and if he accepts within 60 days of the date of the letter, there is a contract.

(D) The homeowner has three months from the date of the letter to accept, because offers from merchants are irrevocable.

Question 16

On Monday, Jim decided to sell his vintage car. Bill had always admired the car and inquired as soon as he saw the for-sale sign. Jim said he was firm at $5,000. Bill thought this was a good price, and told Jim he wanted it, but needed to check with his wife before spending such a large amount of money. In the meantime, Bill pulled a $100 bill from his pocket and gave it to Jim, saying, "Here's a down payment. See you tomorrow!" Jim replied, "Okay, it will be here." On Tuesday morning, Bill approached Jim with a check written out for $4,900. Jim said, "Sorry, but you're too late. I accepted an offer last night for $10,000."

In an action by Bill against Jim for breach of contract, how should the court rule?

(A) For Jim, because $100 is insufficient to create an option contract for a $5,000 car.

(B) For Jim, because Bill's language was insufficient to create a valid option contract.

(C) For Bill, because Jim created an option contract, which is irrevocable at least until the following day.

(D) For Bill, because the UCC precludes Jim from selling the car to anyone other than Bill before Wednesday.

Question 17

The owner of a lakefront house had leased the house to a renter for the past three summers. Last year, on October 1, the owner sent the renter a letter stating, "Because you have been such a great tenant, I will rent you the house on the same terms as last year. However, I need your answer by February 1." The renter, uncertain as to when he would be taking his annual vacation, decided to put the letter aside for the time being, intending to respond to it by February 1.

On January 15, the owner received an offer from the renter's cousin to rent the house at a higher price than the renter had paid the prior year. The owner accepted. On January 20, after learning about his cousin's rental, the renter telephoned the owner and said, "I have decided that I want the house for the summer." The owner replied that he had already accepted an offer to rent the house from the renter's cousin. The renter then filed a lawsuit seeking to enforce the contract.

If the renter is unsuccessful in his lawsuit, which of the following provides the best reason?

(A) The contract with the cousin indirectly revoked the offer to the renter.

(B) The contract with the cousin terminated the offer to the renter.

(C) There was no mutual assent, because the renter was unsure whether he wanted to vacation at the lake.

(D) A common law offer cannot extend beyond three months without consideration.

Question 18

On December 1, Arnold, who had purchased two tickets for a holiday magic show, sent the following email to his three friends, Baker, Charlie, and Dora:

"Dear Baker, Charlie, and Dora: I have two tickets for the upcoming holiday magic show. If any of you are interested in buying my tickets, I will let you have them for a reasonable price, but I must have your reply by December 20.

s/Arnold"

The tickets, which cost Arnold $10, were now selling for between $50 and $70. On December 19, Arnold received an email from Baker that stated, "I accept your offer and will pay you $50 for the two tickets." Arnold did not immediately respond to Baker's email. On December 22, Arnold received the following text message from Charlie: "I am dying to go to the concert…will pay $70 for your seats." The next day, Arnold sent a reply text to Charlie which read: "The tickets are yours. You may take delivery upon payment of the $70." Dora did not respond to Arnold's letter. Baker tendered the $50 to Arnold within a reasonable time, but Arnold refused to sell the tickets to him.

In an action by Baker against Arnold for breach of contract, judgment should be for whom?

(A) Arnold, because his email of December 1 and Baker's reply were too indefinite to constitute an offer and acceptance.

(B) Arnold, because his email was not an offer, but rather, an invitation to bargain, and he was free to accept either Baker or Charlie's offer.

(C) Baker, because he accepted Arnold's offer first.

(D) Baker, because Arnold's offer lapsed on December 20, and therefore, Charlie's attempted acceptance was invalid.

Question 19

A seller sent an email to a potential buyer offering to sell his patio furniture to her for $5,000. The buyer immediately responded via email asking whether the offer included the umbrella that was sitting in the garage. The seller emailed back: "No, it does not; just what is sitting on the patio. If you want an umbrella, you will have to buy one." The buyer then ordered an umbrella that would fit on the table and matched the color of the chairs. Later that day, the buyer replied to the seller: "I accept your offer." The seller then wrote back, "I have changed my mind, I've decided to keep the furniture."

If the buyer sues the seller claiming there was a valid contract, who is likely to prevail?

(A) The buyer, because she accepted the seller's offer within a reasonable amount of time and before the seller revoked his offer.

(B) The buyer, because her ordering the umbrella is a sufficient act in reliance on the seller's offer.

(C) The seller, because the offer lapsed after the buyer did not accept the original offer.

(D) The seller, because the buyer's initial email was a counteroffer which terminated her power of acceptance.

Question 20

A famous football player had his dog stolen from his yard. He immediately went to social media and implored anyone with details to contact him. He put a description of the dog, where it was last seen, and said that he would be forever indebted to whomever found his dog.

One particular fan immediately went out looking for the dog in the area surrounding the player's home. A few days passed and the player became desperate, so he offered a $5,000 reward for finding the dog. After several days of looking, the fan finally saw the dog tied to a bench. He untied the dog and went onto the player's website to contact him. The fan then saw the reward offer and returned the dog, demanding the reward. The player refused to pay the fan the $5,000.

Is the player liable to pay the fan the reward money?

(A) No, because the fan did not know of the reward before he found the dog.

(B) No, because the player was unaware that the fan had accepted the offer.

(C) Yes, because the fan found the dog as requested.

(D) Yes, because the fan learned of the reward before he returned the dog.

Essays

Essay Question 1

IE13JUL001

ISSUE SPOTTING EXERCISE

Consider the fact pattern below and then answer the questions that follow:

A lifelong stamp collector was proud of the large and valuable collection he had amassed. Many of his stamps were extremely rare and highly coveted by others.

On numerous occasions, the collector had rejected offers to sell his prized collection. Finally, on December 1, the collector sent his neighbor, who was also an avid stamp collector, the following letter:

"I've decided to finally sell my stamp collection. Because I want it to go to someone who will appreciate it, I'll sell you my entire collection for $75,000. You have until December 15 to make up your mind."

The neighbor received the letter the next day. On December 5, the collector sold his stamps to his cousin for $100,000. On December 6, the neighbor saw the collector's cousin with the collection, and immediately called the collector to accept his offer.

1. *What was the legal effect of the collector's December 1st letter?*

2. *What was the legal effect of the neighbor's December 6th call to the collector?*

ISSUE 1

Identify the primary legal concept being tested in this issue:

Which part of the prompt provides you with the most information with regard to the legal significance of the December 1st letter?

ISSUE 2

Identify the primary legal concept being tested in this issue:

Identify two facts from the prompt that help you to determine the legal significance of the December 6th phone call:

1.

2.

Essay Question 1

IE13JUL001

RULE RECOLLECTION EXERCISE

A good rule statement will demonstrate your understanding of the law and provide the foundation for your analysis. This exercise is intended to help you practice: (1) recalling the relevant rules of law; (2) organizing rules of law; and (3) explaining legal concepts completely and concisely.

- PUT AWAY YOUR NOTES for this exercise and practice actively trying to recall the relevant rules.
- In FIFTEEN minutes, write out rule statements for the following issues.
- WRITE THESE RULES OUT IN FULL; do not merely jot down concepts, topics, or fragments.

DECEMBER 1st LETTER

Controlling Law

Offer

Firm Offer

DECEMBER 6th PHONE CALL

Revocation

Termination of Power of Acceptance

Communication of Offeror's Revocation

Essay Question 1

IE13JUL001

ANALYSIS EXERCISE

Connect law (rules) to fact, and draft your analysis paragraph for each issue below.

DECEMBER 1st LETTER

Controlling Law

Offer

Firm Offer

DECEMBER 6th PHONE CALL

Revocation

Termination of Power of Acceptance

Communication of Offeror's Revocation

Essay Question 2

IE13JUL002

Ed is the owner of the newly opened Ed's Custom Car Wash, which was located 20 miles outside of Ed's hometown. One day, while grocery shopping, Ed was greeted by his childhood friend, Alice. The two chatted for some time, and as he was leaving, Ed said, "Come on by my new business tomorrow, and I'll give you a free car wash." Alice replied, "Thanks. By the way, we've got a few extra tickets for the game tonight; if you want them, they're yours."

A few minutes later, Ed ran into Officer Brown, who worked in Ed's hometown. Ed told him, "Officer Brown, would you mind driving by my house soon and making sure everything is okay? If you do, I'll give you a free car wash tomorrow." Officer Brown, who was already about to begin patrolling Ed's neighborhood, replied, "I accept your kind offer." Officer Brown then left the store and began his routine patrol, which, as always, promptly took him by Ed's house, where everything was in order.

When Ed eventually returned home from shopping, he saw his next-door neighbor, Charlie. Ed waved at Charlie and said to him, "Charlie, I'll give you a free car wash tomorrow at my new car wash." Charlie replied, "Thanks, I'll take you up on that."

As Ed arrived at work the next day, he found a long line of cars already waiting at the car wash. He called Alice and Officer Brown and told them that he would not be able to give them free car washes. He then saw Charlie, who had left work and driven for a half-hour to get to Ed's car wash, was waiting in line. Ed immediately went up to Charlie and told him, "I'm sorry, but I am not going to give you a free car wash."

Does Ed have an enforceable obligation to Alice, Officer Brown, or Charlie? Discuss.

KAPLAN BAR REVIEW

Criminal Law

Exercise Set 1

Question 1a

Identify the four types of murder:

Question 1b

Identify the two types of manslaughter:

Question 2

Identify the defenses to murder:

For the following exercises, you are given a question prompt. After reading the question prompt, consider the applicable rules. Then, brainstorm possible issues that could be raised or tested based on the given question prompt.

Question 3

If charged with victim's death, which of the following is the most serious crime the defendant committed?

Question 4

Can the defendant be found guilty of murder?

Question 5

What is the defendant's best defense to the murder charge?

Question 6

If the man is prosecuted for manslaughter, what would be his best chance for acquittal?

For each of the following fact patterns and question prompts, write out the relevant issues and their corresponding rule statements.

Question 7

At a party for coworkers at the defendant's home, the victim accused the defendant of making advances toward his wife. The victim and his wife left the party. The next day at work, the defendant saw the victim and struck him on the head with a heavy paperweight. The victim fell into a coma and died two weeks after the incident.

Can the defendant be found guilty of murder?

Question 8

A two-year-old girl was brought into an emergency room by a babysitter, and the doctors there diagnosed the child as having meningitis. However, because her parents were skeptical of modern science and medicine, her parents ignored the doctor's urgent advice and refused to have her admitted into the hospital. Instead, they brought their child home and gave her home-brewed remedies that they found during an internet search. The daughter died of the illness within a week. An autopsy determined that the child would not have died if she had been provided appropriate medical care sooner.

What is the most serious crime for which the parents could be found guilty?

Question 9

After deciding to destroy her dilapidated building in order to collect the insurance money, a woman carefully searched it to make sure no one was inside. However, she failed to notice a vagrant asleep in an office closet. Not aware of the man's presence in the building, she started a fire. As a result, the building was destroyed, and the vagrant died from burns a week later. Two days after the fire, the woman filed an insurance claim in which she stated that she had no information about the cause of the fire. In this jurisdiction, arson is defined as the malicious burning of a structure.

What is the most serious crime committed by the woman

Question 10

One evening, a husband came home from work and slapped his wife several times across the face because he didn't like what she had made for dinner. He then stormed out of the home and went out to a local bar. A couple of hours later, the wife was looking out the window when she saw her husband staggering across the street. He was visibly intoxicated and clearly had trouble keeping his balance. When the husband reached the middle of the street, he collapsed and fell down on the pavement. Seeing her husband lying in the street, the wife's initial reaction was to go outside and assist him. However, she decided not to because she was still angry because of the beating she had received earlier in the evening. Minutes later, a car traveling at an excessive rate of speed struck and killed the husband.

What is the most serious crime for which the wife may be properly convicted?

Exercise Set 2

Question 1

Complete the following chart with the specific actus reus and mens rea for each of the different types of murder.

Intent-to-kill murder		
Intent-to-inflict-serious-bodily-injury/harm murder		
Depraved-heart murder		
Felony murder		

Question 2

Complete the following chart with the type of manslaughter that corresponds to the given actus reus and mens rea.

	Actual and proximate cause of another person's death.	Recklessness or criminal (gross) negligence.
	Actual and proximate cause of another person's death.	An intent to kill that arises from an honest but unreasonable belief that deadly force is necessary to protect oneself or another from an attack.
	Death of another person occurs during the commission or attempted commission of an unlawful act.	An intent to commit an unlawful act (other than an inherently dangerous felony).
	Actual and proximate cause of another person's death.	An intent to kill in circumstances where a reasonable person would not be able to control or resist their homicidal impulse.

For the following fact patterns, complete the chart with the relevant facts that correspond to the rule(s) provided.

Question 3

The defendant works in midtown Manhattan, near the Empire State Building. One day, during her lunch hour, she went up to the Empire State Building's Observatory Deck in order to celebrate the birthday of the famous scientist, Galileo, by replicating this scientist's famous gravity experiment. And so, from the Observatory Deck, the defendant dropped a bowling ball and a small marble to test whether the differently weighted objects did indeed fall at the same rate of speed. Unfortunately, a passing pedestrian was accidentally struck in the head by one of these falling objects. The pedestrian was killed instantly.

If, as a result of the pedestrian's death, the defendant is charged with murder, will she be found guilty?

RULE	RELEVANT FACTS
Depraved-heart murder	

Question 4

David went to a local bar to watch a college football game. During the game, he had a few beers. Near the end of the game, he got into a fight with a fan of a rival school's football team. This bar brawl ended when one of David's punches caught the fan square on the jaw. The fan fell over backwards. Unfortunately, when the fan's head hit the floor, he suffered an injury that ultimately proved to be fatal.

Is David guilty of murder?

RULE	RELEVANT FACTS
Misdemeanor manslaughter	

Question 5

Joe hated his rich uncle and wanted to destroy the portrait of him that hung in his uncle's mansion. The mansion had a second-floor window through which the portrait could be seen hanging in his uncle's den. Joe took out a rifle and pointed it at the window, using the rifle's scope to take aim at the portrait. Joe fired the rifle. The bullet went through the window, but hit the bottom of a chandelier and glanced off to the left of the portrait, hitting the uncle's butler in the chest and killing him instantly.

What is the most serious crime for which Joe can be found guilty?

RULE	RELEVANT FACTS
Depraved-heart murder	

Question 6

Denise went to a local bar to watch a college football game. Angry at her team's poor play, she decided to take out her anger on a nearby fan of a rival school's team, whacking the fan in the back of the head with a beer bottle. Although momentarily dazed by this unprovoked attack, the fan turned around to see Denise getting ready to swing the beer bottle at his head again. In self-defense, the fan flung himself at Denise and tackled her, hoping only to thwart Denise from injuring him further. In the ensuing melee, Denise honestly believed that the fan was trying to put her in a lethal chokehold and that her only means of escape was to counter with her own lethal chokehold. The melee ultimately ended with Denise injured but victorious, the fan fatally injured with a broken neck, and the police arriving on the scene to take Denise away in handcuffs.

Is Denise not guilty of any criminal homicide because she acted in self-defense?

RULE	RELEVANT FACTS
Voluntary manslaughter (imperfect self-defense)	

Question 7

A driver was speeding on a highway when he lost control of his car. Before he was able to regain control, it clipped the rear-left of another car, which crashed into a barrier. A passenger in this other car died as a result of injuries sustained in this crash.

What is the most serious crime for which the driver can be found guilty?

RULE	RELEVANT FACTS
Involuntary manslaughter	

For each of the following fact patterns and question prompts, identify the applicable rules and complete the chart with the relevant facts.

Question 8

One evening, a woman was obeying the speed limit and exercising due care while driving home. As she was driving down a residential street near her home, another automobile suddenly pulled out of a driveway immediately in front of her. The woman's car struck this automobile broadside. The driver of the other car was killed as a result of the collision. Police later discovered that the woman was driving without insurance, which is a misdemeanor in this jurisdiction.

If the woman is prosecuted for manslaughter, what would be her best chance for acquittal?

RULES	RELEVANT FACTS

Question 9

A teenager joined a neighborhood gang. As part of the initiation process, the leader ordered the teenager to kill a member of a rival gang. The teenager refused, saying that he no longer wanted to be part of the group. The leader, with the approval of the other members, told the teenager that he had become too involved with the gang to quit now, and that they would kill him if he did not commit the murder. The next day, the teenager was armed with a gun when he saw the rival gang member sitting on a motorcycle outside a restaurant. The teenager at first hesitated, but then shot and killed the rival gang member. In this jurisdiction, first-degree murder is defined as the intentional, premeditated killing of another.

If the teenager killed the rival because of the threat to his own life, should the teenager be found guilty of first-degree murder?

RULES	RELEVANT FACTS

Question 10

While walking home one evening, an off-duty police officer was accosted by a stranger. The stranger had been drinking, and mistakenly thought the off-duty police officer was a man having an affair with his wife. Intending to frighten the off-duty officer but not harm him, the stranger pulled out a knife, screamed obscenities, and told the off-duty officer that he was going to kill him. Frightened and reasonably believing that the stranger was going to kill him and that using deadly force was his only salvation, the off-duty officer took out his service revolver and shot the stranger, killing him. The off-duty officer was charged with murder.

If the off-duty officer claims self-defense, how should the court rule?

RULES	RELEVANT FACTS

Quiz 1

Question 1

A defendant had an argument with his neighbor. As they were quarreling, the defendant pulled out his penknife intending only to frighten the neighbor. The defendant accidentally slightly nicked the neighbor's arm with the knife. Unknown to the defendant, his neighbor was a hemophiliac who then died from the cut.

What is the most serious crime of which the defendant can be convicted?

(A) Murder.

(B) Voluntary manslaughter.

(C) Involuntary manslaughter.

(D) Battery.

Question 2

A defendant wished to see his high school basketball team win the state championship. During an important game, the defendant pulled out a gun and shot at the leg of a key player on the opposing team. The defendant intended only to inflict a slight wound so that the opposing player would be unable to complete the game. When the defendant fired the shot, he unintentionally hit a player on his own high school team in the chest, killing him instantly.

What is the most serious crime of which the defendant can be convicted?

(A) Murder.

(B) Voluntary manslaughter.

(C) Involuntary manslaughter.

(D) Battery.

Question 3

A defendant hated his boss, who had recently demoted him to a less prestigious position. Late one afternoon, the defendant saw his boss walking down the hallway. The defendant pulled out a gun and fired four shots at his boss. Although none of the bullets directly hit his boss, one of the shots ricocheted against a wall and struck the boss in the head, killing him instantly.

What is the most serious crime of which the defendant can be convicted?

(A) Murder.

(B) Voluntary manslaughter.

(C) Involuntary manslaughter.

(D) Battery.

Question 4

One afternoon, a man was driving his car in the downtown section of a city. Already late for a business appointment, he was becoming very upset because of the heavy traffic. Suddenly, he decided to drive his car along the sidewalk to avoid the traffic jam. While he was speeding down the sidewalk, people were hastily scurrying to avoid his car. His car struck a pedestrian, who had tripped trying to get out of his way, killing her.

Which of the following is the best theory regarding the man's criminal liability?

(A) Felony murder, because he was committing an assault with a deadly weapon.

(B) Transferred intent, because one is presumed to intend the natural and probable consequences of his acts.

(C) Intentional killing, because the man's conduct was a substantial factor in causing the pedestrian's death.

(D) Commission of an act highly dangerous to life, without an intent to kill but with disregard for the consequences.

Question 5

A man's mother has lived with him for 20 years, and for the past several months she has been suffering from terminal cancer. Tired of her constant demands, the man begins to add a small amount of poison to his mother's liquid medication each day. When the mother dies, the medical examiner determines that the cancer would have killed her within a few days, but that her death was hastened by the poison.

If the man is prosecuted for murder, what should the result be?

(A) The man should be convicted, because his actions showed a depraved indifference to the value of human life.

(B) The man should be acquitted, because his mother was ill and in pain.

(C) The man should be acquitted, because his mother would have died almost immediately from cancer.

(D) The man should be acquitted, because the man's actions alone would not have caused the death.

Question 6

A husband came home early from work one day. He walked to the bedroom and, upon opening the door, saw his wife and another man in bed together. Visibly upset, the husband told the other man to leave. As the man was reaching for his pants, he pulled out a gun, fearing that the husband was about to attack him. When the husband saw the gun, he jumped on the man and angrily twisted his neck, breaking it and killing him.

The husband is guilty for which, if any, of the following crimes?

(A) Murder.

(B) Voluntary manslaughter.

(C) Involuntary manslaughter.

(D) No crime.

Question 7

A defendant was walking through a park when he decided to rob someone. He hid behind a tree, lying in wait for a victim to approach. Shortly thereafter, a girl was strolling in the park when the defendant suddenly jumped from his hiding place and accosted her. Although the defendant intended only to rob his victim, he punched her in the mouth and she fell to the ground. The defendant then grabbed her purse and fled. Unknown to the defendant, the girl suffered a fractured skull when her head struck the pavement. She subsequently died from her head injuries.

Which of the following is the most serious crime for which the defendant can be found guilty?

(A) Murder.

(B) Felony murder.

(C) Involuntary manslaughter.

(D) Voluntary manslaughter.

Question 8

One night, two teenagers, ages 17 and 18, were walking home from their jobs at a pizza shop. As they passed a large house, the older boy told the younger one that as a kid, he had worked in a hotel for the family that owned both that house and the hotel in which he worked. He also told the younger boy that when he had worked at the hotel, rumor had it that the hotel owner skimmed most of the cash off the top of his businesses, and that he had accumulated more than $500,000 in cash, which he kept hidden in the basement of his home. The younger boy grew extremely excited at the thought of all that cash there for the taking. They spontaneously decided to sneak into the house and steal the money. They jumped the fence surrounding the property and crept through the backyard of the house. They were attempting to jimmy the downstairs window when they heard the owner yelling, "Hey, who's there?" Frightened, the boys began running away, chased by the incensed homeowner. However, before he could catch up to them, the homeowner suffered a heart attack from the excitement and extreme physical exertion and died.

If the teenagers are charged with homicide, they will likely be found guilty of what crime?

(A) Felony murder.

(B) Involuntary manslaughter.

(C) First-degree murder.

(D) No crime, because they intended no death.

Question 9

A defendant was charged with felony murder as a result of his setting fire to the victim's house. The victim was upstairs sleeping when the fire was set, and he died in his bedroom during the fire.

If the defendant can prove the facts to support his defense, which of the following assertions would least likely remove liability for felony murder?

(A) The defendant did not intend to kill the victim.

(B) The defendant was insane when he set the fire.

(C) The defendant was coerced by another to set the fire.

(D) The victim died in his sleep before the fire spread to his bedroom.

Question 10

A legislature, determined to do something about impatient drivers who put others at risk, enacts a law that driving in the breakdown lane without a legitimate reason to do so is a misdemeanor. The same act, if it proximately causes serious injury, is a felony. Several months later, the defendant was stuck in traffic and tried to go around the traffic bottleneck by driving in the breakdown lane. After driving in the breakdown lane for about a quarter of a mile, the defendant's vehicle crested a hill. Just past the crest, he saw a stalled car in the breakdown lane. The defendant could not stop in time, so he tried to swerve back into the right-hand lane of the highway. His car struck a minivan in the right-hand lane, which flipped over, killing the driver.

What is the most serious crime of which the defendant can be convicted?

(A) Involuntary manslaughter.

(B) Depraved-heart murder.

(C) Intent-to-cause-serious-bodily-injury murder.

(D) Felony murder.

Question 11

A father took his son to an outdoor concert put on by a famous pop singer. The father left his son in his seat and went to the bathroom. While in the bathroom, the father saw a man placing what he believed to be a bomb inside a trash can. The father immediately went back to his seat, grabbed his son, and left the concert. On the way to his seat and to the exit, the father passed several security guards, but said nothing to them as to what he had seen.

Shortly after leaving, the bomb exploded, killing several concertgoers and injuring dozens more. The father felt bad for what transpired, and confessed to a police officer, who then arrested him. In this jurisdiction, homicide is defined as at common law.

Which of the following is most accurate?

(A) The father is guilty of manslaughter, because his failure to act was grossly negligent.

(B) The father is guilty of depraved-heart murder, because his conduct evidenced a wanton disregard for the value of human life.

(C) The father is guilty of murder, because he believed the man was placing a bomb inside the garbage can.

(D) The father is not guilty of any crime.

Question 12

The defendant considers himself the greatest and most inventive practical joker on earth. He plans a dinner party incorporating an elaborate joke to spook his guests. The planned joke involves a timed fire near the dining room door, set to go off as the defendant's guests are eating dinner. The defendant has treated the walls, door, ceiling, and floor of the room with a special fireproof finish to prevent them from igniting, and the fire is set to burn for only 45 seconds. On the night of the dinner party, the defendant is electric with anticipation; he cannot wait to see the terrified looks on his friends' faces. However, when the fire goes off as planned, a woman, one of the guests, panics and runs from the room through the only doorway, which is precisely where the flames are. As the woman runs through the flames, her clothes catch fire, and she dies from her injuries.

The defendant should be convicted of which of the following crimes?

(A) First-degree murder.

(B) Involuntary manslaughter.

(C) Voluntary manslaughter.

(D) No crime.

Question 13

A senior associate in a law firm was conducting spot checks of other associates as they left the office to determine who had taken some documents that were missing from the firm's library. A young associate was leaving his office for the day when he was stopped by the defendant, who asked him to open his briefcase. The senior associate explained that some files from the law office had been stolen. Startled, the young associate refused to permit the senior associate to look in his briefcase. The young associate said that he had personal papers in his briefcase and he didn't want the senior associate to see them. Having his suspicions aroused, the senior associate raised his clenched fist and exclaimed, "If you don't hand over that briefcase, I'm going to punch you in the mouth." The young associate, who, unknown to the senior associate, suffered from a serious heart condition, had a seizure and died as a result of fright produced by the threatened attack.

Which of the following is the most serious crime for which the senior associate should be found guilty?

(A) Assault.

(B) Voluntary manslaughter.

(C) Involuntary manslaughter.

(D) Murder.

Question 14

A gang member got into a fight with another young man. Their friends broke up the fight. The gang member, however, remained angry. Later that day, he decided he would kill the young man. The gang member placed a loaded gun in his coat pocket and went outside looking for the young man. He had no idea where to find the young man, so he decided to patrol the neighborhood. After an hour or so, he passed a local bar and decided to go inside and have a drink. While at the bar, he consumed twelve bottles of beer and became very intoxicated. He left the bar and began his search again. Ten minutes later, the gang member ran into the young man on the sidewalk. The two men got into a verbal argument during which the young man threatened to cause bodily injury to the gang member's parents and siblings. The gang member became angry and pulled out his gun and shot the young man to death. When the gang member woke up the next morning, the effect of the alcohol had mostly worn off. He had only a hazy recollection of what happened the night before, and he could not remember killing the young man.

What is the most serious crime of which the gang member could be properly convicted?

(A) Voluntary manslaughter, because he acted under adequate provocation.

(B) Depraved-heart murder, because he acted with a wanton indifference to human life.

(C) Second-degree murder, because his intoxication prevented him from acting with premeditation or deliberation.

(D) First-degree murder, because he acted with premeditation and deliberation.

Question 15

After weeks of deliberation, the defendant decided to rob a local liquor store. The defendant purchased a ski mask and then went into the liquor store, put his gun into the face of the clerk, and demanded the money from the register. Terrified, the clerk gave him the money from the register. The defendant pocketed the money, grabbed a bottle of tequila off the shelf for his celebration, and then ran back to the car and drove off. About an hour later, the defendant was slowly approaching his hideout in the outskirts of town when a young child suddenly darted in front of the defendant's car. He applied the brakes but couldn't stop in time. The car struck the child, killing her.

For the child's death, the defendant should be found guilty of which, if any, of the following crimes?

(A) Felony murder.

(B) Involuntary manslaughter.

(C) Voluntary manslaughter.

(D) No crime.

Question 16

A defendant shot and killed a victim at close range with a revolver. After the shooting death, the defendant was arrested and charged with first-degree murder. In this jurisdiction, first-degree murder is defined as "knowingly or willfully causing the death of another human being."

Which of the following situations, if believed by the jury, would most likely result in the defendant's acquittal of the first-degree murder charge?

(A) The victim, who was the defendant's brother, suffered from an incurable case of cancer and asked the defendant to kill him to put an end to his pain and suffering.

(B) The killing was not done with premeditation or deliberation.

(C) The defendant intended to kill himself, but the bullet grazed his head and struck and killed the victim.

(D) The defendant intended to kill another man, but the victim unknowingly stepped in front of the other man and was struck and killed by the bullet.

Question 17

A victim was leaving his favorite local watering hole and contemplating a late night cheeseburger when he tripped over his own feet and fell on the sidewalk. A few moments later, the victim got up in a daze and stepped into the street, where he was struck by a car driven by the defendant, who was driving 35 miles per hour, and could not brake in time to avoid the victim. The posted speed limit was 25 miles per hour. The victim died in the hospital two hours later.

What is the most serious crime for which the defendant can be found guilty?

(A) Felony murder.

(B) Involuntary manslaughter.

(C) Voluntary manslaughter.

(D) Depraved-heart murder.

Question 18

A breeder and owner of vicious guard dogs trained his dogs to attack strangers at night. He often sold and leased his guard dogs to various business and factory owners who used the guard dogs to frighten away intruders from entering their premises at night. One evening, the breeder was in the back yard of his home training three of his guard dogs. The back yard was enclosed with a chain link fence and a latched gate that prevented the dogs from running out. After the training session, the breeder opened the gate and permitted the dogs to run loose in his front yard. Minutes later, a man was walking along the sidewalk in front of the breeder's house when he was attacked by one of the dogs. The man suffered severe injuries and died as a result of the attack.

The breeder should be found guilty of what crime?

(A) Murder.

(B) Involuntary manslaughter.

(C) Voluntary manslaughter.

(D) Reckless endangerment.

Question 19

One evening, the defendant was playing football with his son in the front yard of his house. The night before, a rainstorm had felled a large branch from a tree in his neighbor's yard, and the branch now lay across the fence that divided the defendant's and his neighbor's properties. When the defendant's wife came outside to tell the defendant and his son that dinner would be ready soon, the defendant launched into a tirade about the fallen branch. His wife responded that she and the neighbor had discussed the branch over coffee that morning, and that she had told the neighbor that the defendant would take care of it. Seething with anger, the defendant made no response and continued playing catch with his son. Several minutes later, the defendant's neighbor stepped outside, and the defendant immediately began yelling about the branch. The irritated neighbor responded, "Your wife is a liar and she shouldn't have told me you'd move the branch if you're not going to." Infuriated, the defendant hurled the football in his hand at the neighbor's head. The football hit the neighbor's neck at an odd angle, breaking his neck and killing him instantly.

Of what crime can the defendant be found guilty?

(A) First-degree murder.

(B) Second-degree murder.

(C) Voluntary manslaughter.

(D) Involuntary manslaughter.

Question 20

A night watchman became annoyed at his next-door neighbor who was remodeling his house. The noise from the jackhammering was so loud that the night watchman could not fall asleep. The night watchman knocked on the door, asked the neighbor to keep it down, and the neighbor simply replied, "Sucks to be you!" Angered, the night watchman went home and got his service revolver. Not intending to shoot anyone, he fired a bullet through the open first floor window at the jackhammer, as he merely wanted to put an end to the noise. The bullet, however, ricocheted off the jackhammer and struck a construction worker in the head, killing him. The jurisdiction makes it a misdemeanor to discharge a firearm in public.

For what crime should the night watchman be found guilty?

(A) Murder.

(B) Involuntary manslaughter.

(C) Voluntary manslaughter.

(D) Discharge of a firearm in public.

Quiz 2

Question 1

A teenage brother and sister had heard that a locally notorious immigrant, who had become extremely wealthy through a number of ethically questionable business ventures, did not trust American banks and kept all his money in a suitcase in his garage. One night, the teenagers decided to sneak into the man's garage and steal the suitcase full of cash. They jumped the fence surrounding his home and attempted to jimmy the garage door. They had just managed to enter the garage when his dog, alerted by the noises coming from the garage area, began barking furiously, causing the man to come out to investigate. In a panic, the brother grabbed a bicycle that was sitting in the garage and beckoned his sister to get on. They rode away as fast as they could, with the sister perched on the bike's handlebars, as the man chased after them yelling for help. As they turned a corner, however, they were met by a policeman who heard the commotion. Sensing that a crime had been committed, he ordered them to stop, but the brother kept pedaling. The policeman fired a shot at the tire of the bicycle in order to stop the fleeing teenagers, but the bullet struck and killed the sister.

Can the brother be charged for his sister's death?

(A) Yes, for felony murder, as they committed a burglary.

(B) Yes, for involuntary manslaughter, because the brother was negligent in causing his sister's death.

(C) No, because they had already left the scene of the felony.

(D) No, because the deceased was a co-felon.

Question 2

A customer has banked with the same area bank for the last 10 years. On several occasions, the bank merged with or was bought out by a larger national bank, but in each instance, the customer was able to iron out the ensuing logistical difficulties and maintain his fee-free banking services, in large part because of a very large account he has at the bank. Now, the bank has merged again. Two days after the merger, the customer receives several statements documenting substantial fees. The customer is enraged. He contacts the newly appointed bank manager, who indicates that that she is not willing to help the customer oppose the fees. The customer requests the name of her supervisor, and the manager tells him that in fact, she herself is the regional manager and oversees the entire state. The manager then hangs up on the customer. Infuriated, the customer walks over to the bank, enters, and walks straight to the manager's office. He fires a single shot at the woman standing in the office, killing her. The woman in the office was not the manager but another customer waiting for the manager to return from the vault. The customer is facing charges for the shooting death.

Of which of the following crimes is the defendant guilty?

(A) First-degree murder.

(B) Second-degree murder.

(C) Voluntary manslaughter.

(D) Involuntary manslaughter.

Question 3

The defendant and the victim have been rivals for years. Their rivalry began when they were teenagers and competed against each other on rival sports teams at schools on opposite sides of the town. Later, the victim broke up the defendant's marriage by having an affair with the defendant's wife. The defendant and the victim are now in rival motorcycle gangs, and each is trying to control the local drug trade. The defendant just learned that the victim has been dating his little sister, and she is now addicted to drugs. To make matters worse, the defendant also learned that after the victim gives the defendant's sister drugs, he passes her around to members of his gang so that they can "do whatever they want with her." The defendant is completely enraged by the victim's conduct. He calls the victim and asks if they can meet for a few beers to discuss a merger of their respective drug trade organizations. The victim agrees, so they meet and talk for an hour or so. Later, the defendant offers the victim a ride home. When they pull up in front of the victim's house, the defendant shoots the victim in the back of the head, stating, "That's for my little sister." The victim dies instantly.

What is the most serious crime of which the defendant can be found guilty?

(A) First-degree murder.

(B) Second-degree murder.

(C) Voluntary manslaughter.

(D) Involuntary manslaughter.

Question 4

A college student was a committed vegan, eating only plant-derived foods, and the thought of all the animals slaughtered to provide meat for people nauseated her. One night, in order to draw attention to the slaughter of innocent animals, the student went to the butcher's section of the supermarket where she worked as produce manager and sprinkled a nausea-inducing chemical on all the meat, fowl, and fish products. Despite being careful, the student accidentally put too much powder in one package of hamburger. When the woman who bought the meat served it to her family, her husband, who was unusually susceptible, died as a result of ingesting the chemical.

In the student's jurisdiction, murder is defined as "the unlawful killing of a human being with malice aforethought. Such malice may be express or implied. It is express when there is manifested a deliberate intention unlawfully to take away the life of another person. It is implied when no considerable provocation appears or when the circumstances attending the killing show an abandoned and malignant heart. All murder which is perpetrated by willful, deliberate, or premeditated killing or which is committed in the perpetration of or attempt to perpetrate arson, rape, robbery, or burglary is murder of the first degree. All other kinds of murders are of the second degree."

If prosecuted for the criminal homicide of the woman's husband, of what crime should the student should be found guilty?

(A) First-degree murder, because she willfully, deliberately, and with premeditation killed the victim.

(B) First-degree murder, because the homicide occurred during perpetration of a felony.

(C) Second-degree murder, because the circumstances show that she acted with an abandoned and malignant heart.

(D) Involuntary manslaughter, because she did not intend to kill anyone.

Question 5

A defendant was a firm believer that psychics have the power to see into the future. She consulted with a practicing clairvoyant before making any major decisions. The clairvoyant told the defendant that she sensed an "evil presence" in the defendant's life that planned to murder the defendant in the near future. The clairvoyant described the evil presence as someone with red hair who was close to the defendant and whom the defendant would never suspect. The only person with red hair the defendant knew was her sister. The following day, the sister visited the defendant on her way home from work. Believing her sister had come to kill her, the defendant struck her sister in the temple with a fireplace poker, killing her instantly. The defendant was subsequently charged with murder. At her murder trial, the defendant claimed that she killed her sister in self-defense because she believed that her life was threatened.

If the jury finds that the defendant honestly believed that she was acting in self-defense, which of the following is true?

(A) The defendant will not be convicted of a crime, because she had a good-faith belief that her life was in danger.

(B) The defendant will be convicted of voluntary manslaughter, because the defendant's belief that her life was threatened was unreasonable.

(C) The defendant will be convicted of involuntary manslaughter, because the defendant honestly believed that her life was in danger.

(D) The defendant will be convicted of murder, because the defendant's life was not actually threatened.

Question 6

A man took two people hostage and arranged for them to play a game. The man blindfold the first hostage and strapped a gun, which was pointed at the first hostage's head, to the second hostage's hand. The man told the second hostage that if he did not pull the trigger, that the man would shoot the second hostage. Not wanting to die, the second hostage pulled the trigger, killing the first hostage.

If the second hostage is charged with the death of the first hostage, how should the jury find the second hostage?

(A) Guilty of murder.

(B) Guilty of manslaughter.

(C) Not guilty, because the second hostage was under duress.

(D) Not guilty, because the killing was done out of necessity.

Question 7

A man and his roommate got into an argument over a loan the man made to the roommate. The roommate called the man a spoiled brat who always got his way. The man slapped the roommate across the face. The roommate then grabbed a carving knife from the kitchen counter and tried to stab the man. The man wrestled the knife away and stabbed the roommate in the chest, killing him.

If the man is charged with homicide, which of the following statements is most accurate?

(A) The man is guilty of murder, because deadly force was not justified.

(B) The man is guilty of manslaughter, because deadly force was not justified.

(C) The man is guilty of murder, because he was the initial aggressor.

(D) The man is not guilty of any crime, because deadly force was justified.

Question 8

A man lived in a duplex and worked at night as a security guard. The man soon became annoyed at his upstairs neighbor, who kept a large number of dogs inside his home during the day while he was at work. The noise from the dogs was so loud that the man could not fall asleep. On several occasions, the man asked the neighbor to do something about the dogs, but the neighbor simply replied, "Get a day job!"

The following day, the man was coming home just as the neighbor was leaving for work and again pleaded with him to keep the dogs quiet, because he had been awake for 24hours straight at that point, and desperately needed sleep. The neighbor simply smiled and got into his car, but said nothing to the man. A short time later, the dogs began to bark, and the man fired three shots through the ceiling of his apartment, as at that point he merely wanted to put an end to the noise. One of the bullets struck the neighbor, who had returned home because he had forgotten his laptop. The neighbor died a week later from the gunshot wound.

For what crime should the man be found guilty?

(A) Murder, because the man intentionally shot into a dwelling.

(B) Involuntary manslaughter, because while the defendant was criminally negligent, he did not act with malice.

(C) Voluntary manslaughter, because a jury could conclude the man was adequately provoked.

(D) Felony murder, because the man intended for the bullet to enter the apartment to cause either damage to the building or injury to the dogs.

Question 9

A man who had recently lost his job decided to seek revenge by committing a fake robbery at his former place of employment. The defendant entered the sporting goods store, picked up a ski mask and replica gun, and approached the clerk. The man pointed the gun at the clerk and demanded the money from the register. Terrified, the clerk closed the register and ran into the back room. The man panicked, ran back to his car, and drove off. As he was approaching a traffic light, he hit the gas and sped through the intersection, causing a truck to swerve out of the way and run over a pedestrian standing on the sidewalk. The pedestrian was rushed to the hospital, but died in surgery as a result of his injuries. This jurisdiction criminalizes speeding in an intersection.

Which of the following is the most serious crime for which the man can be convicted?

(A) Felony murder.

(B) Involuntary manslaughter, because no robbery occurred.

(C) Misdemeanor manslaughter, because speeding in an intersection is a crime.

(D) Robbery, because the truck swerving into the pedestrian was a superseding cause.

Question 10

A sailor got into a fight with a marine while at a bar. The fight was quickly broken up by some other patrons. The sailor, however, remained angry. The sailor went back to the same bar the following night. While inside the bar, someone put a substance in the sailor's soda that made him extremely intoxicated. He soon left the bar and, 10 minutes later, ran into the marine on the sidewalk. The two men got into a verbal argument, during which the marine threatened to cause bodily injury to the sailor's girlfriend. The sailor became angry and pulled out a gun, shooting the marine to death. When the sailor woke up the next morning, the effect of the alcohol had mostly worn off. He had no recollection of what happened the night before. He did not remember having a gun, or using it to shoot the marine. This jurisdiction defines all murder as second-degree murder, but elevates intentional killings and those committed during an inherently dangerous felony to first-degree murder. Manslaughter is defined as at common law.

Which of the following statements is most accurate?

(A) The sailor is guilty of first-degree murder, because he intentionally killed the marine.

(B) The sailor is guilty of second-degree murder, because, due to his intoxication, he could not formulate the specific intent to kill.

(C) The defendant is guilty of voluntary manslaughter, because there was sufficient adequate provocation by the marine due to the threats made concerning the sailor's girlfriend.

(D) The defendant is not guilty of homicide, because he lacked the state of mind required to commit the crime.

Question 11

An off-duty police officer came home early from work one day. He walked up to his bedroom and, upon opening the door, saw his wife and another man in bed together. Visibly upset, the husband grabbed his service revolver and shot the man to death. He then went to a local bar, had several drinks, returned home, and killed his wife.

The husband is guilty for which of the following crimes?

(A) Murder of both his wife and the other man.

(B) Voluntary manslaughter of both his wife and the other man.

(C) Murder of the other man, and voluntary manslaughter of his wife.

(D) Murder of his wife and voluntary manslaughter of the other man.

Question 12

A man has been arrested and charged with homicide for the intentional killing of a neighbor. At trial, the prosecution argued that the man committed murder, and the defendant, in turn, claimed that he should be found guilty of voluntary manslaughter.

Regarding voluntary manslaughter, which of the following statements is most accurate?

(A) Provocation is only adequate if the criminal defendant was actually provoked and if it would have caused a reasonable person to lose self-control.

(B) Provocation is adequate if it would cause the defendant to lose self-control.

(C) As long as the man was still laboring under the heat of passion from the incident, it is irrelevant whether a reasonable person would have cooled off.

(D) A showing by the man that he was intoxicated would reduce a charge of murder to manslaughter.

Question 13

A man and his friend decided to rob a bank. They entered the bank and quickly got into a shootout with the security guard. While the man was taking the money from the vault, the security guard was struck by a bullet and killed. The two men then left and, as the man was following his friend to the car, the man shot the friend in the back. This jurisdiction defines all murders as second-degree murder unless deliberation and premeditation can be shown, in which case the crime is elevated to first-degree murder. Manslaughter is defined as at common law. This jurisdiction also follows the agency theory for felony murder.

Which of the following statements is most accurate?

(A) The defendant is guilty of first-degree murder of the security guard and second-degree murder of the friend under the agency theory.

(B) The defendant is guilty of first-degree murder of security guard and the friend under the agency theory.

(C) The defendant is guilty of second-degree murder of the security guard and first-degree murder of the friend.

(D) The defendant is guilty of second-degree murder of both the security guard and the friend, because both were killed during the felony, and neither death was premeditated.

Question 14

A baseball fanatic became enraged when a fan for the other team reached out into the field of play and touched a ball, causing the winning run to score. As the spectators were leaving the stadium, the fanatic saw the other fan, who had touched the ball, walking to his car. The fanatic walked up behind the other fan and punched him in the back of the head. The other fan, who had been drinking all day, was immediately knocked out and died as soon as his head hit the pavement. This jurisdiction defines assault as: (1) the causing of physical harm to another (categorized as felony assault); or (2) acting in a threatening manner to put another in fear of immediate harm (categorized as misdemeanor assault).The fanatic was arrested for homicide of the other fan.

Which of the following is the most serious crime for which the fanatic should be found guilty?

(A) Assault.

(B) Voluntary manslaughter.

(C) Involuntary manslaughter.

(D) Felony murder.

Question 15

A defendant had an argument with a patron in a bar over a game of pool. As they were quarreling, the defendant pulled out his knife, intending only to frighten the patron. The knife was six inches long, and the defendant held it out towards the patron. The patron immediately retreated from the pool table, telling the defendant that he was a hemophiliac and that he did not want any trouble. Wanting to have some fun at the patron's expense, the defendant drew near and swung the knife in the patron's direction. The defendant got a little too close to the patron and unintentionally nicked the patron's arm. The bar was far from a hospital, and by the time the patron arrived at the emergency room, he had died from his injury.

What is the most serious crime for which the defendant could be convicted?

(A) Murder.

(B) Voluntary manslaughter.

(C) Involuntary manslaughter.

(D) Battery.

Question 16

One evening, the defendant was playing horseshoes with his son in the front yard of his house. One of the horseshoes went too far and landed on the neighbor's lawn, breaking the neighbor's bird bath. Immediately after hearing the crash, the neighbor stepped outside and began yelling about the bird bath. The neighbor said that the defendant's son was going to be a lousy sport, just like his dad. Infuriated, the defendant hurled the horseshoe in his hand at the neighbor's head. The horseshoe hit the neighbor in the temple, killing him instantly.

Of what crime can the defendant be found guilty?

(A) Murder, because the defendant's actions were malicious.

(B) Murder, because the defendant was the initial aggressor.

(C) Voluntary manslaughter, because the neighbor's insults caused the defendant to react violently.

(D) Involuntary manslaughter, because the defendant did not intend to kill his neighbor.

Question 17

The defendant wanted to steal some documents from his wife's divorce attorney's computer, and so he arranged to have a late-night meeting at the attorney's office. He took with him a small vial filled with a drug used to sedate animals for surgery. The drug was odorless and colorless. When the attorney left the room to take a phone call, the defendant put a small dose of the drug into his drinking cup. After he returned, the attorney took a drink and soon passed out in his chair. The defendant then accessed several documents on the attorney's computer and left. The defendant was unaware that the attorney had severe allergies which were exacerbated by the drug, causing him to suffer a heart attack and die.

This jurisdiction defines first-degree murder as the intentional killing of another human being with premeditation, and all other murders are classified as second-degree murder. Manslaughter is defined as at common law. This jurisdiction limits felony murder to inherently dangerous felonies and defines those as at common law.

What is the most serious offense of which the defendant can be convicted?

(A) First-degree murder.

(B) Second-degree murder.

(C) Voluntary manslaughter.

(D) Involuntary manslaughter.

Question 18

A private investigator who does a great deal of divorce and pre-divorce work recently obtained evidence that a wealthy and volatile husband had been cheating on his wife. When the husband learned of the investigator's discovery of the evidence, he came to the investigator's office and initiated a series of screaming matches with him. The investigator always believed the husband to be an idiot because, even though he had several inconspicuous cars at his disposal, he always drove an absolutely unique classic car when he went to meet his lover. One night, when the investigator was crossing the street, he saw the husband's car coming directly at him. When the car came within 20 feet of him without slowing down or swerving, the investigator pulled out his gun and shot at the husband. The husband died from the gunshot wound the next day. Prior to his death, the husband was heard to repeatedly say, "Why did that man shoot me? He could have gotten out of the way. My brakes failed, and I couldn't stop." The investigator, in turn, told the police that he thought that the husband was trying to hit him with the car to get revenge.

Of what crime, if any, is the investigator likely to be convicted with regard to the husband's death?

(A) Murder, because the investigator intended to cause the husband's death.

(B) Manslaughter, because the investigator thought that the husband was trying to kill him.

(C) Murder, because the investigator acted with wanton and willful disregard for human life.

(D) No crime.

Question 19

A man owned a home security business. In addition to selling personal defense devices, he also trained dogs to attack strangers at night. He sold and leased his guard dogs to various business and factory owners, who used the guard dogs to frighten away intruders from entering their premises at night. One evening, the man was in the backyard of his home training three of his guard dogs. The backyard was enclosed with a chain-link fence and a latched gate that prevented the dogs from running out. After the training session, the man opened the gate and permitted the dogs to run loose in his front yard. Minutes later, a bicyclist got a flat time in from of the man's home and was attacked by several of the dogs. The bicyclist suffered severe injuries and died as a result of the attack. At trial, it was conceded that the man's dogs attacked a postal worker two weeks prior to this incident.

For what crime should the man should be found guilty?

(A) Murder, because the man's actions were malicious.

(B) Involuntary manslaughter, because the man did not command the dogs to attack the bicyclist.

(C) Voluntary manslaughter, because the dogs could have reasonably believed the bicyclist was an intruder.

(D) Reckless endangerment, because the dogs killing the victim was a superseding cause.

Question 20

A man decided to take his own life and went to the roof to jump to the street below. On his way up the stairs, he told his neighbor what he was planning to do. The neighbor had a strong belief that anyone who committed suicide would not enter Heaven. Therefore, he snuck up behind the man as he was readying to jump off the rooftop. After the man jumped, the neighbor shot him once in the back before the man struck the sidewalk below.

At trial, the medical examiner testified that the man died of a gunshot wound, and that in all likelihood, the fall would not have killed the man. The jury also found that the neighbor's religious belief was honestly held.

If the neighbor is prosecuted for murder, what should the result be at trial?

(A) The neighbor should be convicted, regardless of the man's intent or the medical examiner's testimony.

(B) The neighbor should be convicted, because the medical examiner testified that the fall would not have killed the man.

(C) The neighbor should be acquitted, because the man intended to kill himself.

(D) The neighbor should be found guilty of a lesser charge, because the jury believed that his religious belief was honestly held.

Essays

Essay Question 1

IE13JUL003

ISSUE SPOTTING EXERCISE

Consider the fact pattern below and then answer the questions that follow:

A husband was supposed to be out of town for a three-day business trip. Because he completed his business sooner than expected, he flew home on Wednesday night instead of Thursday afternoon. The husband arrived home and let himself into the house. After entering, he heard noises coming from the bedroom, and, upon investigation, was shocked to find his wife in bed with his best friend. The friend dressed quickly and took off out the back door. The husband screamed at the wife for a period of time, and then began to drink. After consuming several drinks, he unlocked the door to his gun cabinet, pulled out a rifle, and loaded it. He then set off for the friend's house.

The husband arrived at the friend's about 10 minutes later. Because he had rushed home so quickly, the friend had neglected to lock his front door, and so the husband walked right in. Finding his friend trembling in the living room, the husband pointed the gun at him. The friend immediately began apologizing, blaming the affair on the wife. As the friend was pleading for his life, he rushed the husband and a struggle ensued, during which the husband fired a single shot at the friend. The bullet struck the friend in the head, killing him instantly. The husband set the gun down, fell to his knees, and began sobbing. A neighbor heard the shot and called the police. They arrived a few minutes later to find the husband still on the floor, distraught and muttering about losing his best friend and his wife in one night.

1. *Can the husband properly be found guilty of having committed murder?*

2. *What defenses may the husband raise, and are they likely to succeed?*

1. **The first interrogatory asks you whether the husband can properly be found guilty of murder. Discussion of this interrogatory requires you to address more than one issue. Explain what those issues are and why you would break the essay up in this way.**

2. **The fact pattern implicates two possible defenses that the husband can assert. List each possible defense along with the facts from the prompt that raise each defense.**

Defense #1:

Facts:

Defense #2:

Facts:

Essay Question 1

IE13JUL003

RULE RECOLLECTION EXERCISE

A good rule statement will demonstrate your understanding of the law and provide the foundation for your analysis. This exercise is intended to help you practice: (1) recalling the relevant rules of law; (2) organizing rules of law; and (3) explaining legal concepts completely and concisely.

- PUT AWAY YOUR NOTES for this exercise and practice actively trying to recall the relevant rules.
- In FIFTEEN minutes, write out rule statements for the following issues.
- WRITE THESE RULES OUT IN FULL; do not merely jot down concepts, topics, or fragments.

MURDER

First-Degree Murder

Second-Degree Murder

DEFENSES

Voluntary Intoxication

Self-Defense

Essay Question 1

IE13JUL003

ANALYSIS EXERCISE

Connect law (rules) to fact, and draft your analysis paragraph for each issue below.

MURDER

First-Degree Murder

Second-Degree Murder

DEFENSES

Voluntary Intoxication

Self-Defense

Essay Question 2

IE13JUL004

One afternoon, Don was walking through his neighborhood. As he passed a home with a high fence, a dog on the other side began to bark violently. Although Don was unable to see the dog through the fence, he was frightened that the dog would break through. Don hurried to pass the property, but before he was able to do so, the dog managed to escape, came after Don, and attacked him.

The dog's owner was planting rose bushes in his front yard when he heard the commotion. The owner rushed out of his front yard in time to see Don on the sidewalk kicking his dog in the head. The owner screamed for Don to stop, and commanded the dog to retreat. However, the dog continued to pursue Don menacingly, and Don continued to kick the dog in the head. The owner, who was still carrying a shovel in his hand, took one wild swing at Don in an attempt to stop him from kicking his dog. The owner's shovel hit Don in the head, knocking him to the ground.

A neighbor, witnessing the commotion, called the police. When the officer, Paul, arrived at the scene, he observed the owner standing over Don, still holding his shovel. Both Don and the dog were lying dead on the sidewalk. This jurisdiction allows for imperfect self-defense, and requires that all dogs be tethered by a leash when on a public sidewalk.

1. *With what crimes, if any, can the owner be charged as a result of Don's death? Explain.*

2. *What defenses, if any, will be available to the owner if he is charged with a crime related to Don's death? Explain.*

Criminal Procedure

Exercise Set 1

Question 1

For purposes of the Fourth Amendment's protection against unreasonable searches and seizure, identify three types of actors that would count as "state actors" for purposes of the state action doctrine.

Question 2a

Identify the constitutional requirements for issuing a valid warrant.

Question 2b

Identify the exceptions to the warrant requirement.

1. **C**____________________

2. **H**____________________

3. **A**____________________

4. **P**____________________

5. **E**____________________

6. _______________**L**____________________

7. _______________**S**____________________

Question 2c

Identify the exceptions to the "fruit of the poisonous tree" doctrine.

For the following exercises, you are given a question prompt. After reading the question prompt, consider the applicable rules. Then, brainstorm possible issues that could be raised or tested based on the given question prompt.

Question 3

Should the court grant the defendant's motion to suppress?

Question 4

Was the warrantless search conducted by the police constitutional?

Question 5

What is the prosecutor's best argument for successfully defeating the defendant's motion to suppress?

Question 6

Is the gun seized after the police's warranted search of the defendant's gym locker admissible into evidence despite the police's admittedly tainted search of the defendant's apartment earlier that same day?

For each of the following fact patterns and question prompts, write out the relevant issues and their corresponding rule statements.

Question 7

Suspecting that Derek had slain his wife, police detectives persuaded one of Derek's employees to remove a drinking glass from Derek's office so that it could be used for fingerprint comparisons with a knife found near the body. After the employee provided the detectives with the drinking glass, a forensics team determined that the fingerprints on the drinking glass matched those found on the knife. At trial, Derek's lawyer filed a motion to suppress the evidence of the fingerprint comparisons, contending that the evidence was acquired unconstitutionally.

How should the court rule on the motion?

Question 8

Police properly obtained a warrant that authorized the search of the defendant's residence for a car of a certain make and model believed to have been used in a recent bank robbery. Upon serving the warrant, one officer entered the home and made his way to the garage, which was accessible from a back room. The other officer lingered near the front door and opened up a coat closet out of curiosity. The first officer found a car that matched the description of the car used in the robbery. The second officer found, inside one of the coats in the closet, a set of keys for the car, as well as several plastic bags with what appeared to be an illegal substance inside. The car, keys, and bags of what proved to be cocaine were all sought to be admitted at the defendant's trial.

Should a motion to suppress this evidence be granted?

Question 9

A jazz trio was on a cross-country tour when tensions between the trio's bassist and drummer began to boil over. Having become resentful of the drummer's financial management of the trio, the bassist, at one particular concert stop, went through the drummer's suitcase in their shared dressing home and found significant amounts of illegal narcotics. The bassist turned the narcotics over to the local police, who then asked the bassist to search through the drummer's private bunk on the tour bus for more evidence. The bassist did so and found a book belonging to the drummer that contained contact information for narcotics dealers around the country. At the drummer's criminal trial, the defense counsel moved to suppress both the narcotics and the book.

Will the court grant the motion?

Question 10

A man ran an illegal casino out of the basement of his house. The police grew suspicious as to his activities after seeing a number of known gamblers entering and exiting the side door of the man's house at all hours of the night. A police officer staking out the house waited until he was sure the man had closed up his operations for the night, and then snuck into the man's basement by opening and entering through a basement window. Inside, the officer saw cards, poker chips, and stacks of cash. The police officer then tracked down one of the gamblers he had seen leaving the man's house. This gambler voluntarily gave a statement that illegal gambling was indeed occurring in the basement and that the police would find cards, poker chips, and cash there. The police officer used an affidavit of the statement to obtain a search warrant for the basement, which the officer then used to enter the basement and seize the cards, poker chips, and cash. At trial, the man brought a motion to suppress the introduction of the seized evidence.

Is the seized evidence admissible?

Exercise Set 2

Question 1

Complete the chart by identifying the exception to the warrant requirement as indicated by both the scope of the warrantless search (or seizure) and the requirements to be met in order to render it constitutional.

WARRANTLESS SEARCH	SCOPE OF THE SEARCH	REQUIREMENTS FOR THE WARRANTLESS SEARCH
	A warrantless search of a person and the area in that person's immediate vicinity ("wingspan") is constitutional if:	the person has been lawfully arrested—that is, the person's arrest was based on probable cause.
	A warrantless search of the vicinity of the lawful arrest (e.g., adjoining rooms, if the arrest occurred in a home) is constitutional if:	there is reasonable suspicion that the arrested person has an armed accomplice.
	A warrantless search or seizure is constitutional if:	• the police are reasonably in pursuit of a fleeing suspect; and • the delay caused by seeking a warrant would allow the suspect an opportunity to escape or to destroy evidence.
	A warrantless search or seizure is constitutional if:	there is an emergency situation in which: • evidence may be lost or destroyed before a warrant can be obtained; or • delay would risk serious injury or death to a person.

Question 2

Complete the chart by describing the scope of a warrantless search (or seizure) and identifying the requirements to be met in order to render it constitutional.

WARRANTLESS SEARCH	SCOPE OF THE SEARCH	REQUIREMENTS FOR THE WARRANTLESS SEARCH
Plain View		
Automobile Exception		
Stop and Frisk (Search Incident to a Lawful Stop)		
Consent		

For the following fact patterns, complete the chart with the relevant facts that correspond to the rule(s) provided.

Question 3

A police officer responded to an all-points bulletin (APB) indicating that an armed suspect was holding people hostage inside his residence. The officer was the first member of law enforcement to arrive on the scene. Upon arriving, shots were fired from the residence, and the armed suspect claimed he would start killing his hostages in 10 minutes if his demands were not met. Deciding not to wait to get a warrant, the officer snuck into the residence through a side entrance, but found only the suspect's hostages and the high-powered rifle that the suspect had just used. Unbeknownst to the officer, the suspect, hearing the officer entering through the side entrance, had escaped out the front door. At the suspect's trial, the defense moved to suppress the rifle seized by the officer.

Should the court grant the motion to suppress?

RULE	RELEVANT FACTS
Exigent Circumstances	

Question 4

A judge provided a tip to the local police that one of his neighbors might be involved in an illegal gambling enterprise. The police began an investigation and, through independent sources, established probable cause to search the neighbor's home. The police secured a search warrant that was issued by the judge who had provided the original tip that had initiated their investigation. Upon executing the search, the police found evidence of criminality and seized it.

Will a motion to suppress this evidence be granted?

RULE	RELEVANT FACTS
Requirements for a Valid Warrant	

Question 5

Based upon probable cause that the defendant was involved in an illegal Ponzi scheme, a warrant was issued for her arrest. The arrest occurred at her home. Upon her arrest, the police searched her person and discovered that she was in possession of cocaine, which they seized. They then proceeded to do a complete search of her bedroom, including its closets, wherein they discovered and seized other illegal drugs as well as the proceeds of a recent store robbery.

Upon the defendant's motion to suppress, should the property police seized from the bedroom closet be deemed inadmissible?

RULE	RELEVANT FACTS
Search Incident to a Lawful Arrest	

Question 6

Because of raging forest fires in the county, law enforcement was stopping all cars headed north on Route 101 to both alert them of the danger and redirect them away from those routes being used by emergency vehicles. On one of these stops, a law enforcement officer saw what looked like fresh blood stains covering the back seat of the car. The driver of the car was told to step out of the vehicle, and the vehicle was then searched. In the trunk of the car, the police found a kidnap victim, bound, gagged, and bleeding, but still alive. The driver was arrested and the car seized.

Was the stop and search of this car constitutional?

RULES	RELEVANT FACTS
Stop and Frisk (Search Incident to a Lawful Stop)	
Automobile Exception	

Question 7

An officer was giving chase of a man who matched the description of an armed robbery suspect. The chase was on foot and involved both the man and the officer running through a residential neighborhood. During the pursuit, the man hopped a fence into a backyard where a family barbeque was taking place. Startled, the family watched stunned as first the man and then the officer ran into their house through the patio door. Moments later, the officer stepped back outside with the man in handcuffs. On the man's person, the officer had found and had seized a gun and a stolen purse.

At trial, should the court grant the defendant's motion to suppress the gun and purse?

RULES	RELEVANT FACTS
Hot Pursuit	
Search Incident to a Lawful Arrest	

For each of the following fact patterns and question prompts, identify the applicable rules and complete the chart with the relevant facts.

Question 8

A homeowner discovered that a lawn chair was missing from her yard, and suspected her neighbor had taken it. The homeowner called a police officer and told him that she believed that her neighbor had the chair, and furthermore, that the chair had a tag on the back of it indicating the specific brand of the chair. The officer went to the neighbor's house and asked if he could look inside. The neighbor agreed to let the officer look around. The officer saw a chair inside covered by a blanket. As soon as the neighbor saw the officer noticing the chair, he told the officer he needed to leave the house immediately. The officer removed the blanket and found the tag on the chair indicating that it was the homeowner's chair. The officer seized the chair.

Did the seizure of the chair violate the neighbor's Fourth Amendment rights?

RULES	RELEVANT FACTS
Consent	
Plain View	

Question 9

A town was suffering a scourge of teenage overdoses from a new designer drug that had become popular in a nearby college. Under political pressure, the town's mayor ordered that the police set up a checkpoint on the road leading into the town from the college, hoping to cut off the supply of the illegal drugs to the town's teenagers. At the checkpoint, police pulled over all cars approaching the town, asked the occupants questions, and led a drug-sniffing dog around the car. During one stop, the dog led police to evidence of drugs inside the car, and the driver of the car, a student, was arrested. At trial, the student made a motion to exclude any evidence gathered at the stop on the grounds that his Fourth Amendment rights were violated.

Will the court grant the motion?

RULES	RELEVANT FACTS
Stop and Frisk (Search Incident to a Lawful Stop)	
Automobile Exception	

Question 10

A police officer was sitting in her squad car when she received a radio message from the police dispatcher that a suspect in a recent robbery had been spotted near her location. Two minutes later, a bartender who matched the detailed description provided by the dispatcher walked by the officer. When the officer got out of her squad car, the bartender began running toward the front door of his home. The officer ran after him and apprehended him before he reached the door to his house. The officer arrested the bartender and advised him of his Miranda rights, which the bartender promptly waived. The officer then asked the bartender, "Is the stuff from the robbery in your house?" The bartender shrugged his shoulders and replied, "It might be." The officer entered the bartender's house and found a briefcase on the kitchen table. When she opened the briefcase, the officer found several thousand dollars, which turned out to be proceeds from the robbery.

At the bartender's trial for robbery, the prosecution sought to admit the briefcase and its contents into evidence. The bartender moved to suppress.

How should the court rule on the bartender's motion?

RULES	RELEVANT FACTS
Hot Pursuit	
Search Incident to a Lawful Arrest	
Consent	
Plain View	

Quiz 1

Question 1

A department store had experienced a growing incidence of shoplifting. At the store's request, the police concealed a woman, who was a detective, at a vantage point above the women's apparel fitting rooms, where she could see into these rooms as customers tried on clothes. The detective saw the defendant enter a fitting room, stuff a dress into her pocketbook, leave the fitting room, and start for the street door. By prearranged signal, the detective notified another police officer near the door, who detained the defendant as she started to go out into the street. The defendant was placed under arrest and the dress was retrieved from her purse. The defendant was subsequently charged with shoplifting. At trial, the defendant moved to prevent the introduction of the dress into evidence.

Will her motion be granted?

(A) Yes, because the police should have secured a search warrant to search her bag.

(B) Yes, because a customer has a reasonable expectation of privacy while using a department store fitting room.

(C) No, because the search and seizure were made incident to a valid arrest based on probable cause.

(D) No, because the detective could see into the room, and thus, the defendant's activities were legitimately in plain view.

Question 2

Late one evening, a police department received a telephone call from an unidentified woman who reported hearing loud shrieks and screams from a neighboring home. The caller furnished the police with the address where the disturbance was taking place. When the police arrived at the home, they discovered the homeowner, bludgeoned to death. The murder weapon was a bloodstained baseball bat found near the victim's body. A subsequent investigation revealed that the homeowner had recently been separated from her husband who had since moved to another city. After questioning several of the victim's friends and relatives, the police concluded that the husband was a prime suspect in the murder. Thus, two detectives went to question the husband about the killing. When they arrived at his apartment, the detectives persuaded the landlord to let them into his apartment. Finding no one inside, they searched the apartment. Before leaving, the detectives took a box of cereal, which they planned to use for a fingerprint comparison. The prints from the cereal box matched those found on the baseball bat. The police presented the fingerprint comparison to the grand jury investigating the murder. The husband is to testify before the grand jury. Before his appearance, the husband files a motion to evidence of the fingerprint comparison, contending that the evidence was illegally obtained.

How should the court rule on his motion?

(A) Granted, because the warrantless search of the husband's apartment was unconstitutional.

(B) Granted, because the grand jury is barred from considering illegally obtained evidence.

(C) Denied, because the exclusionary rule has not been extended to grand jury hearings.

(D) Denied, because the landlord had the apparent authority to authorize the search of the husband's apartment.

Question 3

Police received reliable information that a homeowner had a stolen x-brand stereo in his possession. The detectives submitted an affidavit to a neutral magistrate setting forth sufficient underlying circumstances for the issuance of a search warrant. Making a determination of probable cause, the magistrate issued a warrant for the x-brand stereo at the homeowner's address. The police arrived at the homeowner's dwelling, showed him the warrant, and came inside. In the living room, they noticed a y-brand stereo, which had the serial number removed. Upon further inspection, the police determined that the stereo had been stolen from a local electronics store during a recent burglary. The police placed the homeowner under arrest and instructed him to remain seated in the living room while they searched the rest of the home. One of the officers proceeded to the basement where she found the stolen x-brand stereo. She then decided to search the upstairs and came upon a stolen z-brand stereo in the homeowner's second-floor bedroom.

The homeowner was subsequently prosecuted for receiving stolen property. At trial, the homeowner moves to prevent introduction of the stereos into evidence.

His motion should be granted with respect to what evidence?

(A) The y-brand stereo.

(B) The z-brand stereo.

(C) The y-brand and the z-brand stereos.

(D) None of the stereos.

Question 4

A detective received a tip from an informant, who had given reliable information many times in the past, that a man was a narcotics dealer. Specifically, the informant said that, two months before, he had visited the man's apartment with a friend and that on that occasion he saw the man sell his friend some heroin. The detective knew that the informant, the man, and the friend were acquaintances. Thereafter, the detective put all this information into affidavit form, appeared before a magistrate, and secured a search warrant for the man's apartment. The search turned up a supply of heroin.

How will the court likely rule on the man's motion to suppress introduction of the heroin into evidence?

(A) Granted, because a search warrant cannot validly be issued solely on the basis of an informant's information.

(B) Granted, because the information supplied to the detective concerned an occurrence too remote in time to justify a finding of probable cause at the time of the search.

(C) Granted, because a search for mere evidence alone is improper and illegal.

(D) Denied, because the informant had proven himself reliable in the past, and the information he gave turned out to be correct.

Question 5

While on routine patrol, police officers observed a driver making an illegal U-turn. After stopping the driver's car, they saw him reach under the driver's seat. They ordered him out of the car and saw a cellophane package protruding from under the seat. The package contained a white powdery substance, which the officers suspected to be cocaine. The officers placed the driver under arrest and put him in the rear of their patrol car. They then proceeded to search the rest of the driver's car. In the trunk they found an assault rifle that was later determined to be the weapon used in a liquor store robbery. Charged with that robbery, the driver moved to suppress the assault rifle as evidence on the grounds that the police did not have a warrant to search the trunk.

What is the best theory that the prosecution can use in support of the admissibility of the assault rifle as evidence?

(A) The police conducted an automobile search.

(B) The police conducted an inventory search.

(C) The search was incident to a lawful arrest.

(D) The search was made under exigent circumstances.

Question 6

After Sally sold heroin to John, he got into his car and drove off. John was later stopped by police for speeding. The police searched John's car and found the heroin concealed under the rear seat. Unbeknownst to Sally, she was being investigated for drug dealing during this time. Eventually, she was charged with illegally selling heroin. At her trial, the prosecutor sought to introduce into evidence the heroin seized from John's car.

If Sally moves to prevent introduction of the heroin into evidence, how should the court rule on the motion?

(A) Granted, because the heroin was not in plain view.

(B) Granted, because the scope of the search was excessive.

(C) Denied, because Sally has no standing to object to the search.

(D) Denied, because the search was proper as incident to a valid full custodial arrest.

Question 7

Police received information from an undercover police officer that she had just seen two men (whom she described) in a red four-door sedan selling marijuana near the city's largest high school. A few minutes later, two police officers saw a sedan fitting the description half a block from the high school. The driver of the sedan matched the description of one of the men described by the undercover officer.

The two officers stopped the sedan and searched the driver. In the pocket of the driver's jacket, the police found a small bottle of pills that they recognized as narcotics. They also looked in the trunk, where they found a quantity of cocaine in a sealed envelope. The driver was arrested and charged with unlawful possession of narcotics. The driver moved to suppress the use of the cocaine found in the trunk as evidence.

How should the court rule?

(A) Grant the motion, because the search was without probable cause or a warrant.

(B) Grant the motion, because the search went beyond the wingspan of the driver.

(C) Deny the motion, because this was a search incident to a lawful arrest.

(D) Deny the motion, because the police had probable cause to search the entire vehicle.

Question 8

A woman was driving her van along a public road one night. A police officer who was driving behind the woman, decided to pull over the woman's vehicle to check the woman's license and registration. The officer pulled the woman's van over to the side of the road and then walked up to the driver's side of the vehicle. When he came alongside the driver's window, the officer asked the woman for her identification. As the woman was thumbing through her wallet, the officer shone his flashlight into the van and spotted a plastic bag containing marijuana lying on the floor under the back seat. The officer then arrested the woman and charged her with possession of marijuana.

At the woman's trial for illegal possession of a controlled substance, her attorney moved to suppress the use of the marijuana as evidence.

How should the judge rule on her motion?

(A) Granted, because the marijuana was the fruit of an illegal search.

(B) Granted, because the police officer did not have probable cause or a reasonable suspicion to believe that the woman's van contained a controlled substance.

(C) Denied, because the marijuana was in plain view when the police officer shone his flashlight inside the van.

(D) Denied, because the marijuana was in an automobile.

Question 9

The police suspected that a teenager, a 16-year-old high school student, had committed a series of burglaries. Two officers went to the teenager's high school and asked the principal to call him out of class and to then search his backpack. While the officers waited, the principal took the teenager into the hall, where she asked to look in his backpack. When the teenager refused, the principal grabbed it from him, injuring the teenager's shoulder in the process. In the backpack, she found jewelry, which she turned over to the officers. The teenager was subsequently charged with committing the burglaries, and now moves to suppress the use of the jewelry as evidence at trial.

How should the court rule?

(A) Deny the motion, because the search was incident to a lawful arrest.

(B) Deny the motion, because school searches are reasonable if conducted by school personnel, on school grounds, on the basis of reasonable suspicion.

(C) Grant the motion, because the search was conducted with excessive force.

(D) Grant the motion, because the search was conducted without probable cause or a warrant.

Question 10

A wife was divorced from her husband. The wife and the husband had a daughter who was 12 years of age. The daughter lived with the wife, but the husband frequently visited his daughter at her house. One morning, the husband came to his ex-wife's home to see his daughter. He and his daughter were outside on the patio chatting when the wife noticed her ex-husband's briefcase lying on the kitchen floor. The husband had entered the house carrying his briefcase, which he placed down before going out to see his daughter on the patio. Seeing the briefcase, the wife decided to open it. Inside she found a large envelope. She decided to keep it, thinking it contained money. Later that night after her ex-husband left, she opened the envelope and found a large amount of cocaine. The wife called the police who came and confiscated the drugs. The husband was subsequently charged with possession of cocaine.

The husband has filed a motion to exclude the cocaine from being introduced into evidence.

How should the court rule on his motion?

(A) Granted, because the seizure violated the husband's right of privacy.

(B) Granted, because the police failed to secure a search warrant before the seizure of the cocaine.

(C) Denied, because the initial seizure was made by a private individual.

(D) Denied, because the husband left the briefcase in the kitchen in plain view.

Question 11

Acting on a tip that a suspected drug dealer was selling drugs out of a hotel room, police asked the hotel manager for permission to enter the room. The manager gave the police permission to enter and a key to the room. When the police entered the room using the key, they found the suspected drug dealer in the middle of packaging bags of a white powder. The police arrested the suspected drug dealer and seized the powder, which subsequent forensic tests showed to be cocaine. When the drug dealer was charged with possession of narcotics with intent to distribute, he challenged the admissibility of the cocaine at trial.

Should the court admit the cocaine into evidence?

(A) Yes, because the cocaine was in plain view.

(B) Yes, because the hotel manager consented to the search.

(C) No, because the drug dealer had a reasonable expectation of privacy in the hotel room.

(D) No, because there were no exigent circumstances present.

Question 12

Police detectives looking for a gun used in the murder of a federal judge received a tip that the gun had been hidden in a storage unit from the manager of the storage unit who had seen the suspect placing a gun in the unit. The suspect was subsequently arrested and jailed on an unrelated charge. While the suspect was in jail, the detectives applied for a warrant to search the storage unit for the gun. Before they could execute the warrant, the storage unit manager told a policeman who was on patrol in the neighborhood about the gun. The patrolling officer broke into the storage unit and discovered the murder weapon. Just after the patrolling officer left the storage unit, the detectives arrived at the storage unit with their valid warrant. Subsequent ballistics testing confirmed that the gun was in fact the murder weapon, and the suspect was charged with murder. At trial, the defendant seeks to have the gun excluded from evidence.

Should the court admit the gun into evidence?

(A) Yes, because the patrolling officer's search was reasonable due to exigent circumstances.

(B) Yes, because of the inevitable discovery rule.

(C) No, because there were no exigent circumstances justifying the patrolling officer's search.

(D) No, because the patrolling officer's search was unreasonable.

Question 13

Police investigating some burglaries received a reliable tip that the stolen goods were being held at 23 Maple Avenue. Based upon the tip and the police investigation, a neutral magistrate issued a warrant. However, a typographical error on the warrant authorized a search of 32 Maple Avenue and not 23 Maple Avenue. Two young officers not previously involved in the investigation executed the warrant at 32 Maple Avenue. In the course of their search, the officers discovered a large bag of heroin on a chair in an upstairs bedroom and then arrested the homeowners for felony possession of an unlawful substance. Before trial, the typographical error was discovered, and the young officers apologized to the homeowners. At trial, the homeowners challenged the admissibility of the heroin.

Should the court exclude the heroin as evidence?

(A) Yes, because the police lacked a warrant to search the home.

(B) Yes, because the police search of the home was unreasonable.

(C) No, because the police acted in good faith when searching 32 Maple Avenue.

(D) No, because the heroin was in plain view and the police thus did not need a warrant.

Question 14

The police had, over time, accumulated reliable information that the defendant operated a large cocaine-distribution network, that he and his accomplices often resorted to violence, and that they kept a small arsenal of weapons in his home. One day, the police received reliable information that a large, brown suitcase with leather straps containing a supply of cocaine had been delivered to the defendant's home, and that it would be moved to a distribution point the next morning. The police obtained a valid warrant to search for and seize the brown suitcase and the cocaine, and went to the defendant's house to execute it.

Upon executing the warrant, the police encountered the defendant in the kitchen holding the suitcase. They seized the suitcase and put handcuffs on the defendant. A search of his person revealed a switchblade knife and a .45-caliber pistol. The police then searched the rest of the house, but found no other people. However, one officer found an Uzi automatic weapon in a box on a closet shelf in the defendant's bedroom. The defendant was subsequently charged with various crimes. The defendant filed a pretrial motion to suppress the use of the Uzi as evidence.

Should the defendant's motion be granted?

(A) Yes, because the search exceeded the scope needed to find out if other persons were present.

(B) Yes, because once the object of the warrant had been found and seized, no further search of the house was permitted.

(C) No, because the police were lawfully in the bedroom and the weapon was immediately identifiable as being subject to seizure.

(D) No, because the police were lawfully in the house and had probable cause to believe that weapons were present.

Question 15

To investigate a suspected large-scale marijuana farming operation, police officers used a helicopter to fly over an isolated and unoccupied large garden shed. The police used a high-resolution heat-sensing camera that is not available for sale to the public to take thermal photographs of the outside of the shed that suggested the presence of heat lamps associated with marijuana cultivation. The police did not enter the shed, but at trial sought to introduce the thermal pictures as part of their evidence of defendant's drug production. Defendant seeks to have the evidence excluded.

Should the court admit the evidence?

(A) Yes, because of the plain view doctrine.

(B) Yes, because the shed was not within the curtilage of a dwelling.

(C) No, because the camera was not generally available to the public.

(D) No, because the defendant had a reasonable expectation of privacy in the shed.

Question 16

The police received a tip that a man was selling drugs on a street corner. Two narcotics officers parked their unmarked car on the opposite side of the street and began to observe the man. He was approached several times by individuals and, after receiving something from them, would reach into his pocket and hand something back, at which point they would walk away.

The officers decided to approach the man. As they neared, the man noticed them and turned to run, tossing a small bag to the ground as he did so. The officers quickly picked up the bag, which they recognized as containing an illegal substance, and gave chase. The man was not particularly fast, and the officers were able to quickly catch up to him and to make their arrest. Upon the arrest, the officers searched the man and found a bag of cocaine in the man's back pocket. At the man's subsequent trial, the man moved to suppress the bag of cocaine.

How should the court rule?

(A) Grant the motion, because the police had not obtained a warrant.

(B) Grant the motion, because the police lacked probable cause.

(C) Deny the motion, because the police had probable cause to arrest the man.

(D) Deny the motion, because the drugs were in plain view.

Question 17

Investigating a 35-year-old suspect believed to be trafficking in child pornography, police detectives arrived at the suspect's house, hoping to interview her. An old man answered the door. He identified himself as the suspect's father and told them that the suspect was not at home. The police asked if they could come in and speak with the father, who let them in. While in the home, the police asked to search for evidence of child pornography. The horrified father again agreed and took the police to the suspect's locked upstairs bedroom. He told them that he never went inside the room because only the suspect had the key. With the father's consent, the police broke down the door to the bedroom. The police searched the bedroom and found hundreds of images of child pornography inside. While the police were searching, the suspect returned home and was arrested.

Have the police violated the suspect's Fourth Amendment rights?

(A) Yes, because the father could not consent to the search of the bedroom.

(B) Yes, because the images were not in plain view.

(C) No, because the images were part of a search incident to an arrest.

(D) No, because the father gave valid consent to the search of the shared premises.

Question 18

A police officer pulled over a car after observing it drive through a stop sign. The officer walked up to the driver's side of the car, ordered the driver out of the vehicle, and told him to place his hands on the trunk of the car. As the driver was getting out of the car, the officer noticed a gun in his waistband. The driver stated that he did not have a permit for the gun. The officer then ordered the passenger in the front seat to also get out of the car and place his hands on the trunk. As the passenger exited the car, he dropped a small bag of heroin on the ground.

The district attorney charged the driver with illegal possession of a firearm and the passenger with illegal possession of a controlled substance. The driver filed a motion to suppress the gun and the passenger filed a motion to suppress the bag of heroin.

How should the court rule on the motions?

(A) Grant the driver's motion, but deny the passenger's motion.

(B) Grant the passenger's motion, but deny the driver's motion.

(C) Grant both motions.

(D) Deny both motions.

Question 19

Police investigating the unlawful sale of copyrighted videos received a tip that much of the copying was taking place in the offices of a small law firm in the suburbs. Based upon the sworn statement of a paralegal at the firm, stating that the copying operation was taking place in the firm's mailroom, police officers obtained a warrant to search the premises for evidence of an illegal video piracy operation. In executing the warrant, the police approached the loading dock area of the firm and, without alerting the occupants of the building, kicked open the back door and burst inside with guns drawn. The subsequent search of the law firm's offices produced a large number of illegally copied videos and the arrest of most of the members of the criminal operation. Before trial, the defendants seek to have the evidence of the search excluded as violating their Fourth Amendment rights.

Must the court exclude the evidence?

(A) Yes, because the police did not knock and announce their presence before executing the warrant.

(B) Yes, because the manner in which the warrant was executed was unreasonable under the Fourth Amendment.

(C) No, because the knock-and-announce rule does not always bar the admission of exclusion of evidence obtained in violation of the rule.

(D) No, because the police do not need to knock and announce their presence before executing a warrant.

Question 20

A man was arrested for assault. Knowing that he was a "three strike" candidate and not wanting to spend the rest of his life in prison, he told the police that his boss sells a substantial amount of professionally stolen merchandise and that he would be willing to help the police obtain evidence against him. The police agreed to work with the man and sent him to the boss's condo with marked merchandise that contained transmitters. When the man left his boss's condo, he no longer had the merchandise. The man had been under surveillance from the time he left the police van until he went in the front door of the condo, and again from the moment he left the condo until he returned to the van.

Once the man returned to the van, the police immediately moved in to arrest the boss for receiving stolen property. They knocked and announced their presence three times, but there was no answer. They then rammed the door and entered, finding the marked stolen property and numerous other items of expected stolen property. They did not find the boss, who had exited by the back stairwell to take his dog for a walk. Upon the boss's return, he was arrested. At trial, the boss's attorney moves to suppress the seized property.

The court should take what action?

(A) Suppress the evidence, because the police had no warrant.

(B) Suppress the evidence, because the items seized were in plain view.

(C) Admit the evidence, because the police knocked and announced their presence before entering.

(D) Admit the evidence, because they had evidence against the boss for the offense.

Quiz 2

Question 1

A police officer has long been suspicious of one of his neighbors. Every time he encounters her, she behaves furtively and seems nervous. Convinced that there is a reason for the neighbor's edginess, the officer decides to investigate further. He knows that the neighbor lives alone, so when she leaves the house with friends one evening, he walks into the open garage and tries the door to the house. Finding it unlocked, he enters the house. In plain view on the coffee table is a large quantity of cocaine and a clear plastic bag containing cash. Looking further, the officer finds records tying the neighbor's sister to the drug operation.

What is the most likely outcome of the neighbor's and her sister's motions to suppress the evidence?

(A) The neighbor's motion will be granted, but the sister's will not.

(B) The sister's motion will be granted, but the neighbor's will not.

(C) Both motions will be granted as to the records, but not as to the items that were in plain view.

(D) Neither motion will be granted.

Question 2

A defendant is wandering down the street in a drunken stupor, periodically stepping off the sidewalk on to the street and into the path of oncoming traffic. A police officer saw the defendant and decided he should help. The officer stopped the defendant and asked his name and how he was doing. The defendant mumbled something about how he "loved her" and how he "shouldn't have done it." Figuring that the defendant was simply drunk, the officer ignored his remarks and decided the best course of action would be to take away any remaining alcohol from the defendant, so that he could sober up.

The officer reached into the defendant's coat pockets and, to his surprise, found a small pistol. "What are you doing with this, man?" the officer asked. When the defendant did not reply, the officer became angry. "I asked you a question," the officer said. "You'd better answer it." The defendant then told him that he had killed his girlfriend and dumped her body in a drainage ditch. The officer arrested the defendant and read him his rights. At the defendant's murder trial, the state moved to admit the evidence of the gun.

How is the court likely to rule?

(A) The evidence will be suppressed, because the officer had no reason to believe that the defendant was armed.

(B) The evidence will be suppressed, because the Terry stop of the defendant was illegal.

(C) The evidence will be admitted, because there was a reasonable suspicion for the Terry stop.

(D) The evidence will be admitted, because guns constitutes a threat to public safety.

Question 3

A defendant, who is divorced, lives with her 11-year-old daughter. One night, the defendant went out to dinner and left her daughter at home. Upon leaving the house, the defendant locked the door to her bedroom.

While the defendant was gone, the daughter found a spare key to her mother's bedroom and opened the door. While rummaging through her mother's dresser, she found a bag containing white powder. Concerned that the bag might contain drugs, the daughter called her father, who still owned the home along with the defendant, to ask his advice. The father instructed her to call the police. The daughter then telephoned the police station and reported what she had found. A patrol car was immediately dispatched to her home.

The daughter allowed the police to come inside the home. The officers then asked her where the bag that she described to the 911 operator was located, and if she could take them to it. The daughter led the officers to the mother's bedroom and gave them the bag, which they took to the station house for a lab test. After the results confirmed that the bag contained cocaine, the defendant was arrested and charged with illegal possession of a controlled dangerous substance. The defendant's attorney filed a motion to prevent the cocaine from being admitted into evidence.

How should the court rule on the motion?

(A) Denied, because the daughter, and her father, as co-owner, had the authority to allow the police inside the home and to make the seizure.

(B) Denied, because the daughter lived with her mother, and she had equal control over the premises.

(C) Granted, because the daughter, as a minor, did not have the apparent authority to permit the police to enter the home.

(D) Granted, because the daughter did not have the apparent authority to permit the police to enter the defendant's bedroom.

Question 4

The defendant owned a large plot of land in a rural area, and his house sat on the middle of the property. On the left side of the defendant's property sat an undeveloped wooded area, and on the right side of the defendant's property sat a guest house and a large garden.

Recently, the defendant was involved in the robbery of a convenience store, which turned deadly when the store clerk was shot. The defendant took the gun that was used in the robbery and hid it in the woods on his property. After following a number of leads, police suspected that the defendant had played a part in the robbery and murder at the convenience store. They went to his house a number of times, but he refused to let them in or talk to them. The police searched the wooded area on the defendant's property without a warrant and found the gun.

Which of the following is true?

(A) The defendant had a Fourth Amendment right to a reasonable expectation of privacy because the gun was not visible from off the property.

(B) The defendant had a Fourth Amendment right to a reasonable expectation of privacy on his entire plot of land, including the wooded area where the police found the gun.

(C) The defendant had no Fourth Amendment right to a reasonable expectation of privacy as to the gun because he had discarded the gun.

(D) The defendant had no Fourth Amendment right to a reasonable expectation of privacy in the wooded area on his property, as it is outside the curtilage of the defendant's home.

Question 5

After a nine-year-old girl was kidnapped while walking home from school, police and community members began to search the neighborhood. While the search for the girl was ongoing, police also launched an extensive investigation of the kidnapping in an effort to identify a suspect. After several days, police identified a neighbor as a suspect in her kidnapping and brought him into the station for questioning. A rookie police officer had heard that after 48 hours the chance of rescuing a kidnapped child alive decreased dramatically. Since more than 48 hours had passed since the girl was kidnapped, the officer became desperate. He asked around until he learned the suspect's identity and took it upon himself to break into the suspect's office and search the files on his computer for evidence. The officer found a document on the computer which appeared to be a detailed description of the kidnapping, so he printed the document and returned to police headquarters. At the same time, pursuant to a search warrant, other officers on the case were conducting a systematic search of the suspect's property beginning with his house and then his office.

Will the computer file be admissible as evidence in the suspect's subsequent criminal trial for the kidnapping?

(A) No, because it is "fruit of the poisonous tree" and therefore tainted.

(B) No, because the officers who had the search warrant were not the ones who discovered the document.

(C) Yes, because there was an urgent need to search the suspect's office in order to locate the girl as quickly as possible.

(D) Yes, because officers would have inevitably discovered the evidence when they searched the suspect's office pursuant to the search warrant.

Question 6

The defendant was driving down the highway, which had a posted speed limit of 65 miles per hour, at 90 miles per hour when a police officer pulled him over for speeding. As per protocol, the officer called for back-up. The closest officer, who responded to the scene, had a drug-sniffing dog in his car. When the back-up officer arrived, they asked the defendant to step out of the car. While the first officer was questioning the defendant, the second officer allowed his dog to sniff the defendant's car. The dog quickly alerted the officer that he smelled drugs in the trunk of the defendant's car.

Which of the following is true?

(A) Allowing the dog to sniff the exterior of the car constitutes a search of the vehicle, subject to Fourth Amendment protections.

(B) Police may only use a drug-sniffing dog when they already have probable cause to search the defendant's vehicle.

(C) Allowing the dog to sniff the exterior of the car does not violate the privacy rights of the suspect.

(D) Allowing the dog to sniff the exterior of the car in this situation violates the privacy rights of the suspect.

Question 7

The police received a report that women dressed as superheroes had robbed a man in his house and stolen many of his valuables. The only way onto or off the island where he lived was a ferry. The last ferry was getting ready to leave for the night when the report came in to the police.

Without attempting to get a warrant, the police stopped all the cars waiting for the ferry. In one vehicle, the police noticed three women fidgeting rather nervously. Upon searching their auto, the police found the victim's stolen property hidden under the front seat. The defendants were immediately placed under arrest.

At their trial for armed robbery, the defendants move to suppress the use of the property confiscated by the police as evidence.

What should the ruling be?

(A) Granted, because the police did not have a warrant to search their car.

(B) Granted, because the police did not have probable cause to suspect that their car contained evidence of the crime.

(C) Denied, because the police had probable cause to search their car and, under the circumstances, no warrant was required.

(D) Denied, because even though the detention was unlawful, the police had reasonable suspicion to believe that their car contained evidence of the crime since they observed the women fidgeting nervously.

Question 8

A competitor of a restaurant owner advised police that the owner had employed illegal noncitizens to work in the kitchen of his restaurant. The competitor snuck in the back door of the kitchen and took pictures of the staff while they were at work. The competitor also stole the time sheets in the file cabinet in the kitchen to prove the working hours and identities of the workers. After obtaining the evidence, the competitor turned it over to the police. The police used the competitor's information to obtain an arrest warrant for the owner. At his trial the owner filed a motion to suppress the evidence obtained by the competitor and quash the arrest.

Should the court grant the motion?

(A) Yes, because the evidence was obtained without a warrant.

(B) Yes, because the competitor had a self-interest in destroying the owner's business.

(C) No, because the initial seizure was made by a private individual.

(D) No, because the evidence was sufficient to establish probable cause to issue the arrest warrant.

Question 9

A reliable police informant telephoned the police to report seeing two men in a blue car selling narcotics outside a local movie theater. The informant gave a detailed description of the two men and the license number of the vehicle. A patrol car was immediately dispatched to the movie theater. A few minutes later, the police saw a car matching the description given parked about two blocks from the movie theater. When the police approached, they saw one man fitting the description provided. The police proceeded to the car and opened the doors of the vehicle. The police then pried open a locked tool case that was situated in the rear of the vehicle. Inside, the police found an envelope that contained about one gram of cocaine. They then placed the driver of the vehicle under arrest. Immediately thereafter, the police opened the glove compartment and found a small amount of marijuana. The driver of the van was subsequently prosecuted and charged with two counts of possession of controlled dangerous substances. He filed a motion to exclude the cocaine and marijuana from evidence.

How will the court most likely rule on his motion?

(A) Granted, as to the cocaine only.

(B) Granted, as to the marijuana only.

(C) Granted, as to both the cocaine and the marijuana.

(D) Denied, as to the cocaine and the marijuana.

Question 10

A police officer sees a robber point a pistol at a couple and take items from them before fleeing on foot. The officer chases after the robber. The robber, with gun still in hand, runs into a nearby apartment. This apartment is being leased by the robber. The officer follows the robber into the apartment and soon realizes that there is no rear exit. The officer begins to search the apartment in an attempt to locate the robber and finds a large quantity of drugs when he opens a hallway closet. The robber is eventually located under a bed in another room. The officer arrests the robber for the armed robbery and possession of drugs with the intent to distribute. At a pretrial motion, the robber's attorney argues that the drugs are inadmissible evidence because the officer did not have a warrant to search the property.

How will the court rule?

(A) The drugs are inadmissible, because the officer needed a warrant to enter the apartment.

(B) The drugs are inadmissible, because the drugs were not in plain view.

(C) The drugs are admissible, because the officer was in hot pursuit.

(D) The drugs are admissible, because there were exigent circumstances.

Question 11

A prominent attorney was suspected of growing marijuana in his home. Based on an anonymous tip, the police went to the lawyer's neighborhood just before dawn. The police could not see into the lawyer's house from the street due to lack of overhead streetlights. Seeing that a neighbor's yard looked directly into the lawyer's home, the officers climbed over a fence and stood in the neighbors' yard and looked through the man's living room window. The officers observed what appeared to be marijuana plants being cultivated under grow lights in the kitchen.

Based on the tip and their observations, the officers then obtained a search warrant which turned up 40 large marijuana plants. Following the lawyer's arrest, he brings a motion to suppress claiming that the evidence supporting the warrant was obtained through a search that violated the Fourth Amendment.

Will the lawyer be successful in his motion to suppress?

(A) No, because the house was searched pursuant to a valid warrant.

(B) No, because the Fourth Amendment does not protect unlawful activities conducted in plain view.

(C) Yes, because the officers' clandestine observation of the plants violated the lawyer's reasonable expectation of privacy concerning activities occurring in his home.

(D) Yes, because no unlawful activities could be observed by the officers from any public vantage point.

Question 12

The United States Post Office received an anonymous tip that heroin would be found inside a large black hat box sent to a local address from Panama. Pursuant to this tip, United States postal employees opened the hat box bound for the local address and found heroin inside. They then resealed the package and left the heroin inside. The local police were notified and watched as the package was delivered to the address.

The police then secured a warrant to search the house for the package. About two hours after the package was delivered, the warrant was executed. The man who opened the door was arrested, and the officers found the package unopened, sitting on the kitchen counter. After seizing the package, the officers looked through the rest of the house. In an upstairs cedar chest, they found a similar hat box that also contained heroin. At trial, the man brings a motion to suppress the heroin found in the cedar chest.

Should the court grant the motion?

(A) Yes, because the search exceeded the authority granted by the warrant.

(B) Yes, because the initial search by the United States Post Office was without probable cause.

(C) No, because, having found the package, the officers had probable cause to believe more narcotics could be located in the house.

(D) No, because the heroin was found pursuant to a valid protective sweep.

Question 13

The defendant owned a 10-acre farm with an old well that was no longer used. His house was located on the middle of the property 1000 yards from the well. An anonymous tip led the police to believe that there was a gun that killed a murdered drug dealer that was hidden in the bottom of that well. The police searched the well on the defendant's property without a warrant and found the gun. The defendant is charged with murder.

Which of the following is true?

(A) The defendant had a Fourth Amendment right to a reasonable expectation of privacy because the gun was not visible from off the property.

(B) The defendant had a Fourth Amendment right to a reasonable expectation of privacy on his entire plot of land, including the well where the police found the gun.

(C) The defendant had no Fourth Amendment right to a reasonable expectation of privacy as to the gun because he had discarded the gun.

(D) The defendant had no Fourth Amendment right to a reasonable expectation of privacy in the well, as it is outside the curtilage of the defendant's home.

Question 14

A man was arrested for sabotaging an electrical plant and causing a blackout in the city. The police suspected that there was another electrical plant that was also a target for sabotage, but could not make the man admit his guilt or help the police in any way. A rookie police officer feared the harm to the community if there was another blackout and searched the man's home and office without a warrant. He found a computer file with information on the next target and how to stop the sabotage. Five minutes later, other police officers who did not know of the rookie police officer's action and pursuant to a search warrant were conducting a systematic search of the man's property beginning with his house and then his office.

Will the computer file be admissible as evidence in the man's subsequent criminal trial for sabotaging the electrical plant?

(A) No, because it is "fruit of the poisonous tree" and therefore tainted.

(B) No, because the officers who had the search warrant were not the ones who discovered the document.

(C) Yes, because there was an urgent need to search the man's office in order to neutralize the threat to the electrical plant as quickly as possible.

(D) Yes, because officers would have inevitably discovered the evidence when they searched the suspect's office pursuant to the search warrant.

Question 15

A man is walking down the street and is weaving down the street in a drunken stupor. A police officer saw the man and asked, "Do you need help?" The man, who reeked of alcohol, said, "Tired. I am going home." The officer ignored his remarks and decided the best course of action would be to take away any remaining alcohol from the defendant so that he could sober up. The officer reached into the defendant's coat pockets and, to his surprise, found a small pistol. "What are you doing with this, man?" the officer asked. When the defendant did not reply, the officer became angry. "I asked you a question," the officer said. "You'd better answer it." The defendant then told him that he had robbed a liquor store. The officer arrested the defendant and read him his rights. At the defendant's robbery trial, the state moved to admit the evidence of the gun.

How is the court likely to rule?

(A) The evidence will be suppressed, because the officer had no reason to believe that the defendant was armed.

(B) The evidence will be suppressed, because the Terry stop of the defendant was illegal.

(C) The evidence will be admitted, because there was a reasonable suspicion for the Terry stop.

(D) The evidence will be admitted, because guns constitute a threat to public safety.

Question 16

A police officer saw a van that had a bumper sticker with the symbol of a rock band that is known to have fans that regularly take recreational drugs during the concert as a way to enhance their enjoyment of the show. The van entered a restaurant parking lot and the driver and her friend walked into the restaurant. The policeman decided to search the van for drugs. He opened the van door in the back which was unlocked and started looking inside. He saw a bag of marijuana. The police officer arrested both the driver and her friend when they came back.

What is the most likely outcome of the driver's and her friend's motions to suppress the evidence?

(A) The driver's motion will be granted, but the friend's will not.

(B) The friend's motion will be granted, but the driver's will not.

(C) Both motions will be granted as to the marijuana, even though the marijuana was in plain view.

(D) Neither motion will be granted.

Question 17

Police received a tip from an informant that a ring of thieves were hoarding stolen property in the house owned by the ringleader's uncle. The ringleader frequented the uncle's house to sell the stolen goods out of the basement and could be found there every evening after 10:00 pm. The police obtained an arrest warrant and went to the uncle's house to arrest the ringleader the next evening. The uncle refused entry to the police, who pushed past him to find the ringleader. When police entered the living room, they observed bricks of marijuana on the table. Police arrested the uncle and the ringleader and charged them both with narcotics offenses. The uncle's motion to suppress the evidence of the drugs was granted. The ringleader files a similar motion seeking suppression of the drugs.

Should the ringleader's motion be granted?

(A) Yes, because the police did not have a valid search warrant for the uncle's house.

(B) Yes, because there was no probable cause to believe that the drugs belonged to the ringleader.

(C) No, because the ringleader had no standing to contest the legality of the search.

(D) No, because the drugs were observed in plain view and there were exigent circumstances.

Question 18

Police officers received a tip from a reliable informant that a night club was operating a drug distribution business out of the basement in the building where the club was located. During a police surveillance of the building, the officers observed a patron leaving the club by the basement stairs and placing what appeared to be a weapon inside his raincoat. The officers stopped the patron on the street who denied that he was ever in the basement of the night club. At that point the officer, fearing for his safety, patted down the outer clothing and felt small tube-shaped vials in the defendant's shirt pocket. The defendant was placed under arrest. The substance in the vials field-tested positive for cocaine. The defendant filed a motion to suppress the cocaine. At the suppression hearing, the arresting officer testified that based on his 20 years of experience, he concluded that the tube-shaped objects were glass vials used by drug dealers to sell narcotics.

If the court believes the officer's testimony, should the evidence of the cocaine be suppressed?

(A) No, because the stop was reasonable in duration and the officer had a reasonable suspicion that the defendant was armed and dangerous.

(B) No, because the officer had probable cause to believe that crime had been committed.

(C) Yes, because the scope of a pat down in a Terry stop is limited to a search for weapons.

(D) Yes, because the informant supplied no information about the patron to police before the stop.

Question 19

A border patrol officer found packages of heroin glued between the soles of gym shoes being exported from Colombia into the United States. Narcotics agents arranged for a controlled delivery of the boxes to the address listed on the packages. After the boxes were delivered to the address, the house was put under surveillance. One week later a woman driving a car with expired plates arrived at the address and began loading the boxes into the trunk of the car. As she drove away the car was stopped by the narcotics agents and the driver was arrested. The agents searched the entire vehicle without first obtaining a warrant. The box was opened and the heroin was found concealed in the soles of the gym shoes. At her trial on charges of possession of heroin and conspiracy, the defendant moved to suppress the search of the trunk.

Should the motion be granted?

(A) No, because the officers had probable cause to search the trunk.

(B) No, because the search was conducted incident to a lawful arrest.

(C) Yes, because the warrantless search was limited to the wingspan of the driver.

(D) Yes, because the agents entrapped the defendant by arranging the controlled delivery.

Question 20

Police observed a customer leave the bar with a plastic cup in his hand and get into his car. The customer pulled into traffic and drove up onto the curb and then made a U-turn going the wrong way on a one-way street. The officer pulled the car over and arrested the driver for DUI. The customer was handcuffed and seated in the back of the police car. The officer then conducted a search of the vehicle and found the plastic cup filled with beer under the driver's seat. The defendant filed a pre-trial motion contesting the legality of the search.

Should the motion be granted?

(A) Yes, because the defendant was already handcuffed and detained in the police car before the search took place.

(B) Yes, because the officer did not have probable cause to look under the driver's seat.

(C) No, because the search was conducted incident to a lawful arrest.

(D) No, because the driver was a recent occupant of the vehicle and the officer had reason to believe that the car contained evidence of the crime for which the defendant was arrested.

Essays

Essay Question 1

IE13JUL012

ISSUE SPOTTING EXERCISE

Consider the fact pattern below and then answer the questions that follow:

Trained narcotics officers were on a routine foot patrol on a block known for frequent drug trafficking. As they approached an intersection, they saw a teenager standing under a streetlight handing something to a woman in exchange for what appeared to be currency. As the officers approached, they heard the teenager saying, "wet, wet," a phrase the officers understood to signify PCP, a powerful narcotic. When the officers attempted to question the teenager, he started to run.

The officers gave chase, and the teenager ran south for three blocks before ducking into a pizza shop. He ran out the back door, scrambled up a fire escape which led to an apartment above the pizza shop, and began climbing into an open window. The officers tackled the teenager when he was halfway through the window into the apartment and tumbled through it into the apartment's living room, in full view of the man who resided in the apartment. The officers arrested the teenager and, upon arresting the teenager, the officers executed a search of the teenager's pockets and found several small foil packets that were seized. Subsequent testing of the contents of these packets determined that the packets contained PCP in its white powder form. After arresting the teenager, one of the officers walked into the kitchen of the apartment and after opening a kitchen drawer, found tiny vials that, to the officer's trained eye, were filled with liquid PCP. Before leaving the apartment, the officers arrested the man who resided in the apartment and seized the tiny vials. Subsequent testing of the contents of the vials determined that the vials contained PCP in its liquid form.

1. *At the teenager's trial, the defense attorney moved to suppress both the foil packets and their contents on Fourth Amendment grounds. How should the court rule on this motion?*

2. *At the man's trial, the defense moved to suppress the vials and their contents on Fourth Amendment grounds. How should the court rule? [For purposes of this question, assume that the officers had entered the man's apartment lawfully.]*

I. **The first interrogatory asks you whether the foil packets found on the teenager should be suppressed. Discussion of this interrogatory requires you to address three different issues. State each issue and list at least three facts that implicate and/or help to resolve each issue.**

Issue #1:

Facts:

1.

2.

3.

4.

Issue #2:

Facts:

1.

2.

3.

Issue #3:

Facts:

1.

2.

3.

II. **The second interrogatory asks whether the vials of PCP found in the kitchen drawer should be suppressed. What sentence in the fact pattern provides you with the most information with regard to the issues being tested?**

Essay Question 1

IE13JUL012

RULE RECOLLECTION EXERCISE

A good rule statement will demonstrate your understanding of the law and provide the foundation for your analysis. This exercise is intended to help you practice: (1) recalling the relevant rules of law; (2) organizing rules of law; and (3) explaining legal concepts completely and concisely.

- PUT AWAY YOUR NOTES for this exercise and practice actively trying to recall the relevant rules.
- In FIFTEEN minutes, write out rule statements for the following issues.
- WRITE THESE RULES OUT IN FULL; do not merely jot down concepts, topics or fragments.

MOTION TO SURPRESS—TEENAGER

Probable Cause

Hot Pursuit

Search Incident to a Lawful Arrest

MOTION TO SURPRESS—MAN

Search and Seizure

Exception—Plain View Doctrine

Exception—Search Incident to Lawful Arrest

Standing

Exclusionary Rule

Essay Question 1

IE13JUL012

ANALYSIS EXERCISE

Connect law (rules) to fact, and draft your analysis paragraph for each issue below.

MOTION TO SURPRESS—TEENAGER

Probable Cause

Hot Pursuit

Search Incident to a Lawful Arrest

MOTION TO SURPRESS—MAN

Search and Seizure

Exception—Plain View Doctrine

Exception—Search Incident to Lawful Arrest

Standing

Exclusionary Rule

Essay Question 2

IE13JUL056

Vic was killed with a knife during a drug deal gone bad. Vic's roommate, who was hiding under a bed during the killing, immediately reported the crime to the police. He also told them that the assailant had taken a kilogram of packaged cocaine marked with a label depicting a scorpion and placed it into his duffel bag. An hour later, the police received a telephone call from an anonymous caller who described a man driving through a neighborhood known for drug activity and said the man was carrying a bloody knife in a duffel bag. Within minutes, a police officer who had been informed about the killing and the telephone call observed Dave driving a vehicle in that location. Dave fit the description given by the anonymous caller.

The officer followed Dave in an unmarked cruiser until Dave arrived at his own apartment building, parked his car, and exited his vehicle holding a duffel bag. The officer was briefly out of sight as he parked his cruiser around the corner. As Dave stood on the public sidewalk, the officer approached with his service weapon drawn but pointed at the ground. He explained the reason for his approach, handcuffed Dave, and opened the duffel bag. The duffel bag contained only the cocaine marked with a scorpion label. The officer said to Dave: "I know you're the one who killed Vic. Where's the knife?" Dave then pointed to some nearby bushes in which he had concealed the knife.

Dave was charged with, among other things, murder and possession of a controlled substance. He has moved to exclude from evidence the cocaine and the knife.

How should the court rule on Dave's motions regarding the following items and on what theory or theories should it rest? For purposes of this question, limit your discussion to Fourth Amendment considerations.

1. *The cocaine. Discuss.*

2. *The knife. Discuss.*

KAPLAN BAR REVIEW

Evidence

Exercise Set 1

Question 1a

What is FRE 401's test for relevancy?

Question 1b

What is the rule for the admissibility of relevant evidence? For the admissibility of irrelevant evidence?

Question 1c

Explain FRE 403's balancing test.

Question 2a

For purposes of hearsay, define "declarant."

Question 2b

For purposes of hearsay, define "statement."

Question 3a

What is the general definition of "hearsay" under FRE 801(c)?

Question 3b

What are the exclusions from the definition of “hearsay” under FRE 801(d)?

Question 4a

What is the general rule against “hearsay” under FRE 802?

Question 4b

Regarding the rule against hearsay, what distinguishes the exceptions to this rule listed in FRE 803 from those exceptions listed in FRE 804?

Question 4c

How can a party establish a declarant's unavailability?

For each of the following exercises, you are given a question prompt (or call) that could appear as part of a multiple-choice question. After reading each question prompt, try to identify rules that would be relevant to answering such a question. Then, based on these relevant rules, brainstorm possible issues that could be raised or tested by the given prompt.

Question 5

How should the court rule?

Question 6

Should the wife's testimony be admitted?

Question 7

Is the homeowner's testimony regarding the neighbor's remarks admissible?

For each of the following exercises, you are now given a question prompt (or call) as well as an accompanying fact pattern. After reading these excerpts, identify a set of relevant rules and the issues that might be tested by such a multiple-choice question.

Question 8

A man lived next door to a woman. Late one night, the man overheard the woman scream, "Ellen, put down the knife, please don't do it!" The next day, the woman was found dead in her bedroom. Ellen was arrested and charged with murdering the woman. At trial, the man proposed to testify to the woman's statement.

Is the man's testimony admissible?

Question 9

An employee was driving a company vehicle, making deliveries to customers. While driving, the employee came upon the scene of a three-car accident. Because he was gawking at the damaged vehicles, the employee did not notice that a victim of the accident was lying on the road. As a result, the company vehicle hit the victim, who subsequently died from her multiple injuries. The next day, the employee was talking to his neighbor about the prior day's events, when he commented, "It is all my fault. I should have been paying more attention to my driving." The victim's estate brought a wrongful death action, suing the employee's company. At trial, the plaintiff called the neighbor to testify that the employee had admitted to him that the accident was his fault.

How should the judge rule on the admissibility of the testimony?

Question 10

At a shareholders' meeting, the CEO of the company announced, "It's been a long road to recovery, but I'm feeling great and ready to guide this company towards future success." The next day, he was found dead. After the insurance company refused to pay on his policy, believing he had committed suicide, the wife sued. At trial, she sought to introduce into evidence the CEO's announcement at the shareholders' meeting.

Should the judge admit the testimony?

Exercise Set 2

Question 1

Complete the following chart by identifying appropriate examples for each column.

STATEMENTS THAT ARE NOT HEARSAY BECAUSE THEY DO NOT SATISFY FRE 801(c)'S GENERAL DEFINITION	STATEMENTS THAT ARE NOT HEARSAY BECAUSE THEY ARE EXCLUDED BY FRE 801(d)

Question 2

Complete the chart based on the specified FRE 803 exception.

FRE 803 EXCEPTIONS	DOES STATEMENT DESCRIBE OR EXPLAIN AN EVENT OR CONDITION?	DOES STATEMENT CONCERN AN EXTERNAL OR A PERSONAL CONDITION?	MUST THE STATEMENT HAVE ANY OTHER CHARACTERISTICS?
Present Sense Impression			
Then-Existing Mental/ Emotional/ Physical Condition			
Excited Utterance			
Made for Medical Diagnosis or Treatment			

Question 3

Complete the chart with the names of the exceptions to the rule against hearsay based on the requirements needed to establish them.

FRE 803 EXCEPTIONS	ELEMENTS OF THE EXCEPTION
	• The record must have been made or adopted by the witness when the matter was fresh in the witness's memory. • The record must concern a matter the witness knew about but now cannot recall well enough to fully and accurately testify.
	• The record must concern an act/event/condition/opinion/diagnosis of the sort that is regularly recorded as part of a regularly conducted activity. • The record must have been made by someone with knowledge of that act/event/condition/opinion/diagnosis. • The record must have been recorded at or near the time of the act/event/condition/opinion/diagnosis.

Question 4

Complete the chart with the requirements needed to establish the following exceptions to the rule against hearsay.

FRE 804 EXCEPTIONS	WHO MADE THE OUT-OF-COURT STATEMENT?	ELEMENTS OF THE EXCEPTION
Former Testimony		
Statement under Belief of Imminent Death		
Statement against Interest		
Statement of Personal or Family History		

Question 5

Fred was shot. He told the investigating officer, "I walked through the door of my house, argued with my wife, Wilma, and then she shot me." At Wilma's trial for battery, Fred testified that when he walked into the house, Wilma was on the couch with a gun pointing at the ground. He then reached to grab the gun, and it went off, hitting him. Fred could not say who caused the gun to go off and testified that he believed it was an accident. The investigating officer testifies at the trial about Fred's statement at the scene. Wilma, the defendant, objects to the officer's testimony as hearsay.

Read the following fact pattern and explain why Craig's testimony about Bill's statement at the scene could be admissible as hearsay that falls within an exception to the rule against hearsay.

Question 6

Audrey sued Bill for a $100 debt. Craig testified that he, Craig, was present when Bill paid Audrey the $100. He testifies, "I saw Bill pay Audrey $100. Bill said that he was repaying his debt to her." Audrey objects to Craig's testifying about what Bill said as hearsay.

For each of the following mini-fact patterns and question prompts, identify the issues to be addressed and the rules relevant to deciding these issues. Then, explain the answer to the question.

Question 7

Pam, who can't remember the details of a conversation with Darla, refers to a memo and then testifies about the conversation.

Is there a hearsay problem presented?

Question 8

On the issue of whether decedent Victor was still alive after the accident, Wanda testified that Victor said: "My head is bleeding and hurts awful bad."

Would the testimony draw a hearsay objection?

Question 9

Pandora sued David for age discrimination. A former district manager employed under Pandora was called to testify that four of David's employees said that Pandora was terminated because of her age and high income level.

Can Pandora testify as to these terminations and the conversations in which they were learned?

Question 10

The state's primary witness to an armed robbery, Scared Witless, testified at trial that he could not identify Dastardly as the robber. Witless was excused subject to being recalled. State then called Top Cop, who will testify that Witless picked Dastardly out of a lineup 10 days after the robbery.

Is Top Cop's testimony admissible?

Quiz 1

Question 1

Two police officers, a sergeant and a lieutenant, were charged with robbery and felony murder. The sergeant's lawyer moved to have the two officers tried separately, and the court granted the motion. The sergeant's trial was held first, and he was acquitted. At the lieutenant's trial, his lawyer called the sergeant's wife as a witness. The sergeant's wife testified that after the sergeant was acquitted, the sergeant told her that he had committed the robbery because he wanted to buy her a new ring and that he felt bad because the lieutenant was not involved.

Should the wife's testimony be admitted?

(A) No, because the sergeant is estopped from contradicting the jury's acquittal verdict.

(B) No, because it is hearsay not within any exception.

(C) Yes, because it is a statement by a co-conspirator.

(D) Yes, because it is a statement against a penal interest.

Question 2

A man was driving to work when his truck collided with a car driven by a woman, who was backing out of her driveway very quickly without looking or yielding to oncoming traffic. The man subsequently filed suit to recover damages from the woman, asserting that he had severely injured his left arm in the accident and that this injury had rendered him unable to work, as he was left-handed. The woman, in turn, claimed that the man's injury was completely unrelated to the car accident and was the result of repetitive-motion syndrome. The man's employer required its employees to have an annual examination. The previous year, three months before the accident, the man had visited the doctor for his yearly exam. During the trial, the man testified that his injury had caused him severe pain and left him physically unable to work. He then called the doctor to the stand to testify that the man had told him during the annual exam that his previous arm problems had gone away.

Should the doctor's testimony be admitted over the woman's objection?

(A) No, because it is hearsay not within any exception.

(B) No, because the man did not make the statement for the purpose of medical treatment.

(C) Yes, because the man made the statement for the purpose of medical treatment.

(D) Yes, as a statement by a party-opponent.

Question 3

A doctor is on trial for battery of a former patient. He claims that he was acting in self-defense, as the client became enraged at the doctor's advice to no longer pursue his dream of attending law school. During trial, the doctor testified that he was warned by two of the patient's friends that the patient had a short temper and to "beware." The prosecution objected.

How should the court rule?

(A) The statement is inadmissible, as hearsay not within an applicable exception.

(B) The statement is inadmissible, as a self-serving statement.

(C) The statement is admissible, as it is not hearsay.

(D) The statement is admissible, under the present sense impression exception to the hearsay rule.

Question 4

A new husband and wife took a ferry ride on their honeymoon. As they were descending the observation deck, the husband slipped on some water on the stairs. The husband alleged that he sustained severe back injuries from the fall, and he sued the ferry owner. Although the ferry owner admitted that the husband was injured by slipping on the water, the ferry owner denied negligence and claimed that the husband was contributorily negligent. The wife died before the trial. At trial, the ferry owner called the ferry captain to testify that just before the husband fell, the captain heard someone call out, "Be careful, the stairs are wet." The husband offered into evidence his wife's deposition testimony that "I did not hear anyone warn my husband about the water on the stairs."

Is the deposition testimony admissible?

(A) No, because the wife is not subject to cross-examination.

(B) No, because the testimony is hearsay not within any exception.

(C) Yes, as a dying declaration.

(D) Yes, as former testimony.

Question 5

Blue, an independent taxi driver, took his car to Aamco Transmissions to have the transmission repaired. Owens, Aamco's employee, was working on the transmission when the hydraulic lift broke. This caused the car to plummet on top of Owens, injuring him. Blue, who happened to be standing nearby, saw the incident and rushed over to help Owens. As Blue tried to free Owens from the metal entanglement, the hydraulic pump (an apparatus connected to the lift) suddenly burst, propelling a sharp metallic fragment into Blue's stomach. Blue received a deep laceration wound but was not otherwise injured. Blue then initiated suit against Aamco based on negligent maintenance of the hydraulic lift. At trial, Blue called the chief inspector for the state Department of Occupation Safety and Health Administration (OSHA), who testified about an official report of the accident as prepared by an OSHA investigator. Blue proposes to introduce a segment of the report that quotes Owens' statement, made to the OSHA investigator in an interview at Aamco's shop, as to the cause of the accident.

Should the trial judge admit the report over Aamco's objection?

(A) Yes, as a past recollection recorded.

(B) Yes, as an opposing party's statement incorporated in a public record.

(C) No, because such documents must be offered in their entirety.

(D) No, because it is hearsay not within any exception.

Question 6

A man sued his company claiming that he was denied his yearly bonus. The CEO claimed that the man was not a bonused employee. To prove this fact, he wished to introduce a record of all bonused employees. The CEO called the secretary who was in charge of payroll to testify to this record. The man objected claiming the report was hearsay.

How should the court rule?

(A) The testimony is inadmissible under the Confrontation Clause.

(B) The testimony is inadmissible, because the business record exception applies only to an actual entry in a business record.

(C) The testimony is admissible as proof of the absence of an entry in a business record.

(D) The testimony is admissible as habit evidence, provided there is corroborating evidence.

Question 7

A college professor is on trial for the murder of her husband. The prosecution alleges that the professor paid one of her students to kill the victim. The student told his girlfriend the day after the husband's death, "We're rich! I just knocked off the old man and made $100,000 for five seconds' work." The student was a bit too exuberant, however, and a neighbor outside overheard every word. The student mysteriously disappeared before trial. Over the professor's objection, the neighbor testified at trial as to the student's remarks.

Why is the neighbor's testimony regarding the student's remarks admissible despite the professor's objection?

(A) It is a statement with circumstantial guarantees of trustworthiness.

(B) It is a statement by an opposing party.

(C) It is a statement against penal interest.

(D) It is an excited utterance.

Question 8

A bookie was arrested and charged with the murder of a gambler. The bookie lived in New York City. The gambler, who resided in Philadelphia, was found shot to death in New York City. During the bookie's murder trial, the prosecution called the gambler's sister to testify. She proposed to testify that the day before the gambler was killed, he told her, "I intend to take the train to New York City tomorrow and pay my bookie the money I owe him."

Is the sister's testimony admissible?

(A) Yes, to show the gambler's intent.

(B) Yes, as a verbal act.

(C) No, because the gambler is not subject to cross-examination.

(D) No, as hearsay not within any recognized exception.

Question 9

A patient sued his doctor for malpractice. The patient called an expert witness to testify that the drugs prescribed by the doctor were so experimental that it constituted negligence under accepted practices in the medical community. On cross-examination, the expert stated that Pharmacology: A Guide for the Practitioner was a reliable authority in her area of specialty. The expert testified that she, however, did not rely on that treatise in forming her opinion. The doctor's attorney then proposed to read a portion from the treatise, which stated that the drugs prescribed by the doctor are widely used by other physicians in treating patients. The patient's attorney objected.

Will the court admit the evidence?

(A) No, because the text of the treatise constitutes inadmissible hearsay.

(B) No, because the expert did not rely on the treatise in forming her opinion.

(C) Yes, as substantive evidence.

(D) Yes, to impeach the expert, but not as substantive evidence.

Question 10

A man was charged with domestic abuse of his wife after police responded to a call from his house. When they arrived, the man's wife told police that her husband had beaten her. While the woman did not testify at the man's trial, the police officer did testify about what she had told him. The man's attorney objected to the admission of the wife's statement to the police.

How should the trial court rule?

(A) The statement is inadmissible, because in criminal cases, all evidence presented against the defendant must be subject to cross-examination in front of the trier of fact.

(B) The statement is inadmissible, because it was testimonial in nature.

(C) The statement is admissible, because it was made while under the stress of a startling event.

(D) The statement is admissible, because it was not testimonial in nature and qualifies as an excited utterance.

Question 11

A truck driver for a local beer distributor was pulling onto the freeway when he collided with a car driven by a bank teller. The bank teller and her passengers were seriously injured in the accident, and they filed suit against the truck driver, alleging that he failed to yield as he entered the freeway from the entrance ramp. They also alleged that he had exceeded by five hours the company's 12-hour limit for drivers per day, and that he should not have been driving at all, as he was taking medication that caused dizziness and fatigue. The truck driver, in turn, claimed that the bank teller was speeding and had failed to make any attempt to avoid the accident even though the two lanes to the left of the entrance ramp were wide open. The truck driver's attorney seeks to introduce the testimony of the state trooper who first arrived on the scene that, when he approached the bank teller's car immediately following the accident, she stated over and over, "I should have slowed down or moved over." The bank teller objects.

Is the trooper's testimony admissible?

(A) Yes, because the trooper overheard the statement during his investigation.

(B) Yes, because the testimony concerns a statement by the bank teller.

(C) No, because the statement does not admit any wrongdoing that is clearly a violation of the motor vehicle law.

(D) No, because it is hearsay.

Question 12

A man was prosecuted for armed robbery of a local convenience store. The robber had been extremely unkempt, with long hair and a scruffy beard. The store clerk identified him in a photo lineup. At trial, the alleged robber wore a suit and tie, was clean-shaven, and had short hair. The prosecutor then showed the store clerk a group of photographs. The clerk testified that she had previously told the prosecutor that the third photograph was a picture of the robber. The third photograph was a picture of the suspect, with long hair and a beard.

Should the clerk's testimony be admitted?

(A) No, because it violates the suspect's confrontation rights.

(B) No, as hearsay not within any exception.

(C) Yes, as a prior identification.

(D) Yes, as a recorded recollection.

Question 13

A man's car broke down, and since he was only a mile from the repair shop, he decided to walk. As he approached the repair shop, he tripped on the cracked front cement step. The man fell and fractured his wrist. A woman who was jogging by rushed up to him and asked, "Are you hurt?" The man said, "Yes." The jogger then exclaimed, "It's horrible that a business would allow its front step to deteriorate to this state!" A few months later, the man filed an action against the repair shop to recover for his injuries.

Is the jogger's statement admissible at trial?

(A) Yes, as a statement by an opposing party.

(B) Yes, as an excited utterance.

(C) No, as hearsay not within any recognized exception.

(D) No, as irrelevant nonhearsay.

Question 14

A man crashed into a woman's car. Shortly after the accident, a police officer arrived at the scene, and the woman told the officer that the man had run the red light and swerved into her car. The police officer wrote her statement in the "Accident Report Form," which he was required to complete after every accident. The woman sued for personal injuries sustained in the accident. On direct examination, her attorney calls her to testify as to her statement to the police officer.

Is the woman's statement admissible?

(A) No, because a party is precluded from introducing their out-of-court statements at a subsequent trial.

(B) No, because it is hearsay not within any exception.

(C) Yes, because it constitutes a prior consistent statement.

(D) Yes, because the woman is in court testifying to an out-of-court statement, and is therefore subject to cross-examination.

Question 15

A plaintiff brought suit against a car owner for personal injuries sustained in an automobile accident. The car was driven by a neighbor, who was angry that the plaintiff would not allow him to date the plaintiff's daughter. Liability is based on a statute that assesses liability on the automobile owner for the negligent actions of those driving with the owner's consent. The plaintiff offers the testimony of his chiropractor's receptionist that the plaintiff told her he needed an appointment for the neck and back pain he has had for several days. The car owner's lawyer objects.

Which of the following is most accurate?

(A) The court should overrule the objection, because the evidence is admissible as a present sense impression.

(B) The court should overrule the objection, because the evidence is admissible as a statement for purposes of medical treatment or diagnosis.

(C) The court should sustain the objection, because a statement of personal history is not appropriate if the declarant is available.

(D) The court should sustain the objection, because the receptionist is not a medical professional.

Question 16

The plaintiff owned a very successful seafood restaurant. At the end of the previous season, the plaintiff had become concerned about competition from a new restaurant approximately two miles away. Now, at the beginning of this new season, the plaintiff was particularly concerned, because the clams and scallops he was receiving from his supplier were not up to their usual standard. The plaintiff believed that the diminished quality was due to changes in water temperatures and environmental conditions, which the plaintiff expected to improve by the start of summer. However, even well into the summer season, the plaintiff found that the seafood continued to be subpar.

Early in July, he hired a secretary, who was previously employed by the supplier, to work in his office. Shortly after the secretary began working for the plaintiff, she told him that the owner of the new restaurant was an old high school buddy of the president and owner of the supplier. The secretary told the plaintiff that the owner of the supplier was a silent partner in the new restaurant, and that at a meeting in March, the secretary overheard them discussing a plan to supply inferior seafood to the plaintiff's restaurant, in order to hurt the plaintiff's reputation and increase business at the new restaurant.

The plaintiff immediately instructed his staff to keep tallies of how many meals containing seafood supplied by the supplier were sent back to the kitchen as a result of customer complaints. In a subsequent action by the plaintiff against the supplier for interference with business relations, the plaintiff moved to introduce the tallies into evidence.

Are the tallies admissible?

(A) Yes, because they constitute a past recollection recorded.

(B) Yes, because they are a business record.

(C) No, because they are hearsay not within any exception.

(D) No, because there is no proof that the meals were sent back because of the inferior seafood.

Question 17

A defendant was on trial for drug distribution. The arresting officer was called by the prosecution to describe in detail the events that led to the defendant's arrest. The officer described the night in question, where he was, and what he observed. He was asked to provide a list of what he confiscated from the defendant after he was arrested. The officer testified that the defendant has a large amount of money and many small packets of drugs in several pockets throughout his clothing. When asked specifically about the number of drugs packets, the officer was unable to recall. The officer was then shown his police report. The officer quickly flipped to the third page of the report, then looked at the prosecutor. The prosecutor asked if the officer was now able to remember how many bags of drugs were taken from the defendant. The officer indicated that he was, but before he could answer the question, the defense attorney objected to the officer's testimony.

How should the court rule?

(A) Sustain the objection, because the officer lacks a present memory of the incident.

(B) Sustain the objection and require the report to be admitted into evidence, because the jury is just as capable as reading the report as the officer.

(C) Overrule the objection, because the officer's memory was refreshed.

(D) Overrule the objection, because the report is admissible as a past recollection recorded.

Question 18

After a large chemical spill at an industrial worksite, an inspector for the Environmental Protection Agency investigated the incident. In his initial visit, the investigator took pictures of the scene and made some notes after conducting interviews. After a three-week vacation, the investigator compiled his findings and submitted them in a report. Two weeks after submitting his report, he died of a heart attack. His conclusion was that the worksite owner and operator was negligent is allowing the spill to happen and suggested that fines and penalties be assessed.

In a subsequent civil case brought by a worker at the site against the owner and operator, the worker seeks to use the investigator's report. The owner objects.

Is the investigator's report admissible?

(A) No, because the report was not created contemporaneously with the chemical spill.

(B) No, because the report was created in anticipation of litigation, and the inspector is now unavailable.

(C) Yes, because the report was created by the inspector, who had a duty imposed by law.

(D) Yes, because the inspector is now unavailable.

Question 19

Four men entered into a lease as tenants of a five-bedroom house. They each had a separate bedroom and used the fifth bedroom as a laboratory to manufacture the illegal drug methamphetamine.

One of the men was the so-called moneyman; he provided the funds to make the rental payments and to purchase the laboratory equipment. One of the other men was the chemist; he had both an undergraduate and graduate degree in chemistry and knew the formula and procedure for producing methamphetamine. Another of the men had sold drugs in the past and knew potential buyers of the methamphetamine. Finally, the fourth man was the enforcer; his role in the scheme was to make sure that no unauthorized persons entered onto the premises of the house.

The four men had been involved in this drug venture for seven months when they were finally arrested and charged with conspiracy to manufacture and distribute methamphetamine, and distribution and manufacture of methamphetamine. During the trial, the prosecution wishes to introduce, as evidence against the moneyman, a statement made by the enforcer to the landlord at the time of the signing of the lease, in which the enforcer said, "No matter what you charge us for rent, you better O.K. it with the moneyman, because he's the one who will really be paying it." The moneyman's attorney objects.

The judge's ruling on admissibility will depend on what fact?

(A) Whether the enforcer actually paid all of the rent.

(B) Whether the enforcer had a legal obligation to pay the rent under the terms of the lease.

(C) Whether the landlord may be considered a party-opponent.

(D) Whether the statement was made during the course of and in furtherance of the conspiracy.

Question 20

A plaintiff was seriously injured in a collision involving three trucks. A sideswipe occurred between the plaintiff's pickup truck and a trailer truck as they passed in opposite directions. The sideswipe caused the plaintiff's truck to careen down the road and into the path of a second trailer truck. The driver of the second trailer truck was immediately killed. Both of the trailer trucks were owned by the same transport company. At trial, the plaintiff called a witness to the collision to testify that he heard an unidentified female witness scream, "Oh my God, that trailer truck sideswiped that little pickup truck."

How should the trial judge rule regarding the witness's testimony?

(A) Admissible, as a declaration of then-existing state of mind.

(B) Admissible, as an excited utterance.

(C) Inadmissible, because it contains inadmissible opinion evidence.

(D) Inadmissible, as hearsay not within any recognized exception.

KAPLAN BAR REVIEW

Quiz 2

Question 1

A man lived next door to a woman. Late one night, the man overheard the woman scream "Ellen, put down the knife, please don't do it!" The next day, the woman was found dead in her bedroom. Ellen was arrested and charged with murdering the woman. At trial, the man proposed to testify to the woman's statement.

Upon objection by the defendant's counsel, how should the court rule on the man's testimony regarding the woman's statement?

(A) Admissible as a dying declaration, if the jury determines that the woman believed that her death was imminent.

(B) Admissible as a dying declaration, if the judge, by a preponderance of the evidence, determines that the woman believed that her death was imminent.

(C) Inadmissible, because the probative value is substantially outweighed by the danger of unfair prejudice.

(D) Inadmissible, as hearsay not within any recognized exception.

Question 2

A defendant was on trial for attempted murder. The alleged victim was called by the prosecution to testify. During her testimony, the victim recounted the incident and described how the defendant savagely beat her with a baseball bat. She was not asked by the prosecution whether she made any statements during the attack. After the victim was excused and left the witness stand, the prosecution called another witness to testify. The witness proposes to testify that when the beating stopped, the victim screamed, "I'm dying. Don't let the defendant get away with this."

Upon objection by the defendant's attorney, how will the court rule on the witness's proffered testimony?

(A) Admissible, as an excited utterance.

(B) Admissible, as a dying declaration.

(C) Inadmissible, as hearsay not within any recognized exception.

(D) Inadmissible, because the victim was not questioned about the statement before being excused.

Question 3

After being passed over for a promotion, an aeronautic engineer became a whistleblower. He contacted a government agency to state that the company for which he worked was submitting false safety reports on newly built aircraft. When the company learned that the engineer was leaking this information to the government agency, he was fired from his job. Afterward, the engineer sued the company for wrongful termination of employment. During the discovery stage of litigation, the engineer was deposed by the company's attorney. In his deposition, the engineer stated that the company submitted false safety reports to the government agency to cover up structural defects in its aircraft. A pilot was injured when one of the company's airplanes he was piloting crashed. The pilot asserted a strict products liability tort against the company. At trial, the pilot sought to introduce into evidence portions of the engineer's deposition from his wrongful termination lawsuit against the company. Assume that the engineer is unavailable to testify at trial.

Upon objection by the company, how should the trial court judge rule on the engineer's deposition?

(A) Admissible, as former testimony.

(B) Admissible, as a vicarious statement.

(C) Inadmissible, as hearsay not within any recognized exception.

(D) Inadmissible, because the company did not have the opportunity to cross-examine the engineer on the liability issue for which the statement is now being offered.

Question 4

A man and a woman were involved in a car accident that occurred when the man abruptly switched lanes in front of the woman without signaling. Unable to stop, the woman hit the man's car into a median. Immediately after the accident, as the two drivers emerged from their vehicles, a pedestrian, obviously emotional and upset from having just observed an accident, ran up to the man and shouted, "You careless driver, you! Didn't you ever learn that you're supposed to use a turn signal when you switch lanes?" The pedestrian was never identified and is not present at trial.

How should the court rule on the pedestrian's statement?

(A) Admissible, as nonhearsay.

(B) Admissible, even though it is hearsay.

(C) Admissible, under the excited utterance exception.

(D) Inadmissible, because the bystander cannot be identified and is not present at trial.

Question 5

A plaintiff sued a defendant for injuries suffered in a fall on the sidewalk of the defendant's home. The plaintiff's complaint alleged that the walk was covered by a thick sheet of ice, which had been negligently left there for several days by the defendant. In his answer, the defendant set forth that the ice formed overnight and that the plaintiff fell before the defendant had a chance to remove it. During the trial, a physician, whose office was next door to the defendant's home, testified that he saw the plaintiff fall and that the ice, which had been there for several days was at least two inches thick. On cross-examination, counsel for the defendant asked the physician the following question: "During your treatment of the plaintiff on the day in question, is it not true that he told you his fall resulted from a loss of equilibrium after he suffered from dizziness?"

Upon objection by the plaintiff's attorney, how should the court rule on the physician's testimony?

(A) Admissible, because it is reasonably pertinent to diagnosis or treatment.

(B) Admissible, because the physician had personal knowledge of the plaintiff's injuries.

(C) Inadmissible, because the defendant's counsel failed to lay a proper foundation.

(D) Inadmissible, because the physician's testimony is not relevant to prove that the plaintiff's alleged injuries are false or exaggerated.

Question 6

A heartsick lover knew he was being foolish, but he just could not stop himself. The woman he was in love with was so beautiful, and she was so lonely with her husband in prison. She had told the lover that her husband was extremely jealous. She said that her husband was in prison because he had shot her last lover when he learned of their affair. About four months after he started seeing the woman, the lover received a telephone call from her. She seemed distraught, and cried, "My husband escaped from prison this evening, and he knows about us!" As expected, the husband called on the lover that evening. The lover shot the husband and was prosecuted for his murder. The lover claims self-defense. At trial, he attempts to testify to the woman's statement that her husband was in prison because he had shot her last lover when he learned of the affair.

If the statement is offered to prove that the husband was in prison because he had shot the woman's lover when he learned of the affair, should the statement be admitted?

(A) Yes, under the state-of-mind exception.

(B) Yes, as nonhearsay.

(C) No, as hearsay not within any exception.

(D) No, because it is self-serving.

Question 7

A man crashed into a woman's car. Shortly after the accident, a police officer arrived at the scene, and the woman told the officer that the man had run the red light and swerved into her car. The police officer wrote her statement in the "Accident Report Form," which he was required to complete after every accident. The woman sued for personal injuries sustained in the accident. On direct examination, her attorney called her to testify and asked her to recall the events of the night.

Is the woman's testimony admissible?

(A) No, because a party is precluded from introducing their own out-of-court statements at a subsequent trial.

(B) No, because it is hearsay not within any exception.

(C) Yes, because the officer wrote down the statement as part of his official duties.

(D) Yes, because the woman has firsthand knowledge of the events of the night in question.

Question 8

A woman was on trial for the murder of her husband. The prosecution alleged that the woman paid one of her neighbors $25,000 to kill her husband. Immediately after the killing, the neighbor boarded a bus and called his roommate. In a lowered voice, he whispered, "Pack your bags, we gotta get out of town for a while 'till the heat cools off. Don't worry about money, I got it covered." The neighbor's conversation was heard by a fellow passenger. The neighbor was arrested at the airport the following day. At trail, the prosecution attempted to call the neighbor to testify, but he invoked his Fifth Amendment right not to testify. The prosecution then called the passenger to testify. The wife objected.

Which of the following is most accurate?

(A) The statement is inadmissible, because it does not directly incriminate the neighbor.

(B) The statement is inadmissible, because it does not directly incriminate the wife.

(C) The statement is admissible, as a statement against interest.

(D) The statement is admissible, as an excited utterance.

Question 9

A heavyset man with long red hair robbed a liquor store. Thereafter, a man was arrested and charged with the armed robbery. At the man's trial, the owner of the liquor store was called to testify. He admitted that he was unable to identify the man, who now had a shaven head, as the robber. The prosecuting attorney then handed the owner six photographs. He proposed to testify, over defense objections, that he had previously told the prosecuting attorney that picture #4, admittedly a picture of the man before he shaved his head, was a picture of the person who robbed his store.

How should the court rule on the owner's proffered testimony?

(A) Admissible, as a prior identification by the witness.

(B) Admissible, as a past recollection recorded.

(C) Inadmissible, as hearsay not within any recognized exception.

(D) Inadmissible, because it is a violation of the man's right of confrontation.

Question 10

While driving her company vehicle near a pedestrian mall, a woman came upon the scene of a three-car accident. She was so busy gawking at the damaged vehicles that she failed to see one of the victims lying on the road in front of her car. She hit and ran over the victim, who survived and sued the woman's company. The victim offers the testimony of a witness to the incident. Referring to the woman, the witness stated, "The driver of that car ran over the victim as he was lying on the ground awaiting an ambulance, and said 'It is all my fault, I should have been paying more attention to my driving.'" Assume for this question that the woman is available to testify.

How should the trial judge rule on the admission of the testimony?

(A) Admissible, as a statement against interest.

(B) Admissible, as a present sense impression.

(C) Admissible, as a statement by a party-opponent.

(D) Inadmissible, as hearsay not within any recognized exception.

Question 11

A patient sued his doctor for malpractice. The patient called an expert witness to testify that the drugs prescribed by the doctor were so experimental that it constituted negligence under accepted practices in the medical community. On cross-examination, the expert stated that Pharmacology: A Guide for the Practitioner was a reliable authority in her area of specialty. At trial, it was also stipulated that the treatise in question was first published at the beginning of the last century and had been reprinted every year since with updates. The doctor's attorney then proposed to enter the treatise as an exhibit, highlighting a passage which stated that the drugs prescribed by the doctor are widely used by other physicians in treating patients. The patient's attorney objected.

Will the court admit the treatise?

(A) No, because the text of the treatise constitutes inadmissible hearsay.

(B) No, because the learned treatise exception requires the relevant sections be read to the jury, but not received as evidence itself.

(C) Yes, as hearsay falling under the learned treatise exception.

(D) Yes, because the jury determines the weight of the evidence.

Question 12

A woman called 911, telling the operator that her husband had hit her, threatened her children, and was now breaking objects in the living room. Once the husband saw her calling 911, he fled, and the caller told the operator where he went. The husband was arrested and charged with assault. At trial, the woman did not testify. Instead, the prosecution called the 911 operator to play the recording of what the woman said in her call. The husband's attorney objected to the admission of the wife's call to the police.

How should the trial court rule?

(A) The statement is inadmissible, because in criminal cases, all evidence presented against the defendant must be subject to cross-examination in front of the trier of fact.

(B) The statement is inadmissible, because it was testimonial in nature.

(C) The statement is admissible, as a statement made while under the stress of a startling event.

(D) The statement is admissible, because it was not testimonial in nature and qualifies as an excited utterance.

Question 13

A man was a convicted of sexual assault and required to register with the county of his residence within 30 days of his release from prison. After being paroled, the man rented an apartment, but failed to register. Three months later, during a routine traffic stop, the man was arrested for failing to register in violation of his parole.

At trial, the prosecutor called the chief clerk of the county in which the defendant's apartment was located to testify. She proposed to testify that she did a diligent search of the country sex-offense registry and that the defendant's name did not appear in the records. The defendant objected, claiming that her testimony was hearsay.

How should the court rule?

(A) The testimony is inadmissible, under the Confrontation Clause.

(B) The testimony is inadmissible, because the business record exception applies only to an actual entry in a business record.

(C) The testimony is admissible, as proof of the absence of an entry in a business record.

(D) The testimony is admissible, because the clerk has firsthand knowledge of the country records.

Question 14

A defendant was on trial for drug distribution. The arresting officer was called by the prosecution to describe in detail the events that led to the defendant's arrest. The officer described the night in question, where he was, and what he observed. He was asked to provide a list of what he confiscated from the defendant after he was arrested. The officer testified that the defendant had a large amount of money and many small packets of drugs in several pockets throughout his clothing. When asked specifically about the number of drugs packets, the officer was unable to recall. The officer was then shown his police report. The officer read over his report for several minutes. The prosecutor then asked if the officer was able to remember how many bags of drugs were taken from the defendant. The officer responded that he could not. At this point, the prosecutor directed the office to page three of his report and asked him to read the fifth line, which said, "Confiscated from the defendant's jacket were three purple packets with an off-white powdery substance, and confiscated from his right front pants pocket were 33 purple packets with an off-white powdery substance, that were placed on property receipt #43567." The defense attorney objected to the officer's testimony.

How should the court rule?

(A) Sustain the objection, because the officer lacks a present memory of the incident.

(B) Sustain the objection, and require the report to be admitted because the jury is just as capable as reading the report as the officer.

(C) Overrule the objection, because the officer's memory was refreshed.

(D) Overrule the objection, because the officer's testimony is admissible as a past recollection recorded.

Question 15

A group of women having a bachelorette party were inside of a club when a shooting occurred behind their table. The bartender was arrested for aggravated assault for the shooting. At trial, the bride-to-be took the stand to testify. She admitted that she did not actually see the shooting but that she heard someone behind her yell, "Watch out! He's got a gun! The bartender's got a gun!" She testified that she heard this being yelled at the same time that she heard the gunshots. There was only one bartender, a male, employed by the bar that night. The person yelling never came forward to speak to the police about the shooting.

Can the bride-to-be testify about what she heard?

(A) No, because the declarant's statement it is hearsay not within any exception.

(B) No, because the declarant is unavailable.

(C) Yes, because the statement describes an event while the declarant was perceiving that event.

(D) Yes, because there is sufficient corroboration presented, therefore this is a question of weight, not admissibility.

Question 16

A man pulled his truck onto the freeway and collided with a car. The driver of the car was seriously injured in the accident, and subsequently filed suit against the truck driver, alleging that he failed to yield as he entered the freeway from the entrance ramp. The truck driver, in turn, claimed that the driver of the car was speeding and had failed to make any attempt to avoid the accident even though the two lanes to the left of the entrance ramp were wide open. The truck driver's attorney called the truck driver to testify that when he approached the car immediately following the accident, the driver of the car stated over and over, "I should have slowed down or moved over." The driver of the car objected.

Should the truck driver be allowed to testify as to the driver of the car's statement?

(A) No, because it is inadmissible hearsay.

(B) No, because the truck driver is an interested party and there is no corroboration of the statement.

(C) Yes, because it shows awareness by the driver of the car that he was speeding.

(D) Yes, because it is a statement by an opposing party.

Question 17

A fan attended a minor league hockey game in his hometown. Unfortunately, he was only able to obtain tickets in the visitor's section. While at the game, he became involved in an altercation with a fan of the visiting team. When the fan cheered for a home team goal, the visiting fan turned around and threatened to kill the home fan if he didn't shut up. The home fan pulled a knife out of his pocket and stabbed the visiting fan in the arm. At his trial for aggravated assault, the home fan wants to introduce a statement from a witness who was standing next to the visiting fan at the game. The statement, which the witness had made earlier in the game when the home fan cheered for the home team, was, "You'd better watch out. At a hockey game last week, the visiting fan put two guys in the hospital when they wouldn't shut up. One of them had 33 stitches after the visiting fan bashed his head against the steps." Assume that the witness's statement is being offered as proof of the effect it produced in the home fan's mind.

In this regard, how will the statement most likely be found?

(A) Admissible, because the testimony is not hearsay as it is not being offered for its truth.

(B) Admissible, as a present sense impression.

(C) Inadmissible, as hearsay not within any recognized exception.

(D) Inadmissible, because the statement is self-serving.

Question 18

After an airplane crash at a small airfield, an inspector for the Federal Aviation Administration investigated the crash. In her initial visit, the investigator took pictures of the scene and made some notes after conducting interviews. One particular interview was with a novice pilot who happened to be at the airfield when the crash occurred. He recalled to the investigator seeing something wrong with the left wing of the crashed plane before it took off, but that he didn't have a chance to warn the pilot. He went on to say that "even a novice like him would have done a quick safety check and spotted the issue before taking off." The investigator then compiled her findings and submitted them in a report. Her conclusion was that the pilot failed to conduct himself as a reasonably prudent pilot.

A ground worker at the airfield who had been burned trying to rescue the pilot brought a civil case against the pilot's estate. The ground worker wanted to introduce the novice pilot's statement from the investigator's report. The estate's attorney objected.

Is the novice pilot's statement admissible?

(A) No, because it is hearsay not falling within any exception.

(B) No, because the estate does not have an opportunity to cross-examine the investigator or the novice pilot.

(C) Yes, as a business record, because the FAA routinely conducts such investigations.

(D) Yes, because it is contained inside of a public record compiled by a government agent under duty of law.

Question 19

A CEO was addressing a large group of shareholders at an annual meeting in which his opening remarks discussed the health of the business, some recent acquisitions, and his personal health. "It was a long trip back," he said, "but I am feeling great, ready to take on the world." This news immediately hit the media and stock prices jumped 2%, as there was speculation that the CEO was suffering from severe depression.

The following morning, the CEO was found dead in his hotel room. After his death, the CEO's wife attempted to collect on his life insurance policy, but her claim was denied due to speculation that the CEO committed suicide.

At trial, the wife sought to use the CEO's statement to the shareholders that he was feeling great and ready to take on the world. The insurance company objected.

Should the trial judge admit the testimony?

(A) No, because there was speculation that he suffered from depression.

(B) No, because it was not made to a doctor.

(C) Yes, because it is relevant to the CEO's medical condition.

(D) Yes, because it is a statement of the CEO's then-existing physical condition.

Question 20

The plaintiff owned a very successful seafood restaurant. At the end of the previous season, the plaintiff became concerned about competition from a new restaurant approximately two miles away, and so he decided to hire a quality-control administrator who would help increase customer satisfaction and profitability. As one of his first new directives, the quality-control administrator created a spreadsheet and instructed the staff to keep tallies of any service-related issues. He had three headings on the spreadsheet: (1) food sent back based on quality; (2) complaints about service in general; and (3) comments about price.

About three months later, the plaintiff learned that his seafood supplier was being paid by the competitor to deliver subpar seafood to the plaintiff and keep the best product for the competitor. The plaintiff then brought suit against the competitor for intentional interference with a business relationship. In order to prove damages, the plaintiff called the quality-control administrator to testify as to the column on the spreadsheet that showed the number of meals that were send back due to food quality.

Is the quality-control administrator allowed to testify as to the spreadsheet?

(A) No, because the purpose of keeping the record was not sufficiently business-related.

(B) No, because the spreadsheet constitutes hearsay not within any exception.

(C) Yes, because the spreadsheet constitutes a past recollection recorded.

(D) Yes, because the spreadsheet is a business record.

Essays

Essay Question 1

IE13JUL034

ISSUE SPOTTING EXERCISE

Consider the fact pattern below and then answer the questions that follow:

An owner of a pizzeria in the downtown area of a large city kept the pizzeria going for twenty years, in spite of difficult economic conditions. One day, a real-estate developer stopped by the pizzeria, and informed the owner that he had just purchased the building in which the pizzeria was located. He said that he planned to evict the pizzeria in place of either a clothing boutique or a bank branch. The developer then ordered a slice of pizza and went on his way. The owner's daughter, who was working the cash register that day, ran down the street after the developer shouting, "My father would like you to come back to the store now, because he wants to give you a piece of his mind."

The developer followed her back into the pizzeria. Once the developer was inside the pizzeria, the owner and the developer began fighting, and the owner grabbed the developer's hand and put it in the hot oven. After the fight, the developer went to a hospital emergency room, where he told the intake nurse, "Some maniacal pizza guy shoved my hand in a hot pizza oven." The police were called, and the pizzeria owner's daughter told the police, "My father never intended to hurt the man, but the man started the fight, then slipped and reached out for the oven." The developer's burns were not severe, but a doctor examining him determined that he needed immediate, unrelated surgery for appendicitis, which carried a small risk of death. Before going into surgery, the developer told his friend, "If I do die during surgery, tell the pizzeria owner I'm sorry I started the fight." The developer died during surgery, and the owner was arrested for criminal battery.

At trial, the daughter testifies that the developer started the fight, and accidentally slipped, causing his hand to be injured. The prosecutor implies that she is lying in order to protect her father.

Analyze the following statements for their admissibility at trial: (1) the daughter's statement to the developer; (2) the developer's statement to the intake nurse; (3) the daughter's statement to the police; and (4) the developer's statement to his friend.

I. **All four statements deal with hearsay. List one fact for each statement that tells you that hearsay is at issue:**

Statement 1:

Statement 2:

Statement 3:

Statement 4:

II. **Each statement implicates a different hearsay exception or exemption. For each statement, state the hearsay exception/exemption that is implicated, and then list the facts that implicate that exemption/exception.**

A. **The daughter's statement to the developer.**

Exemption/Exception:

Facts:

B. The developer's statement to the intake nurse.

Exemption/Exception:

Facts:

C. The daughter's statement to the police.

Exemption/Exception:

Facts:

D. The developer's statement to his friend.

Exemption/Exception:

Facts:

Essay Question 1

IE13JUL034

RULE RECOLLECTION EXERCISE

A good rule statement will demonstrate your understanding of the law and provide the foundation for your analysis. This exercise is intended to help you practice: (1) recalling the relevant rules of law; (2) organizing rules of law; and (3) explaining legal concepts completely and concisely.

- PUT AWAY YOUR NOTES for this exercise and practice actively trying to recall the relevant rules.
- In FIFTEEN minutes, write out rule statements for the following issues.
- WRITE THESE RULES OUT IN FULL; do not merely jot down concepts, topics, or fragments.

DAUGHTER'S STATEMENT TO THE DEVELOPER: OPPOSING PARTY'S STATEMENT

DEVELOPER'S STATEMENT TO THE INTAKE NURSE: STATEMENT MADE FOR MEDICAL DIAGNOSIS OR TREATMENT

DAUGHTER'S STATEMENT TO THE POLICE: PRIOR CONSISTENT STATEMENT

DEVELOPER'S STATEMENT TO HIS FRIEND: STATEMENT UNDER THE BELIEF OF IMMINENT DEATH

Essay Question 1

IE13JUL034

ANALYSIS EXERCISE

Connect law (rules) to fact, and draft your analysis paragraph for each issue below.

DAUGHTER'S STATEMENT TO THE DEVELOPER: OPPOSING PARTY'S STATEMENT

DEVELOPER'S STATEMENT TO THE INTAKE NURSE: STATEMENT MADE FOR MEDICAL DIAGNOSIS OR TREATMENT

DAUGHTER'S STATEMENT TO THE POLICE: PRIOR CONSISTENT STATEMENT

DEVELOPER'S STATEMENT TO HIS FRIEND: STATEMENT UNDER THE BELIEF OF IMMINENT DEATH

Essay Question 2

IE13JUL035

Victoria was robbed of her purse and cellphone at gunpoint. During the robbery, the gun fired, and Victoria was killed. When the police arrived at the crime scene, they activated a cellphone GPS locator application from their computer. By following the GPS tracking signal, the police captured Sam, a suspect who matched the perpetrator's description and was in possession of the victim's purse and cellphone. Sam was charged with felony murder and armed robbery. At a pre-trial conference, the prosecutor advised the court she will offer the following evidence:

1. *Testimony of Sam's 18-year-old daughter that 2 days before the robbery, Sam told her that they were desperate for money and he would "do anything" to support her.*

2. *Testimony of the first aid responder that before she died, the victim stated, "If I do not make it, my attacker had a rose tattooed on his right arm."*

3. *The records from Victoria's cellphone company tracking the location of her cellphone.*

4. *Testimony of Oscar, a police officer in Springfield, where Sam lives, that he would not be surprised if Sam robbed Victoria because he was known as a "troublemaker."*

You are the trial judge's law clerk and are assigned to write a memorandum advising the judge how the evidentiary issues raised by the parties should be resolved and why.

PREPARE THE MEMORANDUM

KAPLAN BAR REVIEW

Federal Civil Procedure

Exercise Set 1

Question 1a

Identify the different types of subject-matter jurisdiction.

Question 1b

Identify the two prongs of analysis for determining whether a federal court can exercise personal jurisdiction over a defendant.

Question 2

Identify the six circumstances under which venue is proper.

For the following exercises, you are given a question prompt. After reading the question prompt, consider the applicable rules. Then, brainstorm possible issues that could be raised or tested based on the given question prompt.

Question 3

Will the court grant the defendant's motion to dismiss for lack of subject-matter jurisdiction?

Question 4

Was removal proper?

Question 5

Was service proper?

For each of the following fact patterns, write out the relevant issues and corresponding rule statements.

Question 6

A North Dakota bank made an unsecured $100,000 loan to a man in South Dakota, who became delinquent in his payments. On March 1, the bank filed suit against the man in South Dakota, and sought to serve the defendant personally so as to establish personal jurisdiction over him. The bank knew that the defendant had been living at the homes of various relatives and doing construction work at various sites in South Dakota for the previous three years. On March 15, the bank learned that the defendant had moved to Nebraska to begin a new job and arranged to have the defendant personally served with a summons at the defendant's new home in Nebraska. On June 1, the defendant appeared in the South Dakota court for the first court date and told the court that, although he had been traveling back and forth between a home in South Dakota and his new home in Nebraska, he now lived exclusively in Nebraska. The defendant added that he began his efforts to relocate to Nebraska well before the bank filed the suit. The defendant argued that, because he is no longer domiciled in South Dakota, the court there does not have personal jurisdiction.

Does the South Dakota court have personal jurisdiction over the defendant?

Question 7

The plaintiff, a resident of State A, entered into a contract with a defendant corporation. Pursuant to the terms of the contract, the defendant would manufacture and distribute a product that was developed by the plaintiff. However, the corporation allegedly breached the contract by refusing to manufacture the product in the manner specified by the plaintiff. The plaintiff brought suit against the defendant-corporation, alleging damages arising from the breach of contract. The plaintiff filed his suit in federal court based on diversity jurisdiction. The defendant's main manufacturing facility was in State A, its place of incorporation was State B, and its corporate headquarters was located in State C. The defendant challenged the diversity jurisdiction.

How should the court rule?

Question 8

The plaintiff, a resident of Red State, has been considered a "pushover" for his entire life, and he is tired of this label. He musters the courage to bring suit against everyone who has wronged him over the years. First, the plaintiff sued a corporation whose principal place of business is Red State and is incorporated in Green State. The plaintiff sued the corporation for $80,000. The plaintiff also sued the driver of a vehicle that hit him when the driver was visiting Red State. The plaintiff's claim was for $75,000 against the driver of the vehicle. The driver resided in Yellow State at the time of the accident, but after the lawsuit was filed, the driver relocated to Red State. The plaintiff also sued an international businessperson, who resided overseas, for $150,000. After the lawsuit was filed, however, the international businessperson moved to Red State. Finally, the plaintiff sued an old friend who allegedly took $55,000 worth of valuable jewelry from the plaintiff when visiting him. The friend resided in Purple State.

Which case can the plaintiff bring in federal court based on diversity jurisdiction?

Question 9

A contractor from one state contracts with a farmer, who lives in another state, to construct a large residential development on the farmer's property. The contract contains a forum selection clause, which provides that any disputes will be litigated in state court. Halfway through the construction of the homes, the contractor defaults. The farmer sues for damages in a state court in the state in which the farm is located, claiming $1 million in damages. The contractor filed a notice of removal to federal court.

What recourse does the property owner have?

Question 10

A husband and wife living in Pennsylvania filed suit in a Maryland state court against a Maryland law firm, alleging legal malpractice. Ten days after filing their initial complaint, the husband and wife filed a motion joining another defendant, an investigative services firm doing business in the state of Virginia. Two weeks after it received notice of the joinder of the second defendant, the law firm filed a notice of removal to federal court on the grounds that the parties were residents of different states and the amount in controversy was in excess of $75,000. The investigative services firm did not object to the removal, but the plaintiffs did.

Should the case be remanded?

Exercise Set 2

Question 1

Complete the chart with the requirements to establish each of the following types of jurisdiction.

Federal-question jurisdiction		
Diversity jurisdiction		
Supplemental jurisdiction		

Question 2

Complete the following chart with the basis for personal jurisdiction that corresponds to the given elements.

BASIS FOR PERSONAL JURISDICTION	ELEMENTS
	• Agreement; • Waiver; or • Engaging in regulated activity.
	• Established minimum contacts with the state. • Claim arises out of defendant's contacts. • Exercise of jurisdiction does not offend traditional notions of fair play and substantial justice.
	• Company is "essentially at home" in state.
	• Resides in the jurisdiction. • Express intent to remain indefinitely.
	• Served while physically present in state. • Presence in state was voluntary.

For the following fact patterns, complete the charts with the relevant facts that correspond to the rules provided.

Question 3

A citizen of State A drove recklessly through State B. As he drove through State B, he ran a red light and hit a pedestrian walking across the street with her championship show dog. The woman, a long-time resident of State B, was seriously injured, and her dog, worth over $200,000, was killed. After spending the night in jail for reckless driving, the driver returned to State A. Several weeks later, after extensive physical therapy and counseling, the pedestrian filed an action in State B for her injuries and the loss of her dog.

Will the federal court in State B have jurisdiction over the claim?

RULES	RELEVANT FACTS
Complete diversity	
Amount in controversy	

Question 4

A cardiologist in State A contracted with a local mechanic to do a complete restoration of his two vintage Italian sports cars. When the cardiologist failed to pay, the mechanic sued. However, since the mechanic moved to State B after the service was completed, he filed the action in State B. The cardiologist's contacts with State B were as follows: (1) on a previous occasion, the cardiologist drove through State B to attend a conference there, and paid for a hotel room and other expenses there; and (2) the cardiologist had also considered moving, and he submitted his resume online to some employers in State B.

Does exercise of personal jurisdiction in State B comport with due process?

RULES	RELEVANT FACTS
Minimum contacts	
Fundamental fairness	

Question 5

Three U.S. citizens and siblings, two from State A and one from State B, entered into a contract with a resident of State B. However, over the course of negotiation, the parties experienced a miscommunication regarding the terms of the contract. As a result, each of the parties believed the others have breached the contract. The three siblings brought suit for breach of contract against the resident of State B. The plaintiffs' claim against the defendant was for $100,000.

Does the federal court have jurisdiction over this action based on diversity of the litigants?

RULES	RELEVANT FACTS
Complete diversity	
Amount in controversy	

Question 6

A teenager was driving while three of the teenager's friends were passengers in the car. The friends were distracting the teenager, and while the teenager was driving on the freeway, his car skidded out of control and crossed the center median. The car crashed head-on into an oncoming vehicle being driven by an elderly man, leaving the elderly man with two broken legs. The accident occurred in the Southern District of State A. The elderly man was a resident of State B and sought to bring suit against the four teenagers for damages arising from the automobile accident. Two of the teenage defendants resided in the Eastern District of State A, one resided in the Northern District of State A, and one resided in the Western District of State A. The elderly man wanted to file his claim in federal court based on diversity of the parties.

The elderly man may file his action in which judicial district(s)?

RULE	RELEVANT FACTS
Venue	

Question 7

A man from State A took a one-day vacation to State B where he visited a casino. There, he placed several bets on sporting events. He quickly lost all his money, and then asked for, and received, a loan from the casino to place further bets. He lost all that money as well and immediately drove back to State A. He had never been in State B before that day and pledged never to return. Several months later the casino filed suit against him in State B court to recover payment on the loan paid to the man. The man argued, however, that the court did not have jurisdiction over him.

Does the State B court have personal jurisdiction over the man?

RULE	RELEVANT FACTS
Personal jurisdiction	

For the following fact patterns, identify the applicable rules and complete the chart with facts that you develop to answer the call of the question.

Question 8

While visiting friends in Georgia, a pedestrian was walking across the street legally in a cross-walk when a car driven by a Georgia resident went through a red light and hit her. The pedestrian was seriously injured and spent months in the hospital. When she got out of the hospital and went home to North Carolina, the pedestrian sued the driver in federal court in North Carolina.

Under what circumstances may the federal district court exercise personal jurisdiction over the driver?

RULES	RELEVANT CONSIDERATIONS

Question 9

A Delaware businessman takes out a $400,000 mortgage against his vacation home in Florida to finance his business ventures. The bank, which is based in Florida, properly records the mortgage. When his business begins to fail, the businessman stops paying the mortgage. After months of non-payment, the bank seeks to foreclose on the vacation home in federal court in Florida.

What is required for the court to have in rem jurisdiction over the vacation home?

RULES	RELEVANT CONSIDERATIONS

Question 10

A husband and wife married in the state of Missouri and lived there for several years. Their marriage was troubled and, when the husband discovered that his wife had been having an affair with husband's best friend, he immediately moved out of the marital home into an apartment across town. When the wife realized that she could not afford to pay the mortgage on their Missouri house by herself, she ceased paying the mortgage and moved in with her parents, who lived in Kentucky. The husband decided to file for divorce.

Which court(s) would have personal jurisdiction over the wife in the divorce action?

RULES	RELEVANT CONSIDERATIONS

Quiz 1

Question 1

Paula and Pete were hit by a truck driven by an employee of the D Corporation, a company that manufactures widgets. The accident occurred in California, where Paula and Pete were living at the time. D Corporation is incorporated in Delaware maintains its principal manufacturing plant in Florida, and is controlled from its offices in Michigan. After the accident, Paula and Pete moved to Miami, Florida, where they planned to retire. After moving, they contacted a lawyer, who filed suit against D Corporation in the appropriate U.S. District Court where Paula and Pete lived, alleging diversity jurisdiction. The suit alleged that each plaintiff had suffered personal injuries in excess of $75,000. D Corporation moved to dismiss the case for lack of subject-matter jurisdiction.

Should D Corporation's motion be granted by the district court?

(A) Yes, because D Corporation's headquarters are in Florida.

(B) Yes, because the plaintiffs were citizens of California when they were injured.

(C) No, because diversity subject-matter jurisdiction exists.

(D) No, because D Corporation is a citizen of Delaware only.

Question 2

The plaintiff, a man from State A, was injured when the defendant, a citizen of State B, ran a red light in State A, causing $40,000 in damages. During an informal interview before any suit was filed, the defendant told a newspaper reporter that the plaintiff was "a drunk who should not be allowed to drive a car, let alone practice medicine." The plaintiff believed that he suffered $50,000 in damages to his reputation as a result of the newspaper article. The plaintiff filed suit against the defendant in a State A federal court. The defendant objects, claiming that the federal court does not have jurisdiction to hear the case.

May the federal court hear the case?

(A) Yes, because defamation actions are properly heard in federal court.

(B) Yes, because the elements for diversity jurisdiction are met.

(C) No, because even though the plaintiff's damages arose out of the same case or controversy, both claims arose from violations of state law.

(D) No, because the plaintiff cannot aggregate unrelated claims.

Question 3

Acme became involved in a labor dispute with the Steamrollers' Union (the entity that ordinarily supplied workers for Acme's plant). Acme commenced an action against the Steamrollers' Union in the appropriate U.S. District Court, claiming $75,000 in damages as a consequence of the union's conduct in harassing and intimidating non-union workers in violation of the Federal National Labor Relations Act. Acme is an Indiana corporation, and the union (an unincorporated association) has members who are domiciled in every state except New York and New Jersey. The Steamrollers' Union answered by denying Acme's allegations and filing a $15,000 counterclaim, which asserted that Acme had deliberately made false accusations about the union to the local papers for the purpose of obtaining favorable press coverage.

If the Steamrollers' Union moves to dismiss for lack of subject-matter jurisdiction, should the court grant the motion?

(A) Yes, because Acme has not claimed monetary damages in excess of $75,000.

(B) Yes, because there is no diversity.

(C) No, because subject-matter jurisdiction is satisfied.

(D) No, because a state claim has been asserted in a federal court.

Question 4

Plaintiff, a citizen of Utah, was involved in an auto accident with Defendant, a citizen of Minnesota. The accident occurred in Utah. Pursuant to the applicable Utah long-arm statute, Plaintiff sued Defendant and Insureco, Defendant's auto insurance company, in a Utah state court of general jurisdiction for $80,000. Insureco, which was joined with Defendant under an applicable state law, is incorporated in Delaware and has its principal place of business in Utah. Both defendants were served with process on the same day. Twenty-nine days after being served, Insureco and Defendant filed a joint notice of removal to the applicable U.S. District Court. Plaintiff then filed a motion for remand.

Should the court grant or deny Plaintiff's motion?

(A) The court should deny Plaintiff's motion, because the amount-in-controversy requirement is satisfied.

(B) The court should deny Plaintiff's motion, because Defendant is not a citizen of Utah.

(C) The court should grant Plaintiff's motion, because the notice of removal was not filed in a timely fashion.

(D) The court should grant Plaintiff's motion, because Insureco's principal place of business is in Utah.

Question 5

Acme is a Georgia corporation that has its principal place of business in Alabama. Polly used to live in Alabama and work at Acme's Alabama plant. However, she was recently terminated from her employment with Acme. She consulted an attorney, who advised her that her termination was wrongful under a law recently enacted by Congress. The lawyer also informed Polly that Georgia had the most liberal procedures for prosecuting this type of action. Polly moved to Georgia, where she is now working as a waitress, and commenced an action in the appropriate state court against Acme for wrongful termination under the applicable U.S. law and a similar Georgia statute. Polly seeks $80,000 in damages. Acme filed a notice of removal in the U.S. District Court in Georgia. Polly then filed a motion for remand back to state court.

How should the court rule on Polly's motion?

(A) The motion should be granted, because there is a lack of diversity.

(B) The motion should be granted, because Polly moved to Georgia only for the purpose of acquiring a more litigationally advantageous forum.

(C) The motion should be denied, because one of Polly's actions is a federal claim.

(D) The motion should be denied, because there is no diversity of citizenship.

Question 6

A man from State B was injured while operating a machine that was manufactured by a State B corporation whose principal place of business was in State A. The man found his home state to be more favorable to his case, and so brought a state-law products liability action against the corporation in State B, claiming damages of $95,000.

One week after being served, the corporation removed the case to federal court. The man now seeks to have the case remanded back to state court.

How should the court rule?

(A) The case should be remanded, because the amount in controversy in a strict liability case in federal court must exceed $100,000.

(B) The case should be remanded, because a federal court lacks subject-matter jurisdiction to hear the matter.

(C) The case should remain in federal court, because the corporation removed within 30 days of being served.

(D) The case should remain in federal court, because the defendant is permitted to remove a case that could have originally been brought in federal court.

Question 7

A woman from State A had worked for a law school in neighboring State B for 30 years. Each week, she would deposit her check into the savings account she maintained at a State B bank. Upon her retirement, the woman moved to State C, where she died five years later. Her daughter, named as executrix of her estate, discovered that the account with the State B bank still existed. This was a surprise to the State B bank as well, because the account statements sent to the woman at her original State A address had come back as undeliverable for the past five years. The bank never learned that the woman moved to State C until the woman's daughter came forward to notify it of the woman's death.

The daughter believes that the bank failed to pay proper interest on the account, and has since sued the bank in State C. The bank claims that it is not subject to personal jurisdiction in State C, as it has no branches there (its only branches are in States A and B) and was not aware that the woman had moved or died.

If the bank's assertions are correct, how should the court rule?

(A) For the bank, because it only has branches in State A and State B.

(B) For the bank, because its contacts with the state are insufficient to support personal jurisdiction.

(C) Against the bank, because the woman maintained her State B account after she moved to State C.

(D) Against the bank, because it is foreseeable that a customer would move to another jurisdiction.

Question 8

Railroad Corporation has brought an action in the U.S. District Court for the Eastern District of Ohio against the United Railroad Firemen's Union ("Union") and against the Union's officers. Railroad is a Pennsylvania corporation that has its principal place of business in New York. The Union is an unincorporated association that has its headquarters in Ohio, which is also the place where the major portion of the Union's administrative work is performed. All of the officers of the Union are citizens of Pennsylvania. The membership of the Union includes railroad employees who reside in Michigan, Pennsylvania, and Ohio. The action asserts that members of the Union destroyed railroad property in Pennsylvania during a strike.

Which of the following is most accurate?

(A) Venue is proper only in Ohio, because that is where the Union is doing business, and would therefore be considered its residence.

(B) The action cannot be brought in a U.S. District Court unless it is based upon a federal claim.

(C) The action is outside the subject-matter jurisdiction of federal courts, because it is an action involving an unincorporated labor organization.

(D) Venue is proper only in Pennsylvania, because all of the officers of the Union are citizens of Pennsylvania.

Question 9

Strong Corporation is in the business of providing exercise instruction and exercise facilities and owns two registered trademarks, "The Strong Way" and "Strong Studios." Strong Corporation wanted to sue The Strong Institute for trademark infringement for naming its business The Strong Institute and for selling videos and other equipment that purported to teach the Strong method. The Strong Institute was incorporated in Delaware and had its principal place of business within the Central District of Pennsylvania. All of The Strong Institute's studios are in Pennsylvania, and it does the majority of its business there. However, within the past six months, The Strong Institute started working on a plan to open studios in New York City. In furtherance of that plan, The Strong Institute had started advertising on New York City buses and sent targeted direct-mail brochures to New York City gyms and gym members. Strong Corporation wants to sue The Strong Institute in the Southern District of New York, where New York City is located and Strong Corporation resides.

Is venue appropriate there?

(A) No, because the majority of the trademark infringement occurred in Pennsylvania.

(B) No, because The Strong Institute, the defendant, resides in the Central District of Pennsylvania.

(C) Yes, because Strong Corporation, the plaintiff, resides in the Southern District of New York.

(D) Yes, because The Strong Institute targeted New York City through its advertising.

Question 10

The plaintiff, a citizen of State A, went on a business trip to State B and stayed in a hotel. While there, he was injured while using an exercise machine in the hotel's gym. He filed a tort suit in State A state court against the hotel and the technician (an independent contractor) who serviced the gym equipment. The man alleged a violation of State B law and sought $100,000 in damages. The hotel and the technician are citizens of State B for the purposes of diversity jurisdiction.

One week after the hotel and technician were served with process, the hotel's lawyer sought to remove the case to federal court, but the technician did not wish to remove the action. Two months later, the plaintiff joined the manufacturer of the exercise machine as a defendant. Several weeks after being served, the manufacturer, a resident of State C, wished to remove the case to federal court and persuaded the technician and hotel to join in a notice of removal. The manufacturer filed a notice of removal exactly four weeks after being served, and the hotel and technician filed a notice that same day joining in the removal.

May the suit be removed under these circumstances?

(A) Yes, because the defendants have the right to remove the action at any time prior to trial.

(B) Yes, because the manufacturer's removal was timely and the hotel and technician were free to join in manufacturer's removal.

(C) No, because the manufacturer waited too long to initiate its removal.

(D) No, because the hotel and technician waited too long to initiate its removal.

Question 11

Former employees of a local college planned to file an action in state court against the college's board of trustees. On April 15, they met with the university president, who was a member of the board, and told him that they were planning to sue. They claimed that they had been unlawfully discharged due to their political beliefs. The plaintiffs filed their complaint on April 25. Three of the 12 defendants were served with process on the same day. The nine others were served on May 19. The first three who were served and eight of the nine others then petitioned for removal to federal court on May 25.

The one defendant who had been served on May 19 but who did not join in the petition for removal on May 25 was the university president. He had been travelling out of state. The president joined in the petition for removal on June 18. April has 30 days, and May has 31 days. This court follows the majority rule regarding such petitions, and did not make any adjustments for weekends.

For the case to be properly removable to federal court, when must the president have joined the petition for removal?

(A) May 25, 30 days from the time the first defendant was served.

(B) June 18, 30 days from the time the president was served.

(C) May 15, 30 days from the time the president knew about the lawsuit.

(D) May 29, 15 days from the time the president was served, because he was served in the second round of service.

Question 12

A Hawaiian plaintiff sued a California defendant for personal injuries which resulted in $100,000 in damages after the defendant negligently pushed her down some stairs while in Hawaii.

The defendant argued that he was not subject to personal jurisdiction in Hawaii, because the sum total of his time in Hawaii was to take the bar (in which he immediately went inactive and only paid yearly dues), to vacation there on two occasions (which were paid for by his company, as he was awarded attorney of the year both of those years), and to rent a car while he was on vacation.

Is the defendant subject to personal jurisdiction in Hawaii?

(A) No, because although the defendant had several contacts, even in the aggregate, they are insufficient to establish personal jurisdiction over him.

(B) No, because the defendant has shown his intent not to remain in Hawaii and has only entered at limited times and with a limited purpose each time.

(C) Yes, because the cause of action arose out of the defendant's contacts with the jurisdiction.

(D) Yes, because entering a contract with a hotel for lodging and with a rental car company is implied consent which subjects him to personal jurisdiction.

Question 13

Paul, a citizen of Idaho, and Greg, a citizen of Oregon, sued Darryl, a citizen of Montana, for breach of contract occurring in Montana. The action was filed in the U.S. District Court in Oregon, and Darryl was improperly served. Upon learning of the suit, Darryl made a successful motion to transfer the case to the U.S. District Court in Montana.

Which of the following is true?

(A) The federal court had the authority to transfer the action to Montana.

(B) The federal court in Oregon should have dismissed the action, because venue in the U.S. District Court in Oregon was improper.

(C) The federal court in Oregon should have denied Darryl's motion to transfer the case, because he was improperly served.

(D) The federal court improperly transferred the action to Montana.

Question 14

While on vacation in Vermont, an Ohio citizen visited an antiques store and saw what was labeled as a packet of Civil War coins. Desperate for a sale, the owner of the store told the Ohio citizen that the coins were rare and worth much more than the $100,000 he was asking for them. However, the woman thought the price was too high.

When the woman returned home to Ohio, she received a call from the store owner reducing the price by 20%, prompting the woman to buy the coins. Once she sent the money to the owner, and after receiving the coins, she discovered that the coins were actually worth only a few hundred dollars. The Ohio woman wished to sue the owner for fraud in Ohio. The store owner argued that the court in Ohio lacked jurisdiction.

Which of the following is true?

(A) The woman can sue in Ohio, because the owner's call provided sufficient minimum contacts to support Ohio's exercise of jurisdiction over him.

(B) The woman can sue in Ohio, because the amount in controversy is more than $75,000.

(C) The woman cannot sue in Ohio, because the man is not subject to personal jurisdiction in Ohio based on a single phone call.

(D) The woman cannot sue in Ohio, because the initial conversation took place in Vermont.

Question 15

D-Corp, a Michigan corporation, sells its automobiles through independent dealers. D-Corp's principal place of business is in Detroit. Each dealer has a separate dealership agreement, which they respectively executed with D-Corp at the time they were appointed to be dealers. Their agreements entitle them to sell all automobiles manufactured by D-Corp in their areas. This year, D-Corp has produced a new sports car that is a radical departure from its previous automobiles. D-Corp decided that it will not sell this car to its existing dealers, but will instead enter into agreements with new dealers to handle the new sports car line. Twelve dealers in California jointly filed actions for breach of contract, seeking an injunction against D-Corp in the appropriate U.S. District Court. D-Corp moved to dismiss the case for lack of subject-matter jurisdiction.

How should the court rule on D-Corp's motion?

(A) The court should grant D-Corp's motion to dismiss, because a party seeking an injunction cannot satisfy the amount-in-controversy requirement of diversity jurisdiction.

(B) The court should grant D-Corp's motion to dismiss, because the plaintiffs are not diverse.

(C) The court should deny D-Corp's motion to dismiss, because a party seeking an injunction does not need to satisfy the amount-in-controversy requirement of diversity jurisdiction.

(D) The court should deny D-Corp's motion to dismiss, because the diversity requirement has been met in this case.

Question 16

A plaintiff wanted to sue two defendants for damages stemming from the defendants' reprinting of her novel in violation of copyright laws. The defendants reprinted and sold the novel in the Northern District of Illinois. One defendant resides in the Eastern District of Michigan, while the other resides in the Western District of Illinois. The plaintiff resides in the Northern District of Iowa.

Where would venue be proper for this action?

(A) The Northern District of Illinois.

(B) The Western District of Illinois or the Eastern District of Michigan.

(C) The Northern District of Illinois, the Western District of Illinois, or the Eastern District of Michigan.

(D) The Northern District of Illinois, the Western District of Illinois, the Northern District of Iowa, or the Eastern District of Michigan.

Question 17

A man and woman attended a local art show. The art show featured a world-renowned photographer who was famous for taking pictures of people he saw on his daily walk around the city. The artist would then paint slogans on the photos. As the man and woman walked around the show, they discovered that the artist had taken a picture of them while they were dressed up in matching American flag shirts. Below the couple was painted the slogan "War Pigs." The woman became so upset that she fainted, injuring herself when she hit the ground. The man and woman joined as plaintiffs under Rule 20 and sued the artist in federal court. The man was a citizen of Connecticut, the woman was a citizen of Rhode Island, and the artist was a citizen of New York. The man's claim was for $10,000 under the Federal Misuse of Likeness Act, which made it a federal crime to use another person's image for monetary gain. The woman's claim was for $20,000 under state laws for intentional infliction of emotional distress. The artist moved to dismiss the woman's claim for lack of subject-matter jurisdiction.

How should the court rule?

(A) The court should grant the motion, because the amount in controversy was only $20,000.

(B) The court should grant the motion, because the woman's claim was based on state law.

(C) The court should deny the motion, because the woman's claim arose from the transaction or occurrence underlying the man's claim.

(D) The court should deny the motion, because the woman's claim, in effect, alleged a violation of a federal law.

Question 18

An Illinois man wanted to gain personal jurisdiction over a California businessman who had been quite evasive in avoiding service in Illinois. He called the businessman's office, lied as to who he was, and asked to speak to the businessman. His secretary said he was not there, mentioned that he was set to board a flight, but said that he had a short layover in Chicago and asked if the businessman could call him back around 3:00 P.M. CST. The man then went online and found the businessman's flight.

The man immediately dispatched a process server to the airport with a copy of the complaint. As the businessman was disembarking from the plane, the process server handed him a copy of the complaint and said, "Welcome to Chicago. You've just been served."

Would an Illinois court have jurisdiction over the businessman?

(A) No, because the tactics used shock the conscience.

(B) No, because the man employed fraudulent tactics to serve the businessman.

(C) Yes, because the businessman was served while in the jurisdiction.

(D) Yes, because the businessman was being evasive, which caused unfair prejudice to the plaintiff.

Question 19

A State A plaintiff sued two State B defendants in State A. The plaintiff's claim against each defendant exceeded $100,000. Ten days after being served, the defendants were served notice that the plaintiff had added a third defendant, who was from State A. All three defendants agreed to remove the case, and did so within the next 10 days. The plaintiff successfully challenged the removal in federal court and the case was remanded back to State A court. Forty days later, the plaintiff settled her case against the State A defendant.

At this point, what recourse do the remaining defendants have?

(A) They can remove the case immediately, because they have 30 days from when the grounds for removal become apparent.

(B) They can remove the case immediately, because this is a diversity case and the date for removal was within one year of when the suit was filed.

(C) They cannot remove, because they are time-barred.

(D) They cannot remove, because although they are not time-barred, removal can only occur once.

Question 20

Tax Inc. franchised thousands of tax preparation offices nationwide. Ten years ago, a franchisee signed a franchise agreement with Tax Inc. granting him the right to operate Tax Inc. franchises in Charleston, West Virginia. Believing that the franchisee breached his original agreement and was using his franchise to further a rival tax preparation business, Tax Inc. filed a request for a permanent injunction in federal court. In its complaint, Tax Inc. correctly identified the franchisee as a citizen of West Virginia and itself as a citizen of Delaware, where it was incorporated, and New York, where it had its primary place of business. In determining the cost of the injunction, Tax Inc. focused on the alleged improper use of the franchise, and valued the stopping of that improper use at $80,000. The franchisee calculated the injunction's cost to be $25,000. He derived this figure from the remaining five years on his franchise agreement, arguing that he had made $5,000 per year in profit for the previous 10 years of the agreement and was likely to continue to do so for the remaining five years. The federal district court then dismissed Tax Inc.'s complaint for lack of subject-matter jurisdiction, finding that it failed to meet the $75,000 amount-in-controversy requirement for diversity jurisdiction. Tax Inc. appealed.

Did Tax Inc.'s complaint meet the necessary amount in controversy to be heard in federal court?

(A) Yes, because the value of an injunction is determined by the plaintiff.

(B) Yes, because the value of an injunction is determined by the larger of the injunction's worth to the plaintiff or its cost to the defendant.

(C) No, because lost profits is the correct way to determine the value of an injunction.

(D) No, because Tax Inc.'s $80,000 figure was too speculative.

Quiz 2

Question 1

An elderly couple, through a Washington State travel agent, purchased passage for a seven-day cruise. The couple paid the fare to the agent, who forwarded the payment to cruise line's headquarters in Miami, Florida, where the cruise line was incorporated and conducted all of its business operations. The cruise line then prepared and sent the tickets to the couple. The back of the tickets stated, "It is agreed by the passenger and carrier that all disputes in connection with this contract shall be litigated before a court in the State of Florida." The couple boarded the ship in Los Angeles, California. While the ship was in international waters off the Mexican coast, the couple was injured when a faulty light fixture fell on their bed. The couple sued the cruise line in Washington, claiming that their injuries were caused by negligence. The cruise line moved to dismiss, arguing it was not subject to the Washington court's jurisdiction.

How should the court rule?

(A) Grant the motion, based on the forum selection clause.

(B) Grant the motion, because the suit was based on a contract formed in Florida.

(C) Grant the motion, because the cruise line lacked sufficient contacts with Washington.

(D) Deny the motion.

Question 2

A man and his wife were injured by a truck driven by an employee of S Corporation, a company that manufactures widgets. The accident occurred in State C, where the man and his wife were living at the time. S Corporation is incorporated in State D, maintains its principal manufacturing plant in State C, and is controlled from its offices in State F. After the accident, the man and his wife moved to State F, where they planned to retire. After moving, they contacted a lawyer, who filed suit against S Corporation in the appropriate U.S. District Court where the man and his wife now lived, alleging diversity jurisdiction. The suit alleged that each plaintiff had suffered personal injuries in excess of $75,000. S Corporation moved to dismiss the case for lack of subject-matter jurisdiction.

Should S Corporation's motion be granted by the district court?

(A) No, because diversity subject-matter jurisdiction exists.

(B) No, because S Corporation is a citizen of State D only.

(C) Yes, because S Corporation's headquarters are in State F.

(D) Yes, because the plaintiffs were citizens of State C when they were injured.

Question 3

The plaintiff, a man from State A, was injured when the defendant, a citizen of State B, ran a red light in State A, causing $60,000 in damages. After a pretrial conference, the plaintiff and defendant were arguing in the parking lot over the cause of the accident. The defendant pushed the plaintiff to the ground and stormed off. The plaintiff sought medical attention after the incident. The plaintiff believed that he suffered $20,000 in damages from the incident in the parking lot. The plaintiff ultimately filed suit against the defendant for negligence and battery in a State A federal court. The defendant objected, claiming that the federal court did not have jurisdiction to hear the cases.

May the federal court hear the case?

(A) No, because even though the plaintiff's damages arose out of the same case or controversy, both claims arose from violations of state law.

(B) No, because the plaintiff cannot aggregate unrelated claims.

(C) Yes, because the court has supplemental jurisdiction over the battery action.

(D) Yes, because the elements for diversity jurisdiction are met.

Question 4

The plaintiff is an Alabama corporation that markets computer products of the defendant, a nationwide computer manufacturer with its headquarters in New York. The marketing agreement contained a forum-selection clause providing that any disputes arising out of the contract could only be brought in a court located in the Southern District of New York. After business relations took a turn for the worse, the plaintiff sued the defendant in the Northern District of Alabama. The complaint alleged that the defendant had breached the dealership agreement, causing more than $1 million in damages. The defendant moved the district court to transfer the case to the Southern District of New York. The Alabama court refused to do so, finding that transfer was controlled by Alabama law and that Alabama did not view contractual forum-selection clauses as enforceable. Specifically, the court found that Alabama disfavored such clauses in order to protect state court jurisdiction.

Was the Alabama court's ruling correct?

(A) Yes, because the Alabama court based its ruling on Alabama law.

(B) Yes, because such forum-selection clauses are invalid.

(C) No, because the clause was evidence of what the parties believed was convenient.

(D) No, because the defendant was a resident of New York.

Question 5

One day, a traffic light in a busy intersection malfunctioned because of an electrical problem which could have been prevented if the state had performed reasonable maintenance. A driver was hit by another car because of the confusion created by the malfunctioning traffic light. While the driver's car was stalled in the middle of the road as a result of the accident, a trucker who had fallen asleep at the wheel crashed into the driver's car. The driver now seeks to bring suit in federal court against the various parties that caused him injury to his person and damages to his car. Assume that all parties are residents of the state except the driver, who lives in a neighboring state.

Under which of the following circumstances would the federal court have jurisdiction over the case?

(A) The lawsuit involves diverse litigants in which the amount in controversy is $55,000.

(B) The lawsuit involves diverse litigants where the amount in controversy is $80,000, which includes property damage and medical expenses against the trucker as well as attorneys' fees and litigation costs in the amount of $10,000.

(C) The lawsuit is a negligence action involving diverse litigants, and the driver has incurred property damages of $30,000 and medical expenses of $50,000.

(D) The lawsuit involves diverse litigants, including the state, the trucker, and the other driver, and the claim against each defendant is $30,000.

Question 6

After an automobile accident, the plaintiff brought suit against the defendant in the United States District Court for State X, where venue was proper. After being served, the defendant consulted his attorney and they felt that a change of venue would be better. The defendant then filed a motion to transfer venue to the United States District Court for the District of State Y. Both parties agreed that venue would have been proper there, and that it would be more convenient for the parties and witnesses. The court scheduled a pretrial conference to settle the issue.

Two weeks later at the pretrial conference, the plaintiff and defendant informed the court that they had agreed that the case should be transferred to the United States District Court for the District of State Z, which all parties agreed was not a proper venue. The plaintiff and defendant each thought that a State Z jury pool would be more sympathetic to their case.

May the court transfer the case to the United States District Court for the District of State Z?

(A) No, because that court is not a court where the case might have originally been brought.

(B) No, because venue is proper in the district where the case was originally filed.

(C) Yes, because all parties have agreed that the court may do so.

(D) Yes, if the court could be convinced that the transfer was also for the convenience of the parties and witnesses, in the interest of justice.

Question 7

A man was injured while riding a bus. The bus company operates nationwide and was concerned that their reputation would be tarnished if the case was litigated, so they settled with the man out of court. In the settlement, the man was given free bus rides anywhere in the country for life.

Several years after the settlement was reached, the National Transportation Safety Board passed a regulation precluding nationwide passenger carriers from providing free transportation. The ruling was retroactive and covered airlines, cruise ships, trains, and bus services. The defendant then notified the man that it could no longer allow him to ride the bus for free as originally agreed upon. The man subsequently brought suit in federal court against the company. The defendant moved that the case should be dismissed because the federal court lacked subject-matter jurisdiction.

Which of the following is true?

(A) The motion should be denied, because the matter involves interstate commerce, which is an exclusively federal power, and therefore should be heard in federal court.

(B) The motion should be denied, because a central issue in the case is the federal statute.

(C) The motion should be granted, because there is no federal question presented.

(D) The motion should be granted, because defendants can remand a case to state court if they choose.

Question 8

A State A resident received a job offer on the other side of the country. He decided to take the offer and move to State C. He went to his local Brand Z car dealer in State A to shop for a new Brand Z. He asked the dealer for advice, stating that he was thinking about driving across the country. Based on the dealer's assertions that the new Brand Z Model X "was perfect for all kinds of weather," the man bought the Model X. On the third day of his trip, some 1,000 miles from either State A or State C, he was involved in an accident in State B. The car slid out of control and smashed into a fence. Due to the nature of his injuries, the man never made it to State C or took the job. The man sued the State A car dealer for $100,000 in a State B state court, alleging a design defect in the car.

Does the State B court have jurisdiction over the car dealer?

(A) No, because the car dealer does not have sufficient minimum contacts with State B.

(B) No, because the car was sold in State A to a resident of State A and the car dealer is a resident of State A.

(C) Yes, because the car dealer knew the vehicle was likely to travel all around the country.

(D) Yes, because as a commercial seller, the car dealer purposefully availed itself of interstate commerce, and so being sued in State B would not offend traditional notions of fair play and substantial justice.

Question 9

A man from State B brought suit against his former employer in an appropriate U.S. District Court, claiming $100,000 in damages as a consequence of the employee's termination in violation of the Civil Rights Act. The man, who is African American, claimed that he was terminated after he brought several safety violations to the attention of state inspectors when the employer's facilities were being investigated for state health-code violations. The employer operates in States A, C, and D and is incorporated in State B. The man's salary was $37,000 annually, and he had two years remaining on his employment contract.

If the employer moves to dismiss the case for lack of subject-matter jurisdiction, should the court grant the motion?

(A) No, because a federal court can hear violations of state employment contract disputes.

(B) No, because subject-matter jurisdiction is satisfied.

(C) Yes, because the federal court lacks diversity jurisdiction.

(D) Yes, because the man's claim amounts to a breach of contract for termination stemming from whistleblowing to state inspectors.

Question 10

A man from State A rented a car and drove to State B for a work meeting. On his way back to State A, the man ran into the back of a State B driver's car, injuring the State B driver. The State B driver then brought suit against the State A man in State B federal court claiming $100,000 in damages. The State A man argued that the case should be dismissed because the State B federal court lacked sufficient jurisdiction over him.

Which of the following statements is most accurate?

(A) The State B court should dismiss the case, because driving the car in State B does not provide sufficient minimum contact for the court to have jurisdiction over the State A man.

(B) The State B court should dismiss the case, because the rental of the car occurred in State A.

(C) The State B court should hear the case, because the man impliedly consented to being sued in State B by driving a car in the jurisdiction.

(D) The State B court should hear the case, because diversity is complete and the amount in controversy is over $75,000.

Question 11

The plaintiff, a citizen of State A, went on a business trip to State B and stayed in a hotel. While there, he received a chemical burn while using the hot tub. He filed a tort suit in State A state court against the hotel and the technician (an independent contractor) who serviced the hot tub and pool. The man alleged a violation of State B law and sought $100,000 in damages. The hotel and the technician are citizens of State B for the purposes of diversity jurisdiction.

Two weeks after the hotel and technician were served with process, the hotel's lawyer sought to remove the case to federal court, but the technician did not wish to remove the action. Two months later, the plaintiff learned that the technician followed the maintenance instructions as provided by the manufacturer of the hot tub. The plaintiff then joined the manufacturer of the hot tub as a defendant. Several weeks after being served, the manufacturer, a resident of State A, wished to remove the case to federal court and persuaded the technician and hotel to join in a notice of removal. The manufacturer filed a notice of removal exactly four weeks after being served, and the hotel and technician filed a notice that same day joining in the removal.

May the suit be removed under these circumstances?

(A) No, because a case can only be removed that could have originally been filed in federal court.

(B) No, because the defendants waited too long to initiate their removal.

(C) Yes, because the defendants have the right to remove the action within 30 days after a reason for removal become apparent.

(D) Yes, because the plaintiff added the manufacturer to prevent the case from being removed.

Question 12

A citizen of State A was injured in an auto accident by a citizen of State B. The accident occurred in State A. Pursuant to the applicable State A long-arm statute, the plaintiff sued the defendant and the defendant's auto insurance company in a State A state court of general jurisdiction for $80,000. The defendant's auto insurance company, which was joined with the defendant under an applicable state law, is incorporated in State D and has its principal place of business in State A. Both defendants were served with process on the same day. Twenty-nine days after being served, both defendants filed a joint notice of removal to the applicable U.S. District Court. The plaintiff argued that a federal court did not have jurisdiction and then filed a motion for remand.

How should the court rule on the plaintiff's motion?

(A) The court should deny the plaintiff's motion, because the amount-in-controversy requirement is satisfied.

(B) The court should deny the plaintiff's motion, because there is complete diversity and the amount in controversy is satisfied.

(C) The court should grant the plaintiff's motion, because the notice of removal was not filed in a timely fashion.

(D) The court should grant the plaintiff's motion, because the defendant auto insurance company's principal place of business is in State A.

Question 13

On January 1, a State A plaintiff sued a State B defendant and a State A defendant in a State A state court. The plaintiff's claim against each defendant exceeded $100,000. The case went through a series of pretrial conferences, and after a long, drawn-out discovery process, the plaintiff settled her case against the State A defendant on January 20 of the following year. The case has now been certified to proceed to trial.

At this point, what recourse does the State B defendant have?

(A) He could remove the case to federal court, because he has 30 days from when the grounds for removal become apparent.

(B) He can remove because the plaintiff, by settling with the State A defendant, provided complete diversity.

(C) He cannot remove at this point, because he is time barred.

(D) He cannot remove the case, because removal can only occur before the close of discovery.

Question 14

Liz, a citizen of California, filed an action in the U.S District Court in Los Angeles against Watchco, a Texas corporation, and Monitinc, a New York corporation, alleging that they were engaged in a conspiracy to fix prices in violation of the Sherman Act, and that her actual damages from the conduct of the defendants was $73,000. Liz further alleged in a second cause of action that Watchco was wrongfully withholding $1,000 that Liz paid to them as a deposit for a computer that was not delivered.

Which of the following statements is true?

(A) The action should be dismissed by the district court, because the value of the aggregated claims does not meet the amount-in-controversy requirement.

(B) The district court may exercise supplemental jurisdiction over the second cause of action, but only if it arises from a common nucleus of operative facts with the first cause of action.

(C) The federal court has subject-matter jurisdiction, because there is complete diversity of citizenship between all plaintiffs and defendants.

(D) The federal court lacks subject-matter jurisdiction, because Sherman Act violations must be tried in the state court where such violations allegedly occurred.

Question 15

HoagieWorld franchised thousands of sandwich shops nationwide. Ten years ago, a franchisee signed a franchise agreement with HoagieWorld granting him the right to operate five franchises in State A. Believing that the franchisee breached his original agreement requiring him to purchase all of his meat, condiments, and bread from approved vendors, HoagieWorld filed a request for a permanent injunction in federal court. In its complaint, HoagieWorld correctly identified the franchisee as a citizen of State A and itself as a citizen of State B, where it was incorporated, and State C, where it had its primary place of business.

In determining the cost of the injunction, HoagieWorld focused on the alleged improper use of the franchise and reputational damage suffered by the brand, and valued the stopping of that improper use at $90,000. The franchisee calculated the injunction's cost to be $5,000. He derived this figure from the increased yearly costs of using approved vendors, rather than local, less expensive vendors. The franchisee filed a motion to dismiss the case, claiming that the federal court lacked subject-matter jurisdiction to hear the case.

How should the court rule on the motion?

(A) Deny the motion, because federal courts have exclusive jurisdiction to hear cases involving copyright violations.

(B) Deny the motion, because there is a sufficient amount in controversy.

(C) Grant the motion, because the case deals with breach of contract, not a federal question.

(D) Grant the motion, because HoagieWorld's $90,000 figure associated with reputational damage was too speculative.

Question 16

A man from State B was injured while driving a vehicle that he purchased from a manufacturer of hybrid technology cars whose principal place of business and place of incorporation were in State A. The man brought a state-law products liability action against the manufacturer in State B, claiming damages of $100,000. Two weeks after being served, the manufacturer removed the case to federal court. The man now seeks to have the case remanded back to state court.

How should the court rule?

(A) The case should be remanded, because it revolves exclusively around state law.

(B) The case should be remanded, because a federal court lacks subject-matter jurisdiction to hear the matter.

(C) The case should remain in federal court, because removal is the right of the defendant.

(D) The case should remain in federal court, because the defendant is permitted to remove a case that could have originally been brought in federal court.

Question 17

A plaintiff brought an action in federal court for assault and battery against a diverse defendant claiming $15,000 in actual damages, $12,500 in pain and suffering, $12,500 in lost wages, and $36,000 in punitive damages. The defendant made a motion to remand the case to state court.

How should the court proceed?

(A) Deny the request, because the amount in controversy is satisfied.

(B) Deny the request, because a plaintiff can aggregate multiple claims against a single defendant.

(C) Grant the request, because punitive damages cannot be used towards the amount in controversy for a case arising out of diversity.

(D) Grant the request, because although punitive damages are counted towards the amount in controversy, they cannot account for the majority of the total amount.

Question 18

A plaintiff wanted to sue two defendants for damages stemming from the defendants' reprinting of her novel in violation of federal copyright laws. The defendants reprinted and sold the novel in the Northern District of State A. One defendant resided in the Eastern District of State A, while the other resided in the Western District of State A. The plaintiff resided in the Northern District of State B.

Where would venue be proper for this action?

(A) The Northern District of State A only.

(B) The Western District of State A or the Eastern District of State A.

(C) The Northern District of State A, the Western District of State A, or the Eastern District of State A.

(D) The Northern District of State A, the Western District of State A, the Northern District of State A, or the Eastern District of State B.

Question 19

A State A plaintiff sued a State C defendant in federal court in State A for personal injuries that occurred in State B which caused an alleged $100,000 in damages. The plaintiff argued that the defendant was subject to personal jurisdiction in State A because the defendant took the bar exam in State A several years earlier, and took several vacations to State A in the last 10 years. Additionally, on the latest vacation, the defendant rented a car. The defendant argued that the sum total of his time in State A was to take the bar (which he failed and never took again) and to vacation on two occasions.

Is the man subject to personal jurisdiction in State A?

(A) No, because although the man had several contacts, even in the aggregate, they are insufficient to establish personal jurisdiction over him.

(B) No, because the man has shown his intent not to remain in State A and has only entered at limited times and with a limited purpose each time.

(C) Yes, because renting a car is implied consent which subjects him to personal jurisdiction.

(D) Yes, because the man, by way of his taking the bar exam, has purposely availed himself of the jurisdiction.

Question 20

A local politician and his girlfriend attended a local art show. The art show featured a world-renowned photographer who was famous for taking pictures of people he saw on his daily walks around the city. The artist would then paint slogans on the photos. As the politician and his girlfriend walked around the show, they discovered that the artist had taken a picture of them while standing in front of a foreign consulate. Below the couple was painted the slogan "Commie Pigs." The girlfriend became so upset that she fainted, injuring herself when she hit the ground. The politician and girlfriend sued the artist in federal court. The politician was a citizen of State C, the girlfriend was a citizen of State B, and the artist was a citizen of State A. The politician's claim was for libel in the amount of $70,000. The girlfriend's claim was for $20,000 under state laws for intentional infliction of emotional distress. The artist moved to dismiss the claims for lack of subject-matter jurisdiction.

Which of the following is most accurate?

(A) The court should deny the motion, because a federal court must hear the case as it involves defamation of a public figure.

(B) The court should deny the motion, because there is complete diversity and the couple can aggregate their claims against the artist.

(C) The court should grant the motion, because the federal court does not have jurisdiction over either claim.

(D) The court should grant the motion as to the girlfriend's claim, because she is not a public figure.

Essays

Essay Question 1

IE13JUL020

ISSUE SPOTTING EXERCISE

Consider the fact pattern below and then answer the questions that follow:

Dolores Huffinger is a celebrity commentator who currently resides in a quiet, rural area in the state of Franklin. However, she grew up in the bustling metropolitan center of the state of Columbia. Everyone who knows Dolores knows that she considers Columbia to be her real home, and that she will return there when she finally decides she cannot live without the city life. She has lived in Franklin for four years now, and she votes, pays taxes, and owns property there (and only there).

Despite living in Franklin, Dolores still publishes her online blog, "Gawking," where she reports on the comings and goings of Columbia's celebrity set. Visitors to "Gawking" can view and download articles, but because the tastefulness of comments proved difficult to control, Dolores does not allow visitors to leave comments on her site. Due to the subject matter of "Gawking," most visitors to and advertisers on the website are from celebrity-obsessed Columbia.

Penelope Posey, a former socialite, is a resident and domiciliary of Columbia. Because she has fallen on hard times, she has had to take work as a celebrity spokesperson for a Columbia-based dog food company, Precious Pets. While Penelope is not as popular as she once was, stories about her still garner attention, and Dolores recently published an article on "Gawking" about Penelope's recently revealed shoplifting addiction.

Worried about their image, Precious Pets fired Penelope as its spokesperson. Penelope contends that she never had a shoplifting problem and that the article Dolores published is entirely false. Penelope asked Dolores to retract the story, but Dolores refused to do so, citing her free speech rights under both the state and federal constitutions.

Penelope then decided to take legal action, and filed a lawsuit in federal district court in Columbia. Penelope is asserting a state-law defamation claim and arguing that neither of the free speech provisions cited by Dolores provides a defense. Penelope is claiming $350,000 in damages based on her lost contract with Precious Pets. Penelope further contends that the federal court has jurisdiction based on federal question and diversity grounds.

Columbia's long-arm statute allows state courts to exercise jurisdiction over out-of-state defendants to the "fullest extent permitted by the Due Process Clause of the United States Constitution."

Dolores has now filed motions to dismiss for lack of subject-matter jurisdiction and lack of personal jurisdiction.

How should the court rule on these motions?

I. **Dolores has filed a motion to dismiss for lack of subject-matter jurisdiction.**

A. **What two issues does this require you to address?**

1.

2.

B. **List the facts from the prompt that will be most helpful in resolving the first issue:**

C. **List the facts from the prompt that will be most helpful in resolving the second issue:**

II. **Dolores has filed a motion to dismiss for lack of personal jurisdiction.**

A. **On what basis will Penelope assert that the court has personal jurisdiction over Dolores?**

B. **List the facts that tell you that this is the most relevant basis for personal jurisdiction:**

Essay Question 1

IE13JUL020

RULE RECOLLECTION EXERCISE

A good rule statement will demonstrate your understanding of the law and provide the foundation for your analysis. This exercise is intended to help you practice: (1) recalling the relevant rules of law; (2) organizing rules of law; and (3) explaining legal concepts completely and concisely.

- PUT AWAY YOUR NOTES for this exercise and practice actively trying to recall the relevant rules.
- In FIFTEEN minutes, write out rule statements for the following issues.
- WRITE THESE RULES OUT IN FULL; do not merely jot down concepts, topics, or fragments.

SUBJECT-MATTER JURISDICTION

Federal-Question Jurisdiction

Diversity

PERSONAL JURISDICTION

Essay Question 1

IE13JUL020

ANALYSIS EXERCISE

Connect law (rules) to fact, and draft your analysis paragraph for each issue below.

SUBJECT-MATTER JURISDICTION

Federal-Question Jurisdiction

Diversity

PERSONAL JURISDICTION

Essay Question 2

IE13JUL072

An architecture firm designed two different buildings for a corporation incorporated in Delaware that made electric bicycles: (1) a building for the corporation's headquarters in Oregon; and (2) a building for the corporation's new factory in Idaho. Currently, the majority of the corporation's work is done in Oregon, but its directors plan to eventually move most of its operations to Idaho. The architecture firm is organized as an LLP with its members residing in Idaho and North Dakota. The firm's work was all done onsite at the locations of the two buildings.

After the architecture firm completed its work in designing the two buildings, it presented the corporation with a bill for $300,000. The corporation, which was having cash-flow issues at the time, offered to provide the firm with 10,000 shares of stock in the corporation in return for lowering the amount due on the bill to $50,000. The firm agreed to the deal, and a new contract was negotiated and signed in Idaho. Six months later, however, the corporation still had not paid the bill, and its stock had fallen in value by 95% due to the fact that several other competitors in the electric bicycle market had surpassed the corporation in popularity.

The architecture firm filed suit in federal district court in North Dakota, where the firm's general counsel was located. The firm alleged that the corporation had violated federal securities laws by making misstatements about the value of the securities at the time the renegotiated contract was signed and that the corporation was liable to the firm for the drop in stock value. The firm further alleged that the corporation had breached its contract with the firm under state law and thus owed the firm $50,000.

The corporation has filed a motion to dismiss both claims for lack of subject-matter jurisdiction and on the basis of improper venue.

1. *Should the court dismiss the firm's securities law claim for lack of subject-matter jurisdiction?*

2. *Should the court dismiss the firm's breach of contract claim for lack of subject-matter jurisdiction?*

3. *Should the court dismiss the action based on improper venue?*

Real Property

KAPLAN BAR REVIEW

Exercise Set 1

Question 1a

Identify the ways a lease can be created.

Question 1b

Identify the four types of leases.

Question 2

Define the following landlord-tenant duties:

1. *Pay rent:*

2. *Waste:*

3. *Repair:*

4. *Delivery of possession:*

5. *Warrant of habitability:*

6. *Covenant of quiet enjoyment:*

For the following exercises, you are given a question prompt. After reading the question prompt, consider the applicable rules. Then, brainstorm possible issues that could be raised or tested based on the given question prompt.

Question 3

What remedy may the tenant seek?

Question 4

Who is responsible for paying rent to the landlord?

Question 5

What type of lease was created between the landlord and tenant?

Question 6

Is the tenant liable for the damage to the property?

For each of the following fact patterns, write out the relevant issues and corresponding rule statements.

Question 7

A tenant leased an apartment from a landlord for a term of three years. Shortly after moving into the apartment, the tenant noticed that the floorboard in the main hallway was severely warped. The tenant was concerned that guests visiting the apartment might trip on the warped floorboard. The tenant repeatedly asked the landlord to make repairs, but the landlord refused to do so. The lease did not address whose responsibility it was to make such repairs.

Is the landlord required to replace the floorboard?

Question 8

A tenant rented an apartment from a landlord. The tenant was an amateur painter, and she decided to paint the walls of the dining room. When she was done, she had painted all four walls. The painting on the walls consisted of an artistic and professional presentation of an outdoor landscape. The landlord told the tenant that he thought the painting showed the tenant's inherent artistic ability. Soon after the tenant finished the painting, she decided to vacate the apartment. The landlord then asked the tenant to pay for the damage she had caused to his structure through her painting. The tenant responded that she had only increased the value of the apartment with the painting and refused to pay any damages.

If the landlord brings an appropriate action seeking to recover damages from the tenant due to her painting, will the landlord prevail?

Question 9

On March 1, a landlord leased a two-bedroom condominium to a dentist for one year, with the occupancy period terminating on February 28 of the following year. On February 15 of the following year, the landlord entered into a one-year lease of the two-bedroom condominium with a bookkeeper, which was to begin on March 1. On March 1, the bookkeeper attempted to take possession of the condo, but discovered that the dentist had not vacated the premises. As a result, the bookkeeper refused to pay the landlord any rent for the month of March. The landlord brought suit against the bookkeeper for the unpaid rent.

Who is most likely to prevail in the suit?

Question 10

A landlord entered into a one-year written lease of a duplex with a tenant, with the tenancy period running from January 1 to December 31 at a monthly rental of $1,000. At the end of September (the ninth month of the lease), the tenant assigned the lease to a teacher. At that point in time, the tenant had made the rent payments for the first nine months of the lease. The teacher took possession on October 1 and made the rent payment to the landlord for that month. However, the teacher did not pay the rent for November and vacated the premises on November 30. The premises remained unoccupied for December and no rent payment was made for that month. Thereafter, the landlord sued the tenant and the teacher for the nonpayment of rent.

What would be the result of this lawsuit?

Exercise Set 2

Question 1

Complete the chart with the requirements to establish the following.

Permissive waste			
Ameliorative waste			
Warranty of habitability			

Question 2

Complete the following chart with the tenancy that corresponds to the given elements.

TYPE OF LEASE	ELEMENTS
	• Set beginning date. • Defined period. • No termination date.
	No fixed duration.
	• Definite beginning date. • Definite end date. • No notice required for termination.
	• Remains in possession. • Lease has terminated.

For the following fact patterns, complete the chart with the relevant facts that correspond to the rules or other terms provided.

Question 3

A landlord agreed in writing to allow a tenant to live in a house on the landlord's property as long as the tenant promised to maintain the property. The tenant immediately moved into the house and began maintaining the property. Several months later, the landlord decided to sell the property to an investor, who intended to live in the house on the property. After the sale was complete, the investor asked the tenant to vacate the property immediately, but the tenant refused. He had been maintaining the property in good condition since he moved onto it.

Will the investor succeed in evicting the tenant from the property?

RULES	RELEVANT FACTS
Tenancy at will	
Method of termination	

Question 4

A landlord and tenant entered into a residential lease agreement which provided that the landlord was required to provide trash pick-up services on a weekly basis. During the entire month of June, trash was not removed from the premises due to a strike by local sanitation workers. The tenant complained to the landlord on numerous occasions about the accumulating trash and the resulting foul odor. The tenant remained in the apartment.

What remedy is the tenant entitled to pursue?

RULES	RELEVANT FACTS
Constructive Eviction	
Damages	

Question 5

A landlord is the owner in fee simple of a tract of land on which is situated a large office building. The landlord leased the land and building thereon to a tenant for a term of seven years, commencing on August 1, 2015 and terminating at midnight on July 31, 2022. The lease contained the following provision:

"(1) The tenant covenants to pay the rent of $750 per month on the first day of each month."

After three years passed, the tenant assigned the entire balance of the lease term to an attorney, who took immediate possession of the leased property. Then, in 2019, the attorney assigned his leasehold interest to a doctor. The doctor went into possession, but failed to pay any rent for two months.

After the doctor failed to make his rent payments for the first two months of his lease, the landlord brought suit against the original tenant to recover for the unpaid rent.

For whom should the court award judgment?

RULES	RELEVANT FACTS
Assignment	
Duty to pay rent	

Question 6

A landlord is the owner in fee simple of a tract of land on which is situated a studio. The landlord leased the land and building thereon to a tenant for a term of seven years, commencing on August 1, 2015 and terminating at midnight on July 31, 2022. The lease contained the following provision:

"(1) The tenant covenants not to assign the leased premises without the consent of the landlord."

After three years passed, the tenant, without the consent of the landlord, assigned the entire balance of the lease period to a dance instructor, who took immediate possession of the leased property. The landlord accepted rent payments from the dance instructor. Then, in 2019, the dance instructor assigned his leasehold interest to a yoga instructor, who took possession of the property. After learning of the dance instructor's assignment to the yoga instructor, the landlord brought suit against the dance instructor to have the assignment declared void.

Will the landlord prevail?

RULES	RELEVANT FACTS
Assignment	
Rule in Dumpor's Case	

Question 7

A landlord was the owner of a two-story house and leased it completely furnished to a tenant for a 10- year period. Toward the end of the seventh year of the term, a violent storm blew off several of the roof shingles. The tenant noticed a leak through the roof where the shingles had blown off, but didn't make any repairs or notify the landlord. One month later, a severe rainstorm occurred and water leaked through the roof, causing damage to the valuable parquet floors in the two rooms below.

In a subsequent proceeding by the landlord against the tenant to recover for the damage to the parquet floors resulting from the leak, liability would most likely be imposed upon which party?

RULE	RELEVANT FACTS
Waste	

For the following fact patterns, identify the applicable rules and complete the chart with the relevant facts.

Question 8

A landlord was the owner of a two-story house and leased it completely furnished to a tenant for a 10-year period. Two years after the tenant entered into the leasehold agreement with the landlord, he subleased the house to his cousin. Thereafter, the cousin defaulted on the rent payments.

If the landlord brings an action to recover the past rent due from the cousin, will the landlord prevail?

RULE	RELEVANT FACTS
Rent obligations	

Question 9

A homeowner owns a home in fee simple and leased it to his cousin for a term of 10 years. By the terms of the lease, the cousin expressly covenanted to pay a monthly rent of $300 and to pay the taxes on the premises during the term of the lease. The lease also stipulated that the cousin, as lessee, could not assign or sublease the said premises.

The cousin and his family lived in the house for two years, at which time the cousin, still owing the homeowner three months' back rent and taxes, assigned his leasehold interest in the property to a friend. The friend was unaware of the prohibition against assignments. This written assignment expressly provided that the friend would pay the homeowner the monthly rent of $300, but was silent concerning the payment of taxes. After the cousin's assignment to the friend, the homeowner sued the cousin to recover the rent and taxes in arrears.

Will the homeowner prevail?

RULES	RELEVANT FACTS

Question 10

A tenant leased an apartment in a northern city from a landlord pursuant to a two-year lease. The lease specified that the landlord would provide adequate heat to the apartment during the winter months. That January, the heat system to the living room failed, and it became so cold in that room that the tenant could not occupy it. The tenant sealed off the living room but continued to occupy the remainder of the apartment. This condition existed for one month before the landlord repaired the heating system.

What are the tenant's remedies under the majority rule?

RULE	RELEVANT FACTS

Quiz 1

Question 1

A landlord and a doctor entered into a written lease agreement for the lease of an apartment owned by the landlord. Under the terms of the lease agreement, the doctor was to rent the apartment from the landlord for a period of one year. On the day the lease commenced, the doctor found he could not gain access to the apartment, because the landlord had changed the locks.

Has the landlord breached his duty to deliver possession of the premises to the doctor?

(A) Yes, under the American rule, because the landlord has not delivered actual possession of the premises to the doctor.

(B) Yes, under the minority rule, because the landlord has constructively evicted the doctor.

(C) No, under the minority (American) rule, because the doctor has a legal right to possess the premises.

(D) No, under the majority (English) rule, because a lease for a term of years may be terminated at will.

Question 2

A landlord and a tenant lived together in an apartment as roommates. The lease agreement between the two parties stated that the tenant would have access to all of the apartment's common areas, including the living room, bathroom, and kitchen. Believing that the tenant had damaged the television in the living room, the landlord removed all of the tenant's personal property from the living room, locked the door to the living room, and told the tenant that the tenant would no longer have access to that room. Although the tenant objected, the tenant continued to reside in the other rooms of the apartment.

To what relief is the tenant entitled under the law of most jurisdictions?

(A) The tenant is relieved of all liability for rent, because he has been actually evicted.

(B) The tenant is relieved of all liability for rent, because he has been constructively evicted.

(C) The tenant is only entitled to a rent abatement, because he has been partially evicted.

(D) The tenant is only entitled to a rent abatement, because he has been constructively evicted.

Question 3

A landlord entered into a residential lease agreement with a tenant. Five months after the commencement of the lease, the leased premises were destroyed by a fire caused by a lightning strike. The lease agreement did not contain any provision addressing natural disasters or acts of God.

Is the tenant required to rebuild the premises?

(A) No, because under the modern contract theory, neither the landlord nor the tenant is required to rebuild the premises in the event of an act of God.

(B) No, because under the common law estate theory, the tenant is required only to make minor repairs.

(C) Yes, because under the common law estate theory, the tenant has a duty to repair without exception.

(D) Yes, because the lease does not address acts of God.

Question 4

A landlord and a tenant entered into an oral lease for a term of six months. After the commencement of the lease term, the ceiling of the leased apartment caved in as a result of renovations the landlord was making to the apartment above. Unable to remain in the apartment, the tenant moved out.

What are the tenant's remedies at common law?

(A) Treat the lease as terminated and withhold rent, because the covenant of quiet enjoyment has been breached.

(B) Reduce the rent payments, because although the covenant of quiet enjoyment has been breached, the lease is not terminated.

(C) Unilaterally terminate the lease and discontinue rent payments.

(D) No remedies exist at common law, because an oral lease does not contain a covenant of quiet enjoyment.

Question 5

A landlord agreed to lease his townhouse to a tenant for a period of one year. The written lease agreement stated that the lease would automatically renew for successive one-year periods unless either the landlord or the tenant gave notice of termination at least one month (and no more than two months) in advance of the end of the period. One year passed after the landlord and tenant executed the lease agreement, and neither gave notice of termination.

After the one-year anniversary of the execution of the lease agreement, what type of tenancy do the landlord and tenant have?

(A) An implied tenancy.

(B) A term of years.

(C) A periodic tenancy.

(D) An at-will tenancy.

Question 6

A landlord and tenant entered into a residential lease agreement, which provided that the landlord was required to provide heat to the apartment during the winter months. During the entire month of December, there was no heat in the apartment, despite the fact that the tenant complained to the landlord on numerous occasions. The tenant remained in the apartment.

Under the majority rule, what remedy is the tenant entitled to pursue?

(A) The tenant may withhold the entire rent, because she has been constructively evicted.

(B) The tenant is entitled to a rent abatement, because the landlord has breached the covenant of quiet enjoyment but is not relieved of all liability for rent.

(C) The tenant may not withhold the entire rent, because the tenant has merely been constructively evicted.

(D) The tenant may not withhold the entire rent, because she remained in the apartment.

Question 7

A stockbroker leased his apartment to a diplomat pursuant to a lease with a one-year term. Shortly after moving into the apartment, the diplomat installed central air conditioning in the apartment. The lease did not address renovations or improvements such as the diplomat's installation of air conditioning.

In most jurisdictions, is the diplomat's action permissible under the lease?

(A) Yes, because the diplomat improved the value of the premises.

(B) Yes, because the lease does not prohibit it.

(C) No, because it constitutes permissive waste.

(D) No, because it constitutes ameliorative waste.

Question 8

A landlord was the owner in fee simple of a tract of land on which was situated a large office building. The landlord leased the land and building thereon to a tenant for a term of seven years, commencing on August 1, 2001 and terminating at midnight on July 31, 2008. The lease contained the following provision: "The tenant covenants to pay the rent of $750 per month on the first day of each month." After three years of the lease had expired, the tenant assigned the entire balance of the lease period to an attorney, who took immediate possession of the leased property. Then, in 2005, the attorney assigned his leasehold interest to a doctor. The doctor went into possession, but failed to pay any rent for two months. After the doctor failed to make his rental payments for the first two months of his lease, the landlord brought suit against the tenant to recover for the unpaid rent.

For whom should the court enter judgment?

(A) The landlord, because the tenant's contractual obligation under the lease survived the assignments.

(B) The landlord, because he did not object to the assignments.

(C) The tenant, because only the doctor, as assignee, would be held liable.

(D) The tenant, because his assignment to the attorney constituted a novation, thereby extinguishing his obligation to pay rent.

Question 9

A retired farmer leased his ranch to a man. When the man arrived to take possession, he found that a ranch hand was occupying the land illegally. The man refused to pay rent to the retired farmer. The retired farmer then sued the man to enforce the lease.

How should the court rule?

(A) For the retired farmer, because the American rule requires the farmer to provide only the right to possess the ranch.

(B) For the retired farmer, because the English rule requires the farmer to provide only the right to possess the ranch.

(C) For the man, because the American rule requires the farmer to provide him with both the right to possess and actual possession of the ranch.

(D) For the man, because the English rule requires the farmer to provide him with both the right to possess and actual possession of the ranch.

Question 10

In a written agreement, a landlord leased his home to a tenant for a term of three years, ending on December 31 of the third year, at the rate of $1,000 per month. The lease provided that the tenant could sublet and assign the lease. The tenant lived in the home for one year and paid the rent promptly each month. After one year, the tenant leased the home to a student for one year at a rent of $1,000 per month. The student took possession of the home and lived there for six months, but because of her unemployment, she never made any rent payments. After six months, the student abandoned the home, which then remained vacant for the balance of that year.

The tenant retook possession of the home at the beginning of the third and final year of the lease term, but made no further rent payments to the landlord. At the end of the lease term, the landlord brought an action against both the tenant and the student to recover $24,000, the unpaid rent for the second and third years of the lease term.

Assuming the landlord is successful, how will the court rule regarding damages?

(A) Against the tenant individually for $24,000, and no judgment against the student.

(B) Against the tenant individually for $18,000, and against the student individually for $6,000.

(C) Against the tenant individually for $12,000, and against the tenant and student jointly and severally for $12,000.

(D) Against the tenant individually for $18,000, and against the tenant and student jointly and severally for $6,000.

Question 11

A landlord and a tenant entered into a residential lease agreement that described the lease term as "continuing until the landlord, in his sole discretion, terminates the lease."

Under the majority rule, what kind of tenancy has been created by the lease agreement?

(A) A periodic tenancy.

(B) A life estate held by the tenant.

(C) An at-will tenancy that may be terminated by the landlord only.

(D) An at-will tenancy that may be terminated by either the landlord or the tenant.

Question 12

A landlady believed that her tenants were like her family, and for this reason, all of her leases contained a prohibition on assignments. An executive signed a lease on Apartment 3 for five years at $3,000 per month rent. The executive paid her rent on time for four years. She then agreed to spend most of the next year setting up her company's latest headquarters in London. The executive entered into an agreement with a dentist for the dentist to move into the executive's apartment and pay the rent for 10 of the remaining 12 months on the lease. The executive intended to return to and resume living in the apartment for the last two months. The dentist moved into the apartment but never paid any rent to the landlady. When the executive returned home, she discovered a note from the landlady demanding the back rent.

Who is liable to the landlady for the rent owed?

(A) The executive, because assignments were prohibited.

(B) The executive, because the dentist was a subtenant.

(C) The executive and the dentist are jointly and severally liable.

(D) The dentist, because he agreed to pay the rent.

Question 13

A landlord leased an office space to a tenant for five years. The lease contained covenants whereby the tenant agreed to pay $750 rent per month to the landlord, and the landlord agreed to repaint the office once each year. At the beginning of the second year, the landlord refused to paint the office.

What are the tenant's remedies?

(A) The tenant may refuse to pay rent due to the landlord's breach of covenant.

(B) The tenant may treat the lease as terminated if he vacates the premises.

(C) The tenant may paint the office space himself and offset his subsequent rental payments by the cost of the paint and labor.

(D) The tenant may not paint the office space, because this would constitute ameliorative waste.

Question 14

On August 1, a student entered into an oral agreement with a landlord to lease an apartment for $500 per month, starting immediately and running through the end of the year. At the end of the year, the student failed to move out, instead paying the rent for the following month on time and directly to the landlord, who accepted the rent by depositing it into his bank account.

What is the relationship between the parties as of January 1?

(A) The student is a tenant at sufferance, and the landlord may immediately evict him.

(B) The student's payment, and the landlord's acceptance, of the rent formed an at-will tenancy, in which either party can immediately terminate the lease.

(C) Because the original lease agreement was not in writing, the Statute of Frauds will operate to invalidate the agreement, resulting in an at-will tenancy.

(D) A month-to-month periodic tenancy has been formed.

Question 15

A chemist owned a house that he leased to a tenant pursuant to a residential month-to-month lease agreement. Five months after executing the lease agreement with the tenant, the chemist assigned his interest in the lease to his mother. The written lease agreement did not address assignments.

What is the status of the lease?

(A) The chemist is the landlord under the terms of the lease, because the assignment is invalid.

(B) The chemist's mother is the landlord under the terms of the lease, because a landlord under either a residential or a commercial periodic lease may assign his lease interest.

(C) The chemist's mother is the landlord under the terms of the lease, because the lease was a residential lease.

(D) Neither the chemist nor his mother is the landlord under the terms of the lease, because the lease terminated upon the chemist's attempted assignment.

Question 16

A landlord and a soft drink manufacturing company entered into a two-year commercial lease agreement for the lease of a factory owned by the landlord. When the soft drink manufacturing company took possession of the factory at the beginning of the lease term, its engineers discovered that there was a high concentration of toxic chemicals in the factory's air due to the manufacturing activities of the previous tenant. The landlord, who was not aware of these toxic chemicals until notified by the soft drink manufacturing company, refused to pay to have the chemicals removed from the air. The soft drink manufacturing company's lawyer wrote a threatening letter to the landlord asserting that it had breached the lease's implied warranty of habitability.

In most jurisdictions, would the lawyer's contention be successful in a court of law?

(A) No, because the landlord did not know about the chemicals at the time it entered into the lease with the soft drink manufacturing company.

(B) No, because the lease is a commercial lease.

(C) Yes, because the tenant notified the landlord of the toxic chemicals within a reasonable time.

(D) Yes, because the lease is not a long-term lease.

Question 17

A landlord owned a three-story home in fee simple and leased it to his friend for a term of 10 years. By the terms of the lease, the friend expressly covenanted to pay a monthly rental of $300 and to pay the taxes on the premises during the term of the lease. The lease also stipulated that the friend, as lessee, could not assign or sublease the said premises. The friend and his family lived in the house for two years. Then the friend, still owing the landlord three months back rent, assigned his leasehold interest in the property to a professor, who was unaware of the prohibition against assignments. This written assignment expressly provided that the professor would pay the landlord the monthly rental of $300, but was silent concerning the payment of taxes. The landlord never objected to this assignment.

Six months after the assignment, the landlord conveyed his property interest in the premises to a new owner. After residing in the house for a year, the professor subleased the third floor to a student for a term of two years; the agreement provided that the professor would receive a monthly rental payment of $100. After the student had made regular rental payments to the professor for the first six months of the sublease, he defaulted. The following month, the professor sent the new owner $200 as payment for rent and notified him that he should collect the remaining $100 from the student, who refused to vacate the premises.

In an action by the new owner against the student to recover the additional $100 for rent due, what is the most probable outcome?

(A) The new owner will recover, because the landlord and sublessee are in privity of estate.

(B) The new owner will recover, even though he never objected to the sublease.

(C) The new owner will not recover, because the professor would only be held liable.

(D) The new owner will not recover, because the professor remains liable.

Question 18

A tenant leased an apartment from a landlord pursuant to a five-year lease. One afternoon, a group of boys including the landlord's son were playing in the street outside the apartment. One of the boys kicked a soccer ball into the front screen door. As a result, the screen door was partially crushed and had a small hole in the area where the ball had hit it. The tenant requested that the landlord repair the broken door, but the landlord refused. The tenant then replaced the door for $150 and deducted the $150 from the next month's rental payment. The lease agreement did not address which party would be responsible for making repairs to the apartment.

Under the common law rule, will the landlord prevail in an action to recover the $150 against the tenant?

(A) Yes, because the lease did not specify that the landlord had the burden of making repairs.

(B) Yes, because although responsibility for repairing the door lies with the landlord, the tenant is not entitled to reimbursement if the tenant chooses to repair the door himself.

(C) No, because the broken door constitutes a partial, constructive eviction.

(D) No, because deduction of the cost of repairs was the appropriate remedy for breach of the warranty of habitability.

Question 19

A landlord and a tenant entered into a written residential lease agreement. The lease included a provision requiring the landlord to make necessary repairs to the leased house within a reasonable time, except for damage caused by ordinary wear and tear. During the lease term, the living room window was broken during an attempted burglary. The tenant informed the landlord of the need to replace the broken window, but the landlord did nothing. A week after the attempted burglary, the tenant severely injured his hand on the jagged glass from the broken window.

On what basis may damages be awarded to the tenant?

(A) Damages may be awarded on the basis of breach of the lease, but not on the basis of the tenant's injuries.

(B) Damages may be awarded on the basis of the tenant's injuries, but not on the basis of breach of the lease.

(C) Damages may be awarded on the basis of breach of the lease as well as on the basis of the tenant's injuries.

(D) Damages may be awarded neither on the basis of breach of the lease nor on the basis of the tenant's injuries.

Question 20

A landlord entered into a lease agreement with a tenant. The jurisdiction in which the leased premises were located had enacted a statute requiring landlords to maintain a temperature of at least 65 degrees Fahrenheit in leased apartments during the winter months. The lease agreement itself contained no such requirement. In January of the first year of the lease, the temperature in the apartment was no higher than 58 degrees. The tenant vacated the apartment and sued the landlord for violating the lease's covenant of quiet enjoyment.

What remedies are available to the tenant in most jurisdictions?

(A) The tenant may treat the lease as terminated and withhold rent, because he has been constructively evicted.

(B) The tenant is entitled only to a rent abatement, because he has been constructively evicted.

(C) The only remedies available to the tenant are those provided for in the statute, because the landlord has not violated the lease.

(D) The only remedies available to the tenant are those provided for in the statute, because the tenant vacated the apartment.

Quiz 2

Question 1

A saleswoman and an architect entered into an agreement whereby the architect would lease an apartment owned by the saleswoman. The architect moved into the apartment as provided under the lease agreement. However, during the first several months of the lease term, and despite numerous requests from the architect, the saleswoman refused to repair a leaky faucet in the apartment's bathroom. The lease did not address whose responsibility it was to make such repairs.

Under the common law, is the saleswoman required to make the repairs?

(A) Yes, because under the common law, the landlord has a duty to repair without exception.

(B) Yes, because a leaky faucet constitutes ordinary wear and tear.

(C) No, because the failure to repair a leaky faucet does not constitute waste.

(D) No, because the saleswoman has no duty to make any repairs to the premises.

Question 2

A landlord lived with his two tenants as roommates in a townhouse. The lease agreements specified that each tenant had private access to one of the bedrooms and access to the shared common areas of the house. One day, due to poor upkeep, one of the pipes burst under the kitchen sink, flooding the kitchen and rendering the entire room unusable. The tenants salvaged what they could of their property from the kitchen and complained to the landlord to fix it, but despite constant promises that he would get to it, the kitchen was never repaired.

Are the tenants entitled to withhold their next month's rent payments?

(A) No, because they are entitled only to a rent abatement.

(B) No, because they did not move out of the townhouse.

(C) Yes, because they have been constructively evicted from part of the premises.

(D) Yes, because the landlord failed to maintain the kitchen in good repair.

Question 3

A tenant entered into a two-year lease with a landlord for an apartment. Six months into the lease, the tenant fell asleep while smoking and caused a fire that destroyed the apartment. As a result, the tenant moved out. The next month, the landlord demanded that the tenant pay rent, but the tenant refused, citing the destruction of the property. The landlord sued to recover the unpaid rent.

Who will prevail?

(A) The tenant, because the property has been destroyed.

(B) The tenant, because he has moved out of the property.

(C) The landlord, because the tenant negligently caused the destruction.

(D) The landlord, because the tenant leased only part of the property.

Question 4

A landlord and a tenant entered into a lease for a period of one year for an apartment. Three months into the lease, the floor collapsed under the living room and part of the bedroom due to work that the landlord was doing in the apartment below. When the landlord told the tenant that it would take at least three months to repair the floors, the tenant moved out. When the tenant refused to pay rent the next month, the landlord sued the tenant.

Is the tenant obligated to continue paying rent?

(A) No, because the covenant of quiet enjoyment has been breached.

(B) No, because the tenant has been actually evicted from the property.

(C) Yes, because although the covenant of quiet enjoyment has been breached, the tenant is only entitled to a rent abatement.

(D) Yes, because the landlord is working to repair the apartment.

Question 5

On December 15, a landlord and tenant entered into a lease for a period of one year, beginning at the start of the calendar year, with rent to be paid on the first of each month. One month before the end of the lease term, the tenant called the landlord and the two agreed to renew the lease for another year at the same terms.

As of January 1, what type of tenancy do the landlord and tenant have?

(A) A term of years.

(B) A periodic tenancy.

(C) A tenancy at-will.

(D) A tenancy at sufferance.

Question 6

A developer owned a strip mall in a busy area of the city, and leased the storefronts to various businesses pursuant to year-to-year periodic lease agreements. Deciding to retire, the developer sold his interests to a business investor and assigned all of his lease agreements to the investor. None of the written lease agreements contained clauses addressing assignments.

Which of the following is true?

(A) The developer remains the landlord under the terms of the leases, because the assignments are invalid.

(B) The investor is now the landlord under the terms of the leases, because a landlord may assign his lease interest.

(C) The investor is the landlord under the terms of the leases, because the leases were commercial.

(D) The leases terminated upon the developer's attempted assignment.

Question 7

A woman leased an apartment from a landlord. When the woman arrived to move in, she found that the former tenant was still in the apartment, and refused to leave. As a result, the woman refused to pay any rent to the landlord. The landlord then sued the woman to enforce the lease.

How should the court rule?

(A) For the landlord, because the American rule requires him to provide only the right to possess the apartment.

(B) For the landlord, because the English rule requires him to provide only the right to possess the apartment.

(C) For the woman, because the American rule requires the landlord to provide her with both the right to possess and actual possession of the apartment.

(D) For the woman, because the English rule requires the landlord to provide her with both the right to possess and actual possession of the apartment.

Question 8

A landlord owned a home in a neighborhood that was zoned for mixed residential/commercial use, and which had been leased out for several years as a doctor's office. Following the doctor's retirement, the landlord rented the house to a family of four, who moved in immediately while the father began renovating the interior. A couple of months later, both of the family's children began getting sick. A subsequent inspection discovered that the doctor and his staff had allowed hazardous chemicals to seep into the floors and walls, and which were slowly evaporating over time. The landlord, who was not aware of the situation until notified by the father, refused to pay to have the floors and walls scrubbed clean of the chemicals. The family sued the landlord, claiming that he had breached the lease's implied warranty of habitability.

Will the family prevail?

(A) No, because the landlord did not know about the chemicals at the time it entered into the lease with the family.

(B) No, because the doctor's lease was a commercial lease.

(C) Yes, because the family notified the landlord of the hazardous chemicals within a reasonable time.

(D) Yes, because the lease is not a long-term lease.

Question 9

On July 1, a college senior entered into an oral agreement with a landlord to lease an apartment near her college campus for $750 per month for a period of one year, starting immediately. At the end of the year, having found a job nearby following her graduation, the college senior began looking for a new apartment. Because she did not find one right away, however, she remained in the apartment through the month of July. She did not, however, pay any rent to the landlord.

What is the relationship between the parties as of August 1?

(A) A month-to-month periodic tenancy has been formed.

(B) Because the original lease agreement was not in writing, the Statute of Frauds will operate to invalidate the agreement, resulting in an at-will tenancy.

(C) The college senior is a tenant at sufferance, and the landlord may immediately evict her.

(D) The landlord cannot evict the college senior without providing at least 30 days' notice, but may collect rent from the senior according to the lease terms.

Question 10

A landlord entered into a lease agreement with a tenant pursuant to which the landlord was required to pump out and empty the house's small septic tank every six months, on January 1 and July 1. During the second year of the lease, the landlord failed to pump the tank in July despite repeated complaints by the tenant, and as a result, the property was suffused with a foul order for the entire month. The tenant remained in the apartment. When the landlord finally arrived to pump the tank at the beginning of August and demanded the previous month's rent, the tenant refused to pay. The landlord then sued the tenant for the unpaid rent.

Under the majority rule, what remedy is the tenant entitled to pursue?

(A) The tenant is entitled to a rent abatement, because the landlord has breached the covenant of quiet enjoyment, but he is not relieved of all liability for rent.

(B) The tenant may withhold the entire rent, because he has been constructively evicted.

(C) The tenant may not withhold the entire rent, because he has merely been constructively evicted.

(D) The tenant may not withhold the entire rent, because he remained in the apartment.

Question 11

A tenant leased a house in a suburban neighborhood from a landlord. The lease was silent as to which party bore the responsibility to make repairs. One day, a group of neighborhood kids were playing baseball in the street when an errant ball went through a second-floor window of the tenant's house. The tenant replaced the broken window pane at a cost of $300 and deducted the amount from the next month's rental payment. The landlord then sued to recover the $300 from the tenant.

Will the landlord prevail in recovering the $300 against the tenant?

(A) No, because deduction of the cost of repairs was the appropriate remedy for breach of the warranty of habitability.

(B) No, because the broken window constitutes a partial, constructive eviction.

(C) Yes, because the lease did not specify that the landlord had the burden of making repairs.

(D) Yes, because the tenant did not notify the landlord of the damage and give the landlord a reasonable time to make repairs.

Question 12

A tenant leased two floors of an office building from a landlord for a 10-year period, with rent due at the start of each month. According to the terms of the lease, the landlord agreed to perform routine maintenance, including but not limited to repairing and painting the walls, replacing carpeting, and maintaining the air conditioning and electrical systems, at the start of each year, after the tenant submitted an itemized list of requests. At the start of the third year of the lease, the tenant submitted the list to the landlord. However, the landlord, after seeing the costs incurred in doing the repairs in the second year, refused to do them.

What are the tenant's remedies?

(A) The tenant may make the repairs himself and offset his subsequent rental payments by the costs incurred.

(B) The tenant may not make the repairs, because doing so would constitute ameliorative waste.

(C) The tenant may refuse to pay rent due to the landlord's breach of covenant.

(D) The tenant may treat the lease as terminated if he vacates the premises.

Question 13

A landlord leased an apartment in a high-rise building to a tenant. The jurisdiction in which the leased premises were located had enacted a statute requiring landlords to provide running water in leased apartments for no less than 25 days out of each month. The lease agreement itself did not contain any term involving running water. In early June, while making repairs on another apartment, the landlord accidently burst a water pipe leading into the tenant's apartment. As a result, the tenant did not have running water for the last three weeks of the month, and was forced to move out of the apartment. The tenant then sued the landlord for violating the lease's covenant of quiet enjoyment.

What remedies are available to the tenant?

(A) The only remedies available to the tenant are those provided for in the statute, because the landlord has not violated the lease.

(B) The only remedies available to the tenant are those provided for in the statute, because the tenant vacated the apartment.

(C) The tenant is entitled only to a rent abatement, because she has been constructively evicted.

(D) The tenant may treat the lease as terminated and withhold rent, because she has been constructively evicted.

Question 14

A landlord entered into a written residential lease agreement with a tenant for a mountain cabin. According to the terms of the lease, the landlord agreed to make any necessary repairs to the cabin within a reasonable time except for ordinary wear and tear, which the tenant was responsible for. Several years later, part of the cabin's roof collapsed during one of the mountain's annual windstorms. The tenant called the landlord and informed him of the damage, but the landlord refused to make the repairs. A couple weeks later, a loosened piece of wood fell from the damaged area and landed on the tenant's shoulder, causing him injury. The tenant sued the landlord.

For what claim(s), if any, may the tenant be awarded damages?

(A) For breach of the lease, but not for the tenant's injuries.

(B) For the tenant's injuries, but not for breach of the lease.

(C) For breach of the lease as well as for the tenant's injuries.

(D) For neither breach of the lease nor the tenant's injuries.

Question 15

A landlord owned several apartment buildings surrounding a college campus, which he rented to students. After several bad experiences, the landlord now includes in all leases a prohibition against assignments. A sophomore rented one of the apartments for a year, beginning July 1, for $1,200 per month. Unless proper notice was given, the lease would renew automatically each year. During the fall semester, the sophomore was accepted into a program allowing her to study abroad in the spring. Not wanting to give up her apartment due to a housing shortage, the sophomore agreed to let her friend take over the lease for the months of January through May. The friend moved into the apartment, but never paid any rent to the landlord. When the sophomore returned in June, she was greeted by a very angry landlord, who demanded the previous five months' unpaid rent.

From whom can the landlord recover the rent owed?

(A) The sophomore, because assignments were prohibited under the terms of the lease.

(B) The sophomore, because the friend was a subtenant.

(C) The sophomore and the friend, because they are jointly and severally liable.

(D) The friend, because he agreed to take over the lease.

Question 16

A landlord leased an office building to a tenant for 10 years. The tenant always paid his rent on time. After four years, the tenant assigned his interest in the building to a medical practice. The medical practice paid the rent on time for the first six months, but then stopped paying the rent. After being in the office building for a year, the medical practice decided to downsize and assigned the lease to a publisher. The publisher never paid any rent. One year later, the landlord sued the tenant, medical practice, and publisher for the accrued unpaid rent.

From whom should the landlord recover damages?

(A) From the tenant or the medical practice for six months' rent, and from the tenant or the publisher for one year's rent.

(B) From the tenant or the medical practice for six months' rent, and from the tenant, medical practice, or publisher for one year's rent.

(C) Only from the tenant for six months' rent, and only from the publisher for one year's rent.

(D) Only from the tenant, for all of the unpaid rent.

Question 17

A landlord and a business executive entered into a written lease agreement for a penthouse apartment for a period of five years, with rent to be paid monthly. Two years later, the executive was reassigned to an office in another state for one year. The executive leased the apartment to a coworker for the duration of his reassignment. The coworker promptly moved in, but never paid any rent. After nine months, the coworker was fired, and he moved out of the apartment and back in with his parents. Upon returning home from his reassignment, the executive had barely unpacked before he was promptly served with a lawsuit filed by the landlord against both the executive and the coworker for the previous year's unpaid rent.

Assuming the landlord is successful, how will the court rule regarding damages?

(A) Against the coworker individually for the full year's rent, and no judgment against the executive.

(B) Against the executive for the full year's rent, and no judgment against the coworker.

(C) Against the executive individually for three months' rent, and against the coworker individually for nine months' rent.

(D) Against the executive and coworker for the full year's rent, because they are jointly and severally liable.

Question 18

A landlord and tenant entered into a residential lease agreement. According to the terms of the agreement, the lease would continue until the landlord, in his sole discretion, terminates it by providing 30 days' notice. Two years later, the tenant received a new job and moved out of state, assigning the lease to a new tenant and notifying the landlord. The landlord then filed an action to evict the new tenant.

What is the most likely outcome?

(A) The landlord will prevail, because the landlord had the discretion to terminate the lease at any time.

(B) The landlord will prevail, because the lease was terminated when the tenant assigned it.

(C) The new tenant will prevail, because the lease did not prohibit assignments.

(D) The new tenant will prevail, because the landlord did not provide the required notice.

Question 19

A university leased a two-story house near the campus to a newly hired professor for a term of five years. According to the terms of the lease, assignments and subleases were prohibited, and the professor agreed to pay $500 per month in rent. The professor moved in with his family and lived there for two years. After two years, the professor had a new child, and decided that he needed more space. The professor moved out and assigned the lease to a student. The student agreed to pay the university the $500 monthly rent. The university did not object to the assignment.

One year later, the student subleased the top floor of the house to a friend for $250 per month, which the friend paid to the student. The friend paid rent for the first six months, but then stopped. The next month, the student paid the university $250 and notified them that they should collect the remainder of the rent from the friend, who refused to vacate the house. The university instead sued the student to collect the unpaid $250 rent.

What is the most probable outcome?

(A) The university will recover, because the student remains liable.

(B) The university will recover, because they did not object to the assignment or sublease.

(C) The university will not recover, because the friend is the party that is liable.

(D) The university will not recover, because the professor remains liable.

Question 20

A man inherited a large estate with a log cabin that had been constructed many generations ago using wood from the surrounding old-growth forest. For over a century, the family had been exploiting the timber on the property by permitting companies to enter and remove trees at a sustainable rate, although never from a five-acre area around the log cabin. Not wanting to give up his life in the city, the man leased the log cabin and the five acres around it to a tenant. In the third year of the lease, a serious rainstorm caused part of the roof and walls of the cabin to collapse. The tenant, wanting to retain the locally sourced nature of the cabin, cut down several trees nearby to use in making repairs. While the repairs kept the log cabin from becoming unusable, the fact that old-growth trees were used for the repairs caused a net loss in the value of the property due to how long it would take for them to be replaced. When the man learned of this, he sued the tenant for the loss in value to the property and the value of the trees that had been cut down.

Will the tenant be required to reimburse the man?

(A) No, because the tenant used the trees to repair the property.

(B) No, because of the open mines doctrine.

(C) Yes, because the tenant committed voluntary waste.

(D) Yes, because the tenant committed ameliorative waste.

Essays

Essay Question 1

IE13JUL005

ISSUE SPOTTING EXERCISE

Consider the fact pattern below and then answer the questions that follow:

Larry was the owner of a two-story building. The top floor was for residential use only, but the bottom floor could be used for either residential or commercial purposes. On January 1, Larry leased the top floor to Able for a five-year term, at a rent of $1,000 per month. On February 1, Larry leased the bottom floor to Barney for a three-year term, at a rent of $1,200 per month. Both leases were in writing and signed by all parties. Able intended to live on the second floor, while Barney planned to operate a sandwich shop on the first floor. These uses were both known to Larry at the time the respective leases were signed.

Able moved into the second floor on January 2, and, after a brief period of construction, Barney's sandwich shop opened for business on March 1. In June, Able noticed that the window on the south wall of his apartment had a crack in it. Able complained to Larry about the cracked window, but Larry took no action. After a month of waiting, Able had the window replaced at a cost of $500.

Business at the sandwich shop was better than Barney expected, so in July, he decided to expand his operating hours and remain open until two in the morning. This resulted in an increase in the noise emanating from the sandwich shop, which prevented Able from getting a full night's sleep. In addition, Barney's staff was not very diligent at cleaning up the garbage left behind by the patrons of the sandwich shop. Trash frequently piled up for several days before being picked up, creating pungent odors that Able found offensive. Able frequently complained about the noise and smell to Larry, but no action was ever taken.

At the end of July, Able decided to vacate the premises, and has refused to pay any further rent. Additionally, Able wants Larry to reimburse him for the $500 that he spent to replace the cracked window.

1. *Is Able entitled to reimbursement from Larry for the $500 that Able spent to replace the cracked window? Discuss.*

2. *Will Larry be able to hold Able liable for the unpaid rent for the duration of the lease? Discuss.*

I. **Able would like to be reimbursed for the cost of replacing the cracked window.**

   A. **On what legal basis can Able argue that Larry is required to reimburse him?**

   B. **List the facts from the prompt that helped you to identify this issue:**

II. **Able moved out of the apartment and has refused to pay any further rent.**

   A. **On what legal theory can Able argue that he is not required to pay further rent?**

   B. **This legal theory should be discussed as two separate issues. List the two issues that should be separately addressed:**

      1.

      2.

   C. **List the facts that will help you to resolve the first issue:**

   D. **List the facts that will help you to resolve the second issue:**

Essay Question 1

IE13JUL005

RULE RECOLLECTION EXERCISE

A good rule statement will demonstrate your understanding of the law and provide the foundation for your analysis. This exercise is intended to help you practice: (1) recalling the relevant rules of law; (2) organizing rules of law; and (3) explaining legal concepts completely and concisely.

- PUT AWAY YOUR NOTES for this exercise and practice actively trying to recall the relevant rules.
- In FIFTEEN minutes, write out rule statements for the following issues.
- WRITE THESE RULES OUT IN FULL; do not merely jot down concepts, topics, or fragments.

REIMBURSEMENT FOR THE $500 (LANDLORD DUTY TO TENANT)

LIABILITY FOR THE UNPAID RENT

Effect of the Cracked Window (Quiet Enjoyment / Constructive Eviction)

Effect of Barney's Sandwich Shop (Quiet Enjoyment / Constructive Eviction)

Essay Question 1

IE13JUL005

ANALYSIS EXERCISE

Connect law (rules) to fact, and draft your analysis paragraph for each issue below.

REIMBURSEMENT FOR THE $500 (LANDLORD DUTY TO TENANT)

LIABILITY FOR THE UNPAID RENT

Effect of the Cracked Window (Quiet Enjoyment / Constructive Eviction)

Effect of Barney's Sandwich Shop (Quiet Enjoyment / Constructive Eviction)

Essay Question 2

IE13JUL006

Oscar owned a two-story building, and lived on the second floor. On January 1, Oscar leased the bottom floor of the building to Tom, who intended to use it to operate a greeting card store. The lease was for a three-year term at a rental rate of $24,000 per year, payable in monthly installments of $2,000 per month. The lease contained a provision that subleases were not permitted "without the written consent of Oscar."

Business at the greeting card store was not what Tom had hoped it would be, and so in July of the first year, Tom told Sally that he would sublease the premises to her. Tom and Sally signed an agreement whereby Sally would lease the space from Tom for the remaining period of the lease and for the same amount that Tom was paying to Oscar. Sally removed all of Tom's furnishings from the bottom floor and, at considerable expense, outfitted the property so that she could operate a bakery. Neither Tom nor Sally consulted Oscar about this arrangement or obtained his written consent. However, because he was living upstairs from the business, Oscar was aware of what was going on.

As was the case with Tom, sales at Sally's bakery were not what she had hoped for, and that October, Sally closed her bakery and abandoned the premises. While all rent had been paid up to that point, beginning November 1, neither Sally nor Tom paid any rent to Oscar. At the end of December, Oscar filed suit against Tom and Sally for the unpaid rent.

Who, if anyone, is liable to Oscar for the unpaid rent? Discuss.

KAPLAN BAR REVIEW

Mortgages Quiz

Question 1

A man purchased a townhouse and obtained a loan from the bank for $220,000 in order to do so in exchange for a mortgage on the property. A few years later, the man lost his job and had trouble making payments to the bank. After three months without receiving a payment, the bank initiated foreclosure proceedings. One month later, a date was set for a public auction on the property. A few days prior to the public auction, the man's friend provided him with a loan that was more than sufficient for the man to pay his mortgage and stop the auction. However, the bank refused to stop the auction and told the man that he was unable to pay the debt due.

Is the bank correct that the man cannot stop the foreclosure proceedings?

(A) No, because the man has the right to redeem the property before foreclosure.

(B) No, because the man has the right to redeem the property up to two years following foreclosure.

(C) Yes, because once the foreclosure proceedings started, the man lost his ability to redeem the property.

(D) Yes, because the bank obtained a court order to conduct a public auction on the property.

Question 2

A real estate developer purchased a piece of real property in State A, a lien theory jurisdiction, to construct much needed housing and a neighborhood park. He obtained a $7 million loan from a bank, which recorded a lien against the property. The bank loan documents specified that installment payments would start within six months of construction. A month later, Frank realized the $7 million loan would not be enough to cover the project, so he took a loan from the city for $2 million for the project. The city subsequently filed a lien against the property. Three months later, Frank is still in the middle of construction and asks the bank to reschedule the installment payments for its loan. The bank agrees to reschedule the installment payments and modifies its senior lien. The city finds out about this modification and claims its junior mortgage now prevails over the bank's senior mortgage.

Is the city's claim correct?

(A) No, because the bank may make any modifications to its loan without losing its senior mortgage status.

(B) No, because the rescheduling of installment payments does not materially prejudice the city.

(C) Yes, because the rescheduling of loan payments is a modification.

(D) Yes, because the rescheduling of loan payments materially prejudices the city.

Question 3

A professional basketball player owned a mansion on 250 acres, where he raised bulls since bulls were his team's mascot. He purchased the property for $1,400,000. He paid the seller a down payment of $400,000 and secured a mortgage from a bank for $1,000,000. In order to secure the loan in a timely manner, he signed documents at closing in which he waived his right to redeem the property in the event of foreclosure. He had an attorney represent him at the closing. For five years, income from his basketball career and product endorsements was sufficient to pay the monthly mortgage payment. Due to a lapse in judgement on the basketball player's part, he was convicted of a crime and lost all of his endorsements. Attorney fees used up most of his savings, and he defaulted on the mortgage loan. The bank commenced foreclosure proceedings. The bank had the property appraised at $3,000,000. After hearing about the appraisal, the basketball player borrowed money from his fellow teammates. The judge granted the bank's motion for summary judgment and set a date for a sheriff's sale. The basketball player tendered a check to the bank in the amount sufficient pay off the mortgage and all debt otherwise due on the loan. The bank refused to accept his payment. His attorney filed a motion to dismiss the foreclosure suit.

Should the motion be granted?

(A) No, because he may only redeem the property after the foreclosure sale.

(B) No, because he waived the equitable right of redemption.

(C) Yes, because he was entitled to redeem the property even after the foreclosure sale.

(D) Yes, because the waiver of the right to redeem was invalid.

Question 4

A dentist owned a parcel of land in an area zoned for commercial development. The dentist hoped to someday build a large dental practice on the land, but was willing to sell the land if the price is right. The dentist had an outstanding bank mortgage of $200,000. An investor offered to buy the land and stated that he would: (1) assume the mortgage; (2) pay the dentist $25,000 in cash; and (3) give the dentist a second mortgage on the land for another $25,000. The proper instruments were executed, the deed specifically stated that the investor assumed the obligation to pay the bank mortgage.

Unfortunately, the investor had unexpected difficulties obtaining the financing and permits necessary to build a proposed strip mall. He was unable to make the mortgage payments due on the property, and the bank properly instituted a foreclosure proceeding on the land. At the last moment before the foreclosure sale was scheduled to be held, the investor borrowed enough money to exercise his right of redemption, and he paid the bank all the funds due under the first mortgage.

The dentist then brought a foreclosure action for the second mortgage of $25,000, under a provision in the promissory note that allowed the dentist to declare the amount immediately due if the investor defaulted on any of the payments due under the bank mortgage.

Who should prevail in the foreclosure action brought by the dentist?

(A) The dentist, because the bank proceeding has no effect on his interest.

(B) The dentist, because it would be inequitable for the investor to use the redemption proceeding to extinguish the rights of one with whom he was in privity.

(C) The investor, because his exercise of the redemption right extinguished all junior interests.

(D) The investor, because the dentist should have intervened in the bank foreclosure action to protect his interests.

Question 5

A nurse bought a new townhouse to live in while she worked for two years at hospital in a city 175 miles away from her own home. At the time that the nurse bought the new townhouse, housing prices were at the top of a cycle. The nurse took out a 15-year mortgage to buy the new townhouse, which the mortgagee promptly recorded, and hoped to get back what she paid for the townhouse in two years. Unfortunately, the housing market declined rapidly after her purchase. At the end of the two years, the nurse sold the new townhouse, but the selling price did not cover her outstanding mortgage debt. The purchaser paid her in cash. The purchaser did not assume the nurse's mortgage, but rather took subject to the mortgage. The nurse promised the purchaser that she would use the cash proceeds to continue making mortgage payments. However, after that date, the mortgagee received no further payments from any party.

What recourse does the mortgagee have?

(A) The mortgagee may foreclose on the property and sue the purchaser for the balance of the mortgage debt.

(B) The mortgagee may foreclose on the property and sue the nurse for the balance of the mortgage debt.

(C) The mortgagee may sue the nurse for the balance of the mortgage debt, but may not foreclose on the property.

(D) The mortgagee may sue the purchaser for the balance of the mortgage debt, but may not foreclose on the property.

Question 6

A man owned property that he used as his residence. The man received a loan, secured by a mortgage on the property, from a bank. Later, the man defaulted on the loan. The bank then brought an appropriate action to foreclose the mortgage, was the sole bidder at the judicial sale, and received title to the property as a result of the foreclosure sale.

Shortly after the foreclosure sale, the man received a substantial inheritance. He approached the bank to repurchase the property, but the bank decided to build a branch office on the property and declined to sell.

If the man prevails in an appropriate action to recover title to the property, what is the most likely reason?

(A) He had used the property as his residence.

(B) He timely exercised an equitable right of redemption.

(C) The court applied the doctrine of exoneration.

(D) The jurisdiction provides for a statutory right of redemption.

Question 7

A man borrowed money from a bank and executed a promissory note for the amount, secured by a mortgage on his residence. Several years later, the man sold the property. As required by the contract of sale, the deed to the buyer provided that the buyer agreed "to assume the existing mortgage debt" on the residence.

Subsequently, the buyer defaulted on the mortgage loan to the bank, and appropriate foreclosure proceedings were initiated. The foreclosure sale resulted in a deficiency. There is no applicable statute.

Is the buyer liable for the deficiency?

(A) No, because even if the buyer assumed the mortgage, the seller is solely responsible for any deficiency.

(B) No, because the buyer did not sign a promissory note to the bank, and therefore has no personal liability.

(C) Yes, because the buyer assumed the mortgage, and therefore became personally liable for the mortgage loan and any deficiency.

(D) Yes, because the transfer of the mortgage debt to the buyer resulted in a novation of the original mortgage and loan and rendered the buyer solely responsible for any deficiency.

Question 8

A landowner was the record title owner of a three-acre tract of land. In order to finance the purchase of the property back in 2005, the landowner borrowed $100,000 from the bank, which secured the loan with a mortgage that amortized principal and interest payments over a 15-year period. The bank promptly recorded the mortgage. This jurisdiction has the following recording statute in effect:

"Any unrecorded conveyance or mortgage is invalid as against a subsequent bona fide purchaser for value without notice who records first."

In 2006, the landowner subdivided the property into three one-acre lots. He sold Lot 1 to his friend for $75,000. The following year, the landowner sold Lot 2 to his brother for $60,000. The landowner continued to reside on Lot 3.

When the landowner sold Lots 1 and 2 to his friend and brother, the deeds did not make any reference to the original mortgage between the landowner and the bank. In 2009, the landowner was laid off from his job and went into default on his mortgage payments. The bank is now about to institute foreclosure proceedings.

Which of the following most accurately states the rights and obligations of the parties?

(A) The bank can foreclose only on Lot 3, because ownership to that lot is retained by the landowner, the original mortgagor.

(B) The bank has the option of foreclosing on Lots 1, 2, or 3, because the mortgage covered the entire three-acre tract.

(C) The bank must first foreclose on Lot 3, and if the proceeds are insufficient, then the mortgagee may foreclose against Lots 1 and 2 in the inverse order of their alienation.

(D) The bank can foreclose on Lot 3, but not on Lots 1 and 2 unless the friend and the brother assumed the mortgage when they purchased their land from the landowner.

Question 9

A banker purchased a home for $500,000 and obtained a loan from a bank. Two years later, the banker obtained a loan from the city in the amount of $50,000 to install solar panels on the property. Both loans require monthly payments with interest, and both were secured by liens against the banker's property. A year later, the banker lost his job and was no longer able to make payments to either the bank or the city. The bank initiated judicial proceedings for a foreclosure sale of the property. The property was eventually sold at a public auction for $500,000. The funds were sufficient to repay the bank, but not the city. When the city challenged this sale, the bank argued that the city's interest was extinguished by the foreclosure sale.

Which argument below is the strongest for the city to show that its interest was not extinguished due to the bank's initiation of foreclosure proceedings?

(A) The bank did not provide the city with notice of the foreclosure proceedings.

(B) The city's loan was not repaid at all by the foreclosure proceedings.

(C) The city did not receive notice of the pending sale of the property.

(D) The city was not made a defendant and did not receive notice of the foreclosure sale.

Question 10

The owner of Blackacre, who held the property in fee simple, borrowed $50,000 from his brother. The owner gave his brother a promissory note for $50,000 and secured the payment of the note by giving the brother a mortgage on Blackacre, which was duly recorded. One year later, the owner sold Blackacre to a friend by quitclaim deed, which was promptly recorded. While the friend was the owner of Blackacre, the mortgage note was not paid when it became due.

At the time of the conveyance from the owner to his friend, the deed contained no reference to the mortgage. The brother sued the friend on the promissory note.

Will the brother be successful?

(A) No, because the friend did not promise to pay the mortgage debt.

(B) No, unless the friend had constructive notice of the existence of the mortgage.

(C) Yes, because an implied delegation of duties resulted from the conveyance from the owner to his friend.

(D) Yes, because the brother is a third-party beneficiary of the conveyance from the owner to his friend.

Question 11

On May 1, the owner of a 20-acre tract of unimproved land sold the property to his neighbor for the purchase price of $40,000 under a quitclaim deed. The neighbor did not record the deed. On May 5, the owner died leaving a valid will by which he devised the property to his son. After the administration of his father's estate, the son, in consideration of the sum of $75,000, conveyed the property to a friend by warranty deed. This transaction took place on August 1. When the friend acquired title, he had no actual knowledge of the neighbor's deed, which was still unrecorded. On August 10, the neighbor recorded his deed. The friend did not record the deed he received from the son until August 15.

This jurisdiction adheres to the following statute: "No conveyance is good against a subsequent purchaser for a valuable consideration and without notice, unless the same be recorded prior to subsequent purchase."

In an appropriate action to quiet title in which all interested parties have been joined, who owns title to the property?

(A) The neighbor, because his deed preceded the friend's deed.

(B) The neighbor, because his deed was recorded prior to the friend's deed.

(C) The friend, because he is protected by the recording statute.

(D) The friend, because he took title by warranty deed and the neighbor took title by quitclaim deed.

Question 12

A gun collector purchases a residence and two acres of land for $100,000 and obtains a mortgage from the bank for $80,000. Two years later, the gun collector decides to turn the property into a firing range and applies for a permit to demolish the residence. The day after the house was demolished, the bank learns of the gun collector's actions and determines that the market value of the property without the residence is $20,000.

If the bank declared the mortgage to be in default, which of the following provides the strongest justification?

(A) The mortgagor has defaulted in making payments on the mortgage.

(B) In a lien theory jurisdiction, the mortgagor receives a lien on the property.

(C) The mortgagor's actions will be defined as waste.

(D) Foreclosure is not an option for the bank.

Question 13

A couple of newlyweds were in the market for a new home, and asked their broker to look for a three-bedroom, single-family home under $150,000. The broker found an appropriate house listed at $148,000 and brought the couple to look at the property. They decided to buy the house and made a full-price offer that was accepted by the seller. To finance the purchase, the newlyweds made an $18,000 down payment and obtained a mortgage from the bank in the amount of $130,000 to finance the balance.

Three years later, the couple was injured in a car accident and could no longer get up and down the stairs in their home. They decided to sell the house and move to a single-story home in a nearby neighborhood. The couple arranged to sell the two-story house to a buyer for $160,000. The terms of the sale provided that the buyer would pay the couple $32,000 and would assume the existing loan and mortgage held by the bank, which now showed a balance due of $128,000. One year after the sale, the buyer became unemployed and stopped making payments on the mortgage. After six months, the bank personally served the buyer with notice of its intent to foreclose and instituted foreclosure proceedings in an appropriate court. The couple was not served with notice of the foreclosure. One week prior to the scheduled foreclosure sale, the buyer quitclaimed the house and lot back to the bank in lieu of foreclosure. At the time of the quitclaim, the property was worth substantially less than the mortgage debt. Assume that the jurisdiction has no statute preventing deficiency judgments.

In an action by the bank against the couple for the deficiency, how should the court rule?

(A) The couple is liable for the mortgage debt, because they couple as surety for the unpaid balance of the mortgage.

(B) The couple is liable for the mortgage debt, because they were not made a party to the quitclaim in lieu of foreclosure conveyance.

(C) The couple is not liable, because they were not served or otherwise notified of the foreclosure action.

(D) The couple is not liable, because by accepting the property in lieu of foreclosure, the bank effectively discharged the obligations of both the couple and the buyer.

Question 14

On February 1, a woman conveyed her farm to a man, and the man duly recorded the conveyance. The following day, the man conveyed the property to his sister; she did not record her deed. Then on February 4, the man executed an identical conveyance of the farm to a friend. The friend gave the man a check for $100,000 for the property and recorded the conveyance, even though he had actual knowledge of the prior conveyance to the sister. The sister, however, recorded her deed on February 6. The friend then conveyed his interest in the farm to a farmer, who gave a purchase price of $115,000 to the friend. On February 5, the farmer purchased the farm without notice of the conveyance to the sister and duly records the deed.

If the property in question was located in a state having a notice-type statute, which of the following parties would ultimately prevail?

(A) The farmer.

(B) The sister.

(C) The friend.

(D) The man.

Question 15

A buyer fell in love with a charming farmhouse that sat on eight rolling acres of fields. The selling price was $240,000, which was more than the buyer could borrow on his current income. The buyer could only qualify for a bank loan of $140,000. The buyer asked whether the seller would be interested in financing the remaining $100,000, and the seller agreed. The buyer obtained the bank loan, and the closing occurred. The seller recorded his mortgage the same day and the bank recorded its mortgages the next day. The jurisdiction has a race-notice recording act. Several years later, the buyer lost his job and defaulted on both loans. The bank and the seller began competing foreclosure actions.

Which loan has priority?

(A) The bank's loan, because it is a purchase-money mortgage.

(B) The seller's loan, because the buyer used seller-financing.

(C) The seller's loan, because the buyer used seller-financing and the seller recorded first.

(D) The loans have equal priority, because they are both purchase-money mortgages.

Question 16

Which of the following is a purchase-money mortgage?

I. A homeowner takes out a home equity line of credit in order to remodel the kitchen.

I. A buyer buys a home and, in the same transaction, borrows money to remodel the kitchen.

II. A buyer buys a home and borrows money to finance the purchase.

(A) I only.

(B) II and III.

(C) III only.

(D) Neither I, II, nor III.

Question 17

A retiree owned six acres of land, part of which was a lovely apple orchard. A passerby saw the apple trees and inquired about buying the property. The retiree agreed to sell it for $300,000, and the parties wrote up a contract to that effect. The closing occurred in July, and the passerby received a general warranty deed, but forgot to record it. The passerby planned to move onto the property in September. The retiree suffered from memory loss issues and, in August, after settling into a retirement home, the retiree again sold the six acres, this time to another resident of the home, receiving $400,000 for it. The resident had viewed the property, found that it was lovely, and planned to bequeath it to his son. The resident also forgot to record his general warranty deed. When the passerby went to move into the property in September, he found someone there taking measurements for new carpet, who said he had been hired by the resident. The passerby filed suit to quiet title to the property. The parties lived in a notice jurisdiction.

Which party will prevail in the quiet title action?

(A) The passerby, because he was first in time, first in right.

(B) The passerby, because the retiree had no interest to sell to the resident.

(C) The resident, because he took possession first.

(D) The resident, because he was a bona fide purchaser for value without notice.

Question 18

A debtor in a large city bought at the top of the housing market, purchasing a lovely home for $180,000 with a mortgage of $175,000. The mortgage was interest-only, so the debtor only paid the interest due every month, without reducing the principle. Several years later, the debtor was "under water" on his mortgage, meaning that the home was only worth $100,000 but the debtor still owed the mortgage of $175,000. The debtor defaulted. The lender began foreclosure proceedings. The debtor tried desperately to sell the home to avoid foreclosure. An investor said that he would buy the home, and the investor gave the debtor $80,000 in exchange for a deed. The debtor took the $80,000 and left town with the money.

On the way out of town, the debtor left off a deed in lieu of foreclosure with the lender, which the lender accepted in lieu of the $175,000. The debtor did this to avoid a deficiency judgment. The lender recorded its new deed to the home the same day. The investor, believing that the debtor had paid the lender the $80,000 as a negotiated pay-off and knowing nothing of the deed in lieu of foreclosure, asked his title company to record his own deed. The title company took five days to record the deed. The parties live in a race-notice jurisdiction.

Which deed has priority?

(A) The lender's deed, because the lender paid value, recorded before the investor, and had no notice of the investor's claim.

(B) The lender's deed, because a deed in lieu of foreclosure takes precedence over other deeds.

(C) The investor's deed, because the investor paid value and gave instructions for recording first.

(D) The investor's deed, because it was the debtor's responsibility to notify and pay the lender.

Question 19

An old house was rumored to be haunted. Unusual sounds were heard at night, and sometimes objects were seen to have moved. An adventurer thought that such a house might be fun to own, and he looked up the owner in the public records. The owner, who lived in another state, agreed to sell the old house for $22,000. The closing occurred, and the adventurer recorded his deed. When the adventurer arrived to take possession, he found a bearded man living in the house. The bearded man showed the adventurer his quitclaim deed from the owner, dated one year previously, which had not been recorded. The adventurer sued to quiet title. The parties live in a notice jurisdiction.

Is the adventurer likely to prevail in his quiet title action?

(A) No, because the adventurer did not pay full value.

(B) No, because the adventurer had notice of the bearded man's claim.

(C) Yes, because the adventurer had no notice of the bearded man's claim.

(D) Yes, because the adventurer paid value and recorded his deed.

Question 20

A married couple advertised their home for sale through a realtor. The home was in a desirable area, with good schools, and two offers came in simultaneously. The realtor presented the offers to the couple, who said that they would sell to the first offeror, a computer technician, if the technician would raise his offer by $10,000. They said that they would sell to the second offeror, a paralegal, if the paralegal would raise her offer by $15,000. Both the technician and the paralegal agreed to raise their offers. The couple signed both contracts and then instructed the realtor to proceed with a closing with the offeror who could obtain financing and proceed all the way to closing. The couple departed for a trip, leaving an executed power of attorney for the realtor to sign all closing documents on their behalf. The realtor became ill, and her duties were taken over by others in her office. Using the realtor's stamped signature, one co-worker sold the home to the technician, while another co-worker unwittingly and simultaneously sold the home to the paralegal. The technician's deed was about to be recorded when the mistake was discovered. The paralegal was informed that her transaction would be rescinded. The paralegal furiously grabbed her new deed and ran to the courthouse, recording first.

In which jurisdictions will the paralegal have title?

(A) A race jurisdiction.

(B) A notice jurisdiction.

(C) A race-notice jurisdiction.

(D) All of the above.

Torts

Exercise Set 1

Question 1

Identify the elements of negligence:

A.

B.

C.

D.

Question 2

Define the following:

A. *Contributory negligence:*

B. *Pure comparative negligence:*

C. *Partial comparative negligence:*

D. *Assumption of risk:*

For the following exercises, you are given a question prompt. After reading the question prompt, consider the applicable rules. Then, brainstorm possible issues that could be raised or tested based on the given question prompt.

Question 3

Will the plaintiff's wrongful death suit be successful?

Question 4

What is the store owner's best defense against the plaintiff's claim?

Question 5

What damages will the plaintiff be able to recover?

Question 6

Which defendant will be liable for the plaintiff's damages?

For each of the following fact patterns, write out the relevant issues and corresponding rule statements.

Question 7

In a wrongful death action brought against the defendant by the decedent's legal representative, the only proofs that the plaintiff offered on liability were that: (1) the decedent, a pedestrian, was killed instantly while walking on the shoulder of the highway; (2) the defendant was driving the car that struck the decedent; and (3) there were no living witnesses to the accident other than the defendant, who denied any negligence on his part. At the end of the plaintiff's case, the defendant moved for a directed verdict.

How should the trial judge rule?

Question 8

The defendant operates a residential rehabilitation center for emotionally disturbed and ungovernable children who have been committed to his custody by their parents or by juvenile authorities. The center's purpose is to modify the behavior of the children through a teaching program carried out in a family-like environment. Though the children are not permitted to leave the center without permission, there are no bars or guards to actually prevent them from doing so. In the state where the center is located, it has been held that persons having custody of children have the same duties and responsibilities that they would have if they were the parents of the children. Carl, a 12-year-old boy who had been in the defendant's custody for six months, left the center one day without permission. The defendant became aware of Carl's absence almost immediately, but made no attempt to locate him or secure his return, though reports reached him that Carl had been seen in the vicinity. Thirty-six hours after Carl left the center, he committed a brutal assault upon Paul, a five-year-old child, causing Paul to suffer extensive permanent injury.

If an action is brought against the defendant on behalf of Paul to recover damages his injuries, will the plaintiff prevail?

Question 9

Landon owns and operates a 12-story apartment building containing 72 apartments, 70 of which were rented. Walker brought an action against Landon alleging that while he was walking along a public sidewalk adjacent to Landon's apartment building, a flowerpot fell from above and struck him on the shoulder, causing him extensive injuries. The action was to recover damages for those injuries.

If Walker proves the foregoing facts and offers no other evidence explaining the accident, will his claim survive a motion for directed verdict offered by the defendant?

Question 10

Peter and Donald were in the habit of playing practical jokes on each other on their respective birthdays. On Peter's birthday, Donald sent Peter a cake containing an ingredient that he knew had, in the past, made Peter very ill. After Peter had eaten a piece of the cake, he suffered severe stomach pains and had to be taken to the hospital by ambulance. On the way to the hospital, the ambulance driver suffered a heart attack, which caused the ambulance to swerve from the road and hit a tree. As a result of the collision, Peter suffered a broken leg.

In a suit by Peter against Donald to recover damages for Peter's broken leg, will Peter prevail?

Exercise Set 2

Question 1

Complete the following chart with the requirements for the following:

Res Ipsa Loquitur			
Vicarious Liability			

Question 2

Complete the following chart with the defense that corresponds to the given elements.

DEFENSE	ELEMENTS
	• The plaintiff did not act as a reasonable person. • The plaintiff's actions bar recovery.
	• The plaintiff had knowledge of and appreciated the danger. • The plaintiff appreciated the specific danger that caused the injury.
	• The plaintiff did not act as a reasonable person. • The plaintiff's recovery is proportionate to his or her fault.
	• The plaintiff did not act as a reasonable person. • The plaintiff's recovery is barred if she or he had the majority of fault.

For the following fact patterns, complete the chart with the relevant facts that correspond to the rules provided.

Question 3

Dora, who was eight years' old, went to the grocery store with her mother. Dora pushed the grocery cart while her mother put items into it. Dora's mother remained near Dora at all times. Peterson, another customer in the store, noticed Dora pushing the cart in a manner that caused Peterson no concern. A short time later, the cart Dora was pushing struck Peterson in the knee, inflicting serious injury.

If Peterson brings an action based on negligence against the grocery store, what would be the store's best defense?

RULE	RELEVANT FACTS
Standard of Care—Business Invitee	

Question 4

Donald fell while attempting to climb a mountain, and lay unconscious and critically injured on a ledge that was difficult to reach. Paul, an experienced mountain climber, was himself seriously injured while trying to rescue Donald. Paul's rescue attempt failed, and Donald died of his injuries before he could be reached. Paul brought an action against Donald's estate for compensation for his injuries.

Will Paul prevail in his action against Donald's estate?

RULES	RELEVANT FACTS
Foreseeable Plaintiff	
Breach of Duty	

Question 5

Dudley parked her car in violation of a city ordinance that prohibited parking within 10 feet of a fire hydrant. Because Grant was driving negligently, his car sideswiped Dudley's parked car. Grant now asserts a claim against Dudley to recover damages for his injuries, basing his claim on Dudley's violation of the parking ordinance.

Will Grant prevail?

RULES	RELEVANT FACTS
Negligence Per Se	
Contributory Negligence	
Comparative Negligence	

Question 6

Doug's dog ran into the street in front of Doug's home and began chasing cars. A woman who was driving a car down the street swerved to avoid hitting the dog, struck a telephone pole, and was injured.

If the woman asserts a claim against Doug, will the woman prevail?

RULES	RELEVANT FACTS
Duty	
Breach	
Causation	
Damages	

Question 7

A man, an inexperienced driver, borrowed a car from a casual acquaintance for the express purpose of driving it several blocks to the local drug store. Instead, the man drove the car, which was worth $12,000, 100 miles to a nearby town, where he stayed overnight. While the man was driving around in the town the next day, the car was hit by a negligently driven truck and sustained $3,000 worth of damages. If repaired, the car would be fully restored to its former condition.

If the acquaintance asserts a claim against the truck driver, will he be successful?

RULES	RELEVANT FACTS
Negligence—Truck Driver	
Negligence—Friend	
Joint and Several Liability	

For the following fact patterns, identify the applicable rules and complete the chart with the relevant facts.

Question 8

A man operated a bank courier service that used armored trucks to transport money and securities. One day, one of the man's armored trucks was parked too close to a street intersection in violation of the law. A woman that was driving her car at an excessive speed skidded into the armored truck while trying to make a turn. The truck was not damaged, but the woman was injured. The woman has brought an action against the man to recover damages resulting from the accident. The jurisdiction follows a pure comparative negligence rule.

In this action, how much should the woman recover?

RULES	RELEVANT FACTS

Question 9

While walking along a public sidewalk, a woman was struck by a piece of lumber that fell from the roof of a man's house. The man had hired a teenager to make repairs to his roof, and the lumber fell as a result of negligence on the teenager's part.

If the woman brings an action against the man to recover damages for the injury caused to her by the teenager's negligence, will the woman prevail?

RULES	RELEVANT FACTS

Question 10

Stella, who played the lead role in a television soap opera, was seriously injured in an automobile accident caused by Dartanion's negligent driving. As a consequence of Stella's injury, the television series was canceled, and Pauly, a supporting actor, was laid off.

In an action against Dartanion, can Pauly recover for his loss of income attributable to the accident?

RULES	RELEVANT FACTS

Quiz 1

Question 1

A taxicab driver stopped at a convenience store to buy a snack. While he was handing his money to the store clerk at the cash register, a police officer entered the store. The taxi driver had received several traffic tickets from the police officer, and he felt that the police officer had been very rude to him. Seeking to gain some revenge, the taxi driver immediately began to taunt and berate the police officer, calling him a variety of profane and insulting names. The police officer was going through a series of personal difficulties and was feeling very emotionally fragile. As the taxi driver's insults rained down on him, the police officer suddenly snapped. He whipped out his gun and fired a shot at the taxi driver. The bullet missed the taxi driver but hit the store clerk, who was standing behind the taxi driver. The clerk survived the shooting but suffered a gunshot wound to his shoulder.

In an action by the injured clerk against the taxi driver to recover for his personal injuries, what is the likely outcome?

(A) The clerk will recover, because the taxi driver's conduct was the proximate cause of the clerk's injuries.

(B) The clerk will recover, because it was foreseeable that the taxi driver's conduct would result in the clerk being shot.

(C) The clerk will not recover, because the shooting was not a foreseeable consequence of the taxi driver's conduct.

(D) The clerk will not recover, because the police officer intended to shoot the taxi driver, not the store clerk.

Question 2

A tall building was under construction in the downtown business district of a city. A lawyer took a car to the downtown area to go to a meeting with a client. She was running late for the meeting and could not find a legal parking spot, so she decided to park illegally in front of a fire hydrant. This was in violation of a local ordinance that prohibited parking within 50 feet of a fire hydrant. The lawyer figured that it was better to get a ticket than to miss her meeting with an important client. The spot where she parked was next to the site of the construction of the new building. While the lawyer was at her meeting, an accident occurred at the construction site. A large crane was being used to lift a load of bricks. A cable on the crane broke, and the bricks fell. Most of them landed on top of the lawyer's car. The load of bricks that fell on the lawyer's car caused the gas tank of the car to rupture and explode. Shrapnel from the explosion flew in all directions and injured a pedestrian who was walking on the sidewalk near the lawyer's car.

If the pedestrian sues the lawyer and relies on the doctrine of negligence per se, which of the following, if true, is the lawyer's best defense?

(A) Payment of a small fine is the only penalty provided in the ordinance for those who park too close to fire hydrants.

(B) The police never issued a ticket to the lawyer for parking in front of the fire hydrant.

(C) The purpose of the parking ordinance was to facilitate access to the hydrant by fire trucks, not to protect against accidents like the one that occurred when bricks fell on the lawyer's car.

(D) The pedestrian would not have been injured if the construction company had properly maintained the crane.

Question 3

A wife and her husband were having dinner at a restaurant when the wife excused herself to go to the bathroom. The restaurant was owned and operated by a chef. As the wife was walking past a table where another customer was seated, she slipped and fell on an egg roll that had been lying on the floor for quite some time, although the chef was unaware that it had fallen onto the floor. When she fell, her head struck a serving tray that was located in the aisle. The fall caused the wife to suffer a severe concussion. The customer knew that the egg roll was on the floor, and although he could have done so, he did not warn the wife.

If the wife asserts a claim against the chef for the injuries she suffered from the fall, what is the most likely outcome?

(A) The wife will recover, because the egg roll on the floor constituted an unsafe condition of the premises.

(B) The wife will recover, because the egg roll was on the floor for a substantial period of time before the accident.

(C) The wife will not recover, because the chef did not know that the egg roll was on the floor.

(D) The wife will not recover, because the customer could have prevented the injury by warning the wife of the presences of the egg roll.

Question 4

A stockbroker became despondent because the economy was terrible and all of his clients had lost substantial amounts of money on their investments. The stockbroker decided to end his life by jumping off a bridge. He walked to the middle of the bridge, climbed over the railing, stood on the tiny ledge on the edge of the bridge, and prepared to jump. A taxi driver who happened to be crossing the bridge at that moment saw what the stockbroker was doing. The taxi driver slammed on his brakes, jumped out of his taxi, started running toward the stockbroker, and yelled, "Don't do it!" Pleased to hear that someone cared about him, the stockbroker changed his mind about committing suicide and decided that he wanted to live.

At that moment, however, the stockbroker started to lose his balance, and his feet began to slip off the small, grimy ledge of the bridge. Just as the stockbroker started to fall, the taxi driver reached him and grabbed the back of his jacket. The taxi driver hung on tightly to the jacket and nearly was pulled over the side of the bridge, but he managed to hang on.

Using every bit of strength he could muster, the taxi driver pulled the stockbroker back up and onto the bridge. The stockbroker was relieved to have been saved from falling. Unfortunately, the taxi driver suffered a severe injury to his back from the strain of hanging on to the stockbroker and pulling him back up onto the bridge. A statute in the jurisdiction makes attempted suicide a crime.

If the taxi driver asserts a claim against the stockbroker to recover damages for his injuries, will he prevail?

(A) No, because the stockbroker did not intend to harm anyone other than himself.

(B) No, because attempted suicide was a criminal offense in the jurisdiction.

(C) Yes, because the stockbroker put himself in a position of peril.

(D) Yes, because he succeeded in saving the stockbroker's life.

Question 5

A popular electronics store is having a Black Friday super sale, with deep price reductions and giveaways for the first five people to make purchases. A man decided to enter the store the night before, hide out in one of the large appliance boxes that were lying in the stockroom, and then be the first person in the store the next morning.

During the night, the man needed to use the restroom, and entered a door marked "Employees Only." The door led to a stairway that had a broken first step, and the man fell, injuring himself. The next morning, he was found with a broken leg, and arrested.

If the man brings a civil suit against the electronics store, what is the likely result?

(A) The man will recover, because he was an invitee who was injured on the premises.

(B) The man will recover, because he was a licensee who was injured on the premises.

(C) The man will not recover, because he was a trespasser on the premises.

(D) The man will not recover, because he was a trespasser in an area marked "Employees Only."

Question 6

A pedestrian was walking in front of a hotel in the downtown area when a chair was thrown from an unidentified window. The chair struck the pedestrian on the head, knocking her unconscious. When the pedestrian recovered consciousness, she found herself in a nearby hospital with a doctor in attendance. An examination revealed that the pedestrian had suffered a concussion and severe head lacerations. A subsequent investigation revealed that the chair had, in fact, been thrown from a window at the hotel. The pedestrian sued the hotel for negligence. At trial, it was conceded by the hotel that it was one of their chairs, that it came from a room on the 12th floor, and that the hotel was fully occupied on the night of the incident. However, none of the hotel's employees or guests admitted culpability for the incident.

Will the doctrine of res ipsa loquitur enable her to recover?

(A) No, because the furnishings of the room are within the control of the guests.

(B) No, because the hotel is not vicariously liable for the tortious conduct of its employees.

(C) Yes, because a chair is not usually thrown from a window in the absence of someone's negligence.

(D) Yes, because it is undisputed that the chair came from the hotel.

Question 7

A plaintiff and defendant were playing basketball. The plaintiff knew that the defendant had a reputation for being an extremely competitive player. During the game, the plaintiff's eye was severely injured when the defendant poked the plaintiff in her face while trying to get a rebound.

If the plaintiff brings a cause of action against the defendant, will the plaintiff prevail?

(A) No, because the defendant did not intend to injure the plaintiff.

(B) No, because the plaintiff impliedly consented to this kind of injury.

(C) Yes, because she suffered a harmful or offensive contact.

(D) Yes, because the defendant's actions fell below the standard of care.

Question 8

A man negligently hit a woman with his car. The woman was rushed to the hospital and sent into surgery. During the course of the operation, the doctor was careless and caused the woman more injuries.

If the woman sued the man, which of the following statements is most accurate?

(A) The woman should recover for all of her injuries, because they were foreseeably caused by the man.

(B) The woman should recover for all of her injuries, because the thin-skulled plaintiff rule provides that a defendant takes their victim as they find them.

(C) The woman should only recover for those injuries sustained in the accident, and she must sue doctor as a separate tortfeasor for the damages sustained during surgery.

(D) The woman should only recover for those injuries sustained in the accident, because it is not foreseeable that a doctor would be negligent.

Question 9

A pilot decided to fly his small airplane to another city for a weekend visit. He invited one of his best friends to join him as a passenger on the trip. Near the end of the flight, the pilot wanted to show off for his friend. The pilot saw a cloud of fog ahead and decided to navigate through it. However, the fog was much thicker than he anticipated and he got lost, crashing the plane into the side of a mountain. The pilot and his passenger were both killed instantly in the crash.

If the passenger's family brings a wrongful death action against the pilot's estate, what is the most likely outcome?

(A) The plaintiffs will recover under strict liability, because the pilot engaged in an abnormally dangerous activity.

(B) The plaintiffs will recover under negligence, because the pilot failed to exercise reasonable care in the operation of his airplane.

(C) The plaintiffs will not recover, because the passenger did not pay to go on the flight.

(D) The plaintiffs will not recover, because the passenger unreasonably exposed himself to a known danger.

Question 10

Two nine-year-old boys, Pete and Victor, were sitting across from each other in their classroom at school. Pete kicked Victor on his shin so lightly that Victor did not immediately feel it. However, minutes later, Victor was crying out in pain due to the injury. Over the next week, the wound swelled and surgery was performed on Victor's shin. The surgeons found that Victor's shin bone was damaged from an earlier sledding accident and the kick that Pete delivered exacerbated the injury, causing bone degradation and irreparable harm to the leg. Due to these events, Victor would never be able to use the leg again. Victor's parents, on his behalf, subsequently brought suit against Pete for the damages that Victor incurred.

What is the most likely outcome?

(A) Victor should recover for all of his injuries, because he was not at fault.

(B) Victor should recover for all of his injuries, because the eggshell plaintiff rule provides that a defendant takes their victim as they find them.

(C) Victor should only recover for those injuries sustained by the initial kick, but not for those attributable to the earlier sledding accident.

(D) Victor should not recover, because a nine-year-old boy cannot be liable for either negligence or intentional torts.

Question 11

While driving to the grocery store, a 45-year-old man was hit from behind by a car that was being negligently driven by a woman. At the hospital, the doctor indicated that the accident itself should only have caused minor injuries. However, the doctor determined that due to a childhood condition, the man's bones did not fully form properly, and as a result, the injuries he suffered were more severe. In fact, it was determined that the man will have to be placed into traction for one year, and that he would never walk again.

To what damages will the man be entitled?

(A) He will be entitled to just those damages that can be attributed to the car accident.

(B) He will be entitled to all damages he sustained as a result of the accident, because a tortfeasor is liable for the full consequences of the injury she causes.

(C) He will be entitled to damages that a normal person would have sustained in a similar accident.

(D) He will be entitled to damages for the traction, but not the paralysis, because of the doctrine of avoidable consequences.

Question 12

A hobbyist went out fishing on a lake at dawn. Few other people were on the lake so early in the morning, and the hobbyist enjoyed the peace and quiet. A short while later, the hobbyist noticed a canoe with one occupant heading in his direction. The canoe stopped about 50 yards away. The hobbyist was glad that the canoe didn't come any closer, because he didn't want the movement of the canoe to disturb the fish. The hobbyist then watched as the canoeist stood up in the canoe and began moving around, apparently attempting to organize his fishing tackle.

Suddenly, the canoeist's canoe overturned. The canoeist, who was not wearing a life preserver, was thrown into the water. At that same moment, the hobbyist felt a strong tug on his fishing line. He didn't want to lose the fish, so he decided to reel in the fish before going to see if the canoeist needed any assistance. The hobbyist figured that, at worst, the canoeist would have to tread water for a few minutes until the hobbyist got to him. Unfortunately, canoeist did not know how to swim, and by the time the hobbyist made his way over to the canoeist and pulled him out of the water, the canoeist was no longer breathing. Although the hobbyist promptly administered CPR and the canoeist was eventually revived by paramedics, he suffered severe brain damage.

If the canoeist's parents sue the hobbyist for the canoeist's injuries, what is the hobbyist's best argument in support of a motion to dismiss their claim?

(A) The hobbyist's delay in assisting the canoeist was reasonable.

(B) The hobbyist had no duty to help the canoeist.

(C) The canoeist was contributorily negligent.

(D) The hobbyist properly administered CPR to the canoeist so that the canoeist could be revived by the paramedics.

Question 13

A concert pianist suffered a strained wrist, so he went to visit a doctor. The doctor explained to her that the fastest way to regain complete use of the wrist was to treat it with a series of injections of a drug that blocked pain and reduced inflammation. The concert pianist had discussed with the doctor her need to be ready for an important recital in three weeks. The drug was known to cause calcium buildup in joint tissue in approximately one to two percent of patients treated with it. For most individuals experiencing this side effect, the calcium buildup did not result in noticeable limitation of movement. If it did, the buildup could be surgically removed, and after a brief recovery period (one to two months), complete movement was restored.

The doctor did not inform the concert pianist of these facts, and she began a course of treatment consisting of three injections per week for three weeks. At the end of the second week, the concert pianist received in the mail the current edition of a popular health magazine. To her dismay, it contained an article describing the dangers of using the drug that the doctor recommended, pointing out that calcium buildup in the knuckles could be devastating to a pianist. The concert pianist discontinued treatment immediately and was not able to perform in her upcoming recital due to pain in her wrist, but not because of any calcium buildup in her knuckles. The concert pianist sought treatment from another physician, who recommended a two-month hiatus from piano playing followed by six months of physical therapy. After that time, the concert pianist was able to resume her playing.

Which of the following would be most relevant in determining whether the concert pianist has a valid cause of action against the doctor?

(A) Whether the concert pianist would not have consented to the use of the drug if she knew about the risks to her mobility.

(B) Whether a reasonable person would have considered the information about calcium buildup important.

(C) Whether the doctor had weighed the risks and benefits of using the drug before prescribing it.

(D) Whether the concert pianist suffered no harm from the use of the drug.

Question 14

Three friends decided to go bowling together. They made a friendly wager on the match, with the winner receiving a free beer from the other two. In the second frame of the first game, the first friend apparently got a strike when he knocked down all 10 pins. However, the second friend accused the first friend of fouling because his foot went over the line. The first friend denied fouling and wanted to mark down a strike on the scorecard. The second friend refused to give the first friend a strike and wrote in a zero on the scoring sheet. The first friend became enraged. The second friend then went to bowl his frame. As the second friend turned his back, the first friend approached from behind with a bowling ball in his hand. The first friend then raised the bowling ball, threatening to hit the back of the second friend's head. The second friend, who had his back turned, did not see the first friend's actions. The third friend saw what the first friend was about to do and could easily have warned the second friend, but the third friend remained silent. The first friend then struck the second friend on the back of the head with the bowling ball, causing a deep scalp wound.

If the second friend asserts a cause of action against the third friend, what is the likely outcome?

(A) The second friend will prevail, because the third friend was aware of the danger.

(B) The second friend will prevail, on account of the third friend's omission to act.

(C) The second friend will not prevail, because the first friend was responsible for his injury.

(D) The second friend will not prevail, because the third friend was under no duty to warn the second friend of the danger.

Question 15

A construction company was doing repairs and replacing portions of a sidewalk and railing next to a lake. The construction crew started tearing out the old sidewalk and railing, but stopped work when it started to get dark. The construction crew left without putting up a warning sign or barrier around the work area. A few hours later, a jogger came along the sidewalk. Not realizing the construction work was in progress there, the jogger stumbled and fell at the spot where the construction crew had torn up the sidewalk and railing. The jogger fell into the lake.

As the jogger was attempting to stay afloat, he began screaming, "Help! Help! I can't swim. I'm drowning." His screams attracted the attention of a person who was passing on his bicycle. The cyclist immediately hurried to assist the jogger. As the cyclist was leaning over the edge of the lake, trying to help the jogger get out of the water, he lost his balance and fell into the lake. Both the jogger and cyclist suffered serious bodily injuries before they were pulled out of the water by police.

In a negligence action by the cyclist to recover for his personal injuries, what is the probable outcome?

(A) The construction company will be held liable, because the cyclist's attempt to rescue the jogger was foreseeable.

(B) The construction company will be held liable, because the construction company would be strictly liable to anyone injured by the failure to put adequate warnings or barriers around the site of the sidewalk repairs.

(C) The construction company will not be held liable, because the cyclist assumed the risk by leaning over the edge of the lake.

(D) The construction company will not be held liable, because the construction company could not foresee that anyone would be hurt while trying to rescue someone from the lake.

Question 16

An absentee landlord owned a run-down apartment building. He made as few repairs as possible. One day, a man visited the landlord's building to see whether he wanted to rent an apartment there. The landlord showed the man the top-floor apartment that was available. The landlord quickly steered the man into the apartment, hoping that the man wouldn't notice that the front door was about to come loose and fall off. The man did not in fact notice the broken door. The man nevertheless decided to rent the apartment, and moved in that Sunday night. The next morning, the tenant in the apartment below the man's heard a loud crash from upstairs. The tenant raced upstairs to find the man on the floor, unconscious. The broken door was lying on the floor near the man. The man sued the landlord for negligence.

If the man prevails, which of the following provides the best reason?

(A) The door represented a patent defect.

(B) The door represented a latent defect.

(C) The contract did not contain any language that stated the man was renting the property "as is."

(D) The landlord breached the implied warranty of habitability.

Question 17

An investor bought a run-down house in a developing neighborhood, which he hoped to fix up and "flip" for a considerable profit. The investor hired a painter to paint the outside of the house. The painter was a friend of the investor's who was trying to start his own painting company. The painter agreed to paint the house at a discounted rate if the investor would allow him to put a sign in the front yard of the house advertising the painter's new business. The investor chose a color and told the painter, "I don't know anything about painting, so just do the job in your usual manner." The investor paid the painter in advance for his services. As the painter was painting the side of the house, he accidentally flung a bucket of paint from the ladder where he was working. The bucket hit the investor's neighbor in the head, causing the neighbor to suffer a concussion. The neighbor has asserted claims against the investor and the painter for his injuries.

If the neighbor recovers from the investor under a theory of vicarious liability, does the investor have any recourse against the painter?

(A) No, because payment by the investor was an acceptance of the work.

(B) No, because the investor selected the painter to do the work.

(C) Yes, because the judgment against the investor was based on vicarious liability.

(D) Yes, because the investor's conduct was not a factual cause of the harm.

Question 18

A supermarket had just reopened after a six-month renovation period. The renovations included the repair, replastering, and repainting of the entire ceiling and walls by the painting company. The day following the reopening of the supermarket, the store's manager noticed small fragments of plaster on the floor, which appeared to have fallen from a part of the ceiling about 10-square-feet in area. The manager immediately posted signs in that area that read: "Caution: Falling Plaster." In addition, the manager promptly called the painting company and requested a repairman to attend to the problem. That afternoon, a shopper was shopping in the supermarket and wanted to purchase some canned goods in the posted area. Moving quickly, the shopper reached for the desired items. At that very moment, a section of the ceiling fell and struck the shopper, injuring her very seriously.

If the shopper asserts a claim against the supermarket, what is the likely outcome?

(A) The shopper will prevail, because the supermarket failed to take adequate precaution to ensure the safety of its patrons against such an unreasonable risk of harm.

(B) The shopper will prevail, because the supermarket is vicariously liable for the negligence of its independent contractor in the performance of a nondelegable duty.

(C) The shopper will not prevail, because the injury was the fault of the painting company.

(D) The shopper will not prevail, because the supermarket posted signs warning customers of the risk of harm.

Question 19

A retired policeman was hired as a night watchman by a manufacturer of large construction machinery. During the watchman's orientation, the manager of the factory emphasized that in the event of any problem, the watchman was to keep himself out of danger and call the police immediately. The night watchman also was warned never to go outside the fence while on duty. One night, a drug addict, whom the watchman recognized from his days on the police force, was walking past the yard. In a rare moment of lucidity, the addict also recognized the former police officer. The addict jeered, "Hey! You a rent-a-cop now?" The watchman ignored the addict for a while, but the addict continued to rant loudly and derisively about the watchman's new career. After several minutes of this, the watchman flew into a rage. He went outside the gate and chased the addict down. The watchman punched the addict several times, giving him a concussion. The addict subsequently filed a lawsuit against the watchman and the manufacturer.

Which of the following is the strongest argument in the manufacturer's defense?

(A) The watchman's act was outside the scope of his employment.

(B) The watchman was defending the manufacturer's property.

(C) The watchman was acting in self-defense.

(D) The watchman was contributorily negligent.

Question 20

A baseball fan purchased two tickets for a World Series baseball game. The fan contacted his best friend and invited him to go to the game. The friend, who was also a baseball fanatic, eagerly agreed. The fan told the friend that the game started at 7:00 p.m. and that he would pick him up at about 5:00 p.m. so they could get there early to watch batting practice. They were driving to the game together when the fan sped up to cross an intersection while the traffic signal was changing from amber to red. As he reached the intersection, the fan was traveling at 50 m.p.h., although the posted speed limit was 25 m.p.h. Simultaneously, a car entered the intersection on red and collided with the fan's vehicle. The friend suffered a broken pelvis in the collision.

This jurisdiction has adopted the following "modified" comparative negligence statute: "A negligent plaintiff is entitled to obtain a recovery provided plaintiff's negligence is not equal to or greater than that of the defendant's; otherwise no recovery is permitted."

Suppose the friend brings suit against the driver of the car that entered the intersection on the red light to recover damages for his injury. A jury returned a special verdict with the following findings: (1) the fan was 55% negligent in speeding; (2) the driver was 45% negligent in driving through the red light; and (3) the friend suffered $100,000 in damages.

As a result, the court should enter a judgment in favor of the friend for what amount?

(A) $100,000.

(B) $55,000.

(C) $45,000.

(D) Nothing, because the fan was more negligent than the driver.

Quiz 2

Question 1

A man was driving to work in the northbound lane of a highway at the same time that a mother was driving her son to school in the southbound lane of the same highway. The son began to cry, which diverted the mother's attention from the road, causing her to drift slightly over the center line of the highway. The man saw the mother's vehicle cross the line and enter his lane. The man did not move over, nor did he decrease his speed. As the mother drew closer, the man could have moved over to avoid the accident, but did not, and the mother's car hit the man's car. The mother was injured and her car suffered damage. The applicable jurisdiction has adopted a rule of contributory negligence. The mother subsequently brought suit against the man for her injuries.

What is the most appropriate result at trial?

(A) The mother cannot recover damages, because she was negligent.

(B) The mother cannot recover damages, because she was negligent per se.

(C) The mother can recover damages, because the man could have slowed down or moved over.

(D) The mother can recover damages, because she acted reasonably given the circumstances.

Question 2

A traffic accident occurred at a road intersection. A motorcycle, a car, and a truck were involved. The motorcyclist was injured and brought suit against the driver of the car and the driver of the truck. The jury returned a verdict finding that the motorcyclist's injuries were caused by negligence on the part of all three of the parties. The jury assigned 55% of the fault for the motorcyclist's injuries to the motorcyclist, 25% to the driver of the car, and 20% to the driver of the truck. The jury found that the amount of the motorcyclist's injuries was $100,000. The motorcyclist enforced the judgment against the driver of the car and collects $45,000 from him. The driver of the car then brought an action against the driver of the truck for contribution.

What should the driver of the car recover?

(A) Nothing, because he was more at fault than the driver of the truck was.

(B) $27,000.

(C) $20,000.

(D) $15,000.

Question 3

A homeowner purchased a new vacuum cleaner. A few days later, the homeowner received a severe electric shock while using the vacuum cleaner. The homeowner realized that there was a short in the wiring of the vacuum cleaner. The homeowner called the store that sold the vacuum cleaner and arranged to return it for a refund. The homeowner was busy, however, and would not have time to make a trip to the store for several days, so he put the vacuum cleaner in a corner in his living room to store it until he had a chance to take it to the store.

The next day, the homeowner had an old friend from out of town arrive for a three-day visit. The homeowner had a spare room and loved to have overnight guests, so he had invited this old friend to come for a visit and was excited to see her. Shortly after the guest's arrival, however, the homeowner had to go to work for a few hours, so he told his friend to make herself comfortable in the house while he went to his office. While the homeowner was away from the house, his friend got hungry and made herself a snack. After finishing the snack, she realized that she had dropped a lot of crumbs on the carpet. Wanting to be a polite guest, she decided to clean up the mess herself before the homeowner returned. She saw the vacuum cleaner in the corner, plugged it in at an electric outlet, and started to vacuum up the crumbs, when she received a very strong electric shock as a result of the vacuum cleaner's faulty wiring.

If the guest asserts a claim against the homeowner, what is the most likely outcome?

(A) The guest will recover, because the homeowner knew about the hazardous condition of the vacuum cleaner and yet failed to warn the guest.

(B) The guest will recover, because the homeowner had a duty to make a reasonable inspection of the home to discover any unknown dangers.

(C) The guest will not recover, because the homeowner did not create the risk of harm.

(D) The guest will not recover, under the family purpose doctrine.

Question 4

A city was experiencing a severe water shortage. To mitigate the problem, the city enacted an ordinance limiting total water use and prohibiting the use of water by private citizens for any purpose other than that of personal hygiene, cooking, and personal consumption. Use of water for landscaping, gardening, washing cars, and the like was strictly prohibited and punishable by fines of up to $5,000.

A homeowner had a thriving vegetable garden which required daily watering. Because she limited her personal water use, she felt justified in limited use of sprinklers to water her garden. The sprinklers were timed to water the garden between 6:00 and 6:20 p.m. every night, before the homeowner got home from work. As her garden was in her backyard, the homeowner was relatively confident that her water use would go unnoticed by town officials, and it did. However, the sprinklers did not escape the attention of a boy and his friend, the seven- and eight-year-old boys who lived on either side of the homeowner. Noting that the homeowner's sprinklers went off like clockwork every night at 6:00 p.m., just when temperatures in the desert town were peaking, the boy and his friend made a habit of putting on their bathing suits and sneaking into the homeowner's backyard to run through the sprinklers, unbeknownst to their mothers and to the homeowner.

One evening, in his enthusiasm, one of the boys tripped over the sprinkler spigot and scratched his ankle. The wound went unnoticed by his mother until several days later, when she saw that her son was limping. She took him to the doctor only to learn that he had developed a staph infection and required immediate hospitalization. The boy was hospitalized for over a month before he recovered sufficiently to be released, but his infected leg remained weak and his medical bills were extensive. The boy's mother filed suit against the homeowner to recover her medical expenses and lost wages, citing the homeowner's violation of the ordinance. The court accepted the statute as written.

Which of the following statements is most accurate?

(A) The boy's mother will prevail, because the homeowner's violation of the ordinance constituted negligence per se.

(B) The boy's mother will prevail, because the attractive nuisance doctrine applies.

(C) The boy's mother will not prevail, because she was negligent in failing to control her child.

(D) The boy's mother will not prevail, because the homeowner did not breach a duty of care or commit negligence per se.

Question 5

Three friends were driving home together from a local tavern. The driver had not consumed any alcoholic beverages at the tavern. On their way home, the three friends observed a man wandering haphazardly across the busy highway. One friend remarked, "I hope that guy makes it home. If he's not careful, he could get killed." The driver said, "That's his problem. I have to get home. I can't be bothered to stop and help him." After being dropped off at his home, the friend felt pangs of guilt and decided to go back and help the man that he'd seen. The friend asked his brother, who had not been drinking, to drive back to find and help the man. When the brothers returned to the area where the man had been, they found him lying on the shoulder of the highway, obviously injured. They helped the man into their car and the brother drove the man to the hospital. When they arrived at the hospital, the man was admitted with a broken leg. The leg had been broken when the man was wandering on the highway and was struck by a vehicle which had left the scene. The broken leg was the man's only injury.

If the man sues the driver of the car the friend had been in on the way home from the tavern for damages for his injuries, will he prevail?

(A) No, because the driver was under no duty to help the man.

(B) No, because the man was involved in an abnormally dangerous activity.

(C) Yes, because a reasonable person would have helped the man.

(D) Yes, because the driver breached his duty to the man.

Question 6

While walking down an escalator in a department store, a man was hit from behind by an employee who was taking some boxes to the trash compactor. The man fell and suffered injuries as a result. While in the hospital, the doctor indicated that the accident itself should only have caused minor injuries. The doctor then determined the man's bones had never healed properly after falling out of a tree as a child and breaking his pelvis and both of his legs. As a result, the injuries the man now suffered were more severe. At trial, the jury made the following findings: (1) the man was 10% at fault; (2) the employee was gainfully employed by the department store at the time of the injury; and (3) the man's childhood injuries were self-inflicted.

To what damages will the man be entitled?

(A) He will be entitled to only those damages that can be attributed to the employee's accident, minus his own percentage of negligence.

(B) He will be entitled to all damages sustained as a result of the accident minus his own percentage of negligence, because the department store is liable for the full consequences of the injuries sustained by the man.

(C) He will be entitled to damages that a normal person would have sustained in a similar accident.

(D) He will recover nothing, because his childhood injuries were self-inflicted.

Question 7

A plaintiff and defendant were playing football. The plaintiff knew that the defendant had a reputation for being an extremely competitive player. During the game, the plaintiff's eye was severely injured when the defendant's finger came into contact with it while trying to catch a pass. The plaintiff sought medical attention, and the doctor diagnosed him with a scratched cornea. The plaintiff subsequently brought a negligence action against the defendant.

Will the plaintiff prevail?

(A) No, because the plaintiff impliedly consented to this type of injury.

(B) No, because the plaintiff voluntarily played the game.

(C) Yes, because the defendant's actions fell below the standard of care.

(D) Yes, because this type of physical injury is beyond the scope of consent.

Question 8

A man invited several friends to come over to his house to watch a movie on television. While they were watching the movie, freezing rain fell outside, coating everything with a thin layer of very slippery ice. When the movie ended, one of the man's guests slipped on the ice as soon as he took a step out of the door and onto the front stoop of the man's house.

Which of the following would best describe the duty of care owed by the man to his guest?

(A) No duty of care.

(B) A duty to inspect the premises for unknown dangers and disclose their existence to others.

(C) A duty to warn of any known dangerous condition on the premises.

(D) An absolute duty of care.

Question 9

Following a three-car accident, a woman sued a man for negligence, claiming that she suffered damages of $100,000. The driver of the third car was uninsured and the woman chose not to join him as a party. At trial, the jury found that the woman was 30% at fault, the man was 40% at fault, and the third driver was 30% at fault. The jury agreed that the woman's damages were worth $100,000.

How much will the woman be able to recover from the man?

(A) $100,000, because pure comparative negligence allows for recovery regardless of the plaintiff's negligence, and the man can sue the third driver.

(B) $70,000, because a negligent plaintiff's recovery should be reduced by her percentage of fault.

(C) $40,000, because that is the man's percentage of fault.

(D) Nothing, because her negligence was equal to the third driver's negligence, precluding her recovery.

Question 10

A construction company was replacing large portions of a sidewalk in the downtown section of a city. The construction crew started tearing out the old sidewalk, and left for the day without putting up warning signs or barriers around the work area. A few hours later, a jogger came around the corner and fell in a hole at the spot where the construction crew had torn up the sidewalk.

As the jogger was attempting to get out of the hole, she began screaming for help. Her screams attracted the attention of a passerby, who immediately hurried to assist the jogger. As the passerby was leaning over the edge of the work area, he too fell into the hole. Both the jogger and the passerby suffered serious bodily injuries before they were pulled out of the hole by police. This jurisdiction has not adopted a "Good Samaritan" statute.

In a negligence action by the passerby and the jogger to recover for their personal injuries, what is the most likely outcome?

(A) The jogger will prevail but not the passerby, because there was no "Good Samaritan" statute requiring him to come to the jogger's aid.

(B) The passerby will prevail because danger invites rescue, but the jogger will not recover because she created her own peril.

(C) Both will recover, because the jogger was injured by the negligence of the construction company and the passerby acted reasonably given the situation.

(D) Neither will recover, because the jogger was running at night and the passerby had no relationship to her.

Question 11

On New Year's Eve, a man negligently hit a woman with his car. The woman was rushed to the hospital and sent into surgery. The surgeon, who was summoned from a nearby party, operated on the woman while intoxicated. As a result, the surgeon failed to remove a drain tube, causing the woman harm and requiring a second operation to remove. The woman has now brought suit against the man for her injuries.

At trial, testimony showed that the woman suffered $100,000 in damages caused to her legs from the accident and $50,000 from complications surrounding the drain tube. At trial, an expert testified that the surgeon's efforts fell below the standard of care that should have been exercised in an operating room as a result of his intoxication. The jury also found that the woman was 25% responsible for the accident.

How much should the woman recover from the man?

(A) $75,000, or the amount of her injuries from the accident minus her own negligence.

(B) $100,000, or the full amount of her injuries from the accident.

(C) $125,000, or the woman's injuries from the accident as well as the doctor's negligence, minus her own negligence.

(D) $150,000, or the full amount of her injuries for both the accident and the doctor's negligence.

Question 12

A man on his bike was run off the road when the driver of a car, who was not paying attention to the road, drifted into the bicycle lane. The man ran into the guardrail, pinning his leg against his bike, but did not fall. After the incident, the man chose not to go to a doctor, as he was a little shaken and sore, but otherwise did not appear injured. The next week, as the man was delivering a package as part of his job, his legs suddenly gave way, causing him to tumble down several flights of stairs. He was then rushed to the hospital, where he was treated for two broken legs and a shattered hip.

If the man now sues the driver of the car, which of the following statements is the most accurate?

(A) The driver is responsible for all injuries sustained by the man, because the driver must take the victim as he finds him.

(B) The driver is responsible for all injuries sustained by the man, because the man's conduct after the accident was reasonable.

(C) The driver is not responsible for all injuries sustained by the man, because the man failed to go to the doctor, who may have warned him to stay off of his feet.

(D) The driver is not responsible for all injuries sustained by the man, under the doctrine of avoidable consequences.

Question 13

A woman brought a negligence claim against her doctor for failing to warn her of the risks associated with an elective surgery. The surgery was a success, but there was a 50% chance that the woman would be unable to have children, something she had mentioned wanting to the doctor on several occasions.

During discovery, several depositions were scheduled, including the plaintiff's, which was scheduled first. At her deposition, the woman recounted conversations she had with the doctor, her memories of the procedure, and admitted that she was currently pregnant. Immediately following the deposition, and before the remaining depositions, the doctor moved for summary judgment on the negligence claim.

How should the court rule on the doctor's motion?

(A) Motion denied, because the doctor's failure to warn caused the woman to consent to the surgery.

(B) Motion denied, because the doctor breached his duty to the woman by failing to warn her of a material issue.

(C) Motion granted, because the doctor's failure to warn did not result in sufficient injury to the woman.

(D) Motion granted, because the surgery was elective.

Question 14

A pedestrian, who was walking along Chestnut Street at 10:20 p.m. on the night of December 3, urgently needed to find a restroom. Just ahead, the pedestrian noticed a private dinner club. As the pedestrian approached the club, he noticed a sign over the front door that read: "ADMITTANCE TO MEMBERS ONLY." Although the pedestrian was not a member of the exclusive club, he entered the dimly lit club, found a door marked "Gentlemen," and entered the restroom.

Which of the following would best describe the pedestrian's legal status when he was in the restroom?

(A) Trespasser.

(B) Guest.

(C) Licensee.

(D) Invitee.

Question 15

A man purchased two tickets for a basketball game. The man then contacted his best friend, who agreed to accompany the man to the game. As they were driving to the game together, the man sped up to cross an intersection while the traffic signal was changing from yellow to red. As he reached the intersection, the man was traveling at twice the posted speed limit. Simultaneously, a car driven by a woman entered the intersection despite having a red light and collided with the man's car. The friend, who was not wearing a seatbelt at the time, suffered a broken arm and collarbone in the collision.

This jurisdiction has adopted a modified comparative negligence statute. This jurisdiction has also adopted a statute requiring all occupants of motor vehicles to wear a safety belt, harness, or strap. The friend subsequently brought suit against the woman of the car that ran the red light to recover damages for his injury.

What is the most appropriate result?

(A) The friend should recover full compensation, because he was not negligent.

(B) The friend should recover full compensation, because he was not in control of either vehicle that caused the accident.

(C) The friend's recovery should be reduced, because he was negligent per se.

(D) The friend should recover nothing, because he was negligent per se.

Question 16

A woman owned a used bookstore. One day, a customer came into the store drinking a large soda. He carelessly dropped it on the floor, and the bookstore owner failed to clean it up. About four hours later, a second customer came into the bookstore, hoping to find a first edition of a book. The second customer, trying to break in a new pair of five-inch heels that were a size too small, could barely walk. As she was teetering up and down the aisles browsing the selection, she slipped on the wet floor and broke her ankle. The second customer sued the bookstore owner, and after the trial, the jury found the second customer 20% at fault, the bookstore owner 40% at fault, and the first customer 40% at fault. This jurisdiction has a modified comparative negligence statute.

Which of the following is most accurate?

(A) The second customer can recover, because she was not more negligent than the owner or the first customer.

(B) The second customer can recover, because she was not more negligent than the owner and the first customer.

(C) The second customer can recover as long as she did not have the last clear chance to avoid the injury.

(D) The second customer cannot recover, because she has contributed to her own negligence.

Question 17

A woman was walking her dog one day around her neighborhood. As she passed a neighbor's house, the neighbor's dog charged out from the side of the property and attacked the woman. A passerby helped get the neighbor's dog off the woman, though she was seriously injured from the attack. The woman later brought a claim against the neighbor for her medical bills. At trial, the neighbor stated that he was diligent in keeping his dog in the backyard, and therefore, someone must have let it out, which was not his fault. The neighbor then filed a motion for judgment as a matter of law.

How should the court rule on the neighbor's motion?

(A) Denied, because the dog was within the control of the neighbor at the time of the injury.

(B) Denied, because the keeper of an animal is strictly liable for injuries that it causes.

(C) Granted, because the neighbor testified that he was diligent in keeping his dog in the backyard.

(D) Granted, because the woman cannot prove that someone else did not let the neighbor's dog out of the backyard.

Question 18

A teenage boy and his friend were playing paintball at the friend's father's farm. The paintballs were designed to break on impact, spraying paint but not physically injuring anyone. The boy pointed his paintball gun at the friend and fired a paintball at him. The paintball missed the friend and instead hit a horse that was grazing nearby. The horse, startled and in pain, started bucking and kicked up a rock that hit the friend in the head, causing him to lose vision in his right eye.

In a negligence action against the boy, will the friend recover?

(A) No, because shooting the gun was not the proximate cause of the friend's injury.

(B) No, because shooting the gun was not the actual cause of the friend's injury.

(C) Yes, because paintball is an adult activity.

(D) Yes, because the boy shot the gun at his friend, which is sufficient for recovery under transferred intent.

Question 19

While on vacation, two friends went scuba diving in the ocean. Each of them was equipped with a spear gun, which they planned to use to kill tuna. As they were swimming, both men saw what appeared to be a large fin entangled in a nearby coral reef. Simultaneously, they shot their spear guns at the projecting wing-like figure. Unbeknownst to either of the friends, it was not a fish but rather another scuba diver. The victim was struck and slightly wounded by one of the spears. The victim asserts a claim for damages against the two friends.

At trial, how should the judge instruct the jury to rule?

(A) In favor of both defendants, if no evidence is presented showing who actually shot the spear that injured the victim.

(B) Against both defendants jointly, unless one of them proves that he did not shoot the spear that struck the victim.

(C) Against each defendant for one-half of the amount of damages, because they both acted independently and not jointly.

(D) Against each defendant for one-half of the amount of damages, because they both shot their spear guns simultaneously.

Question 20

A man negligently set fire to apartment building. The fire caused a panic and residents rushed to try to escape the burning building. In the rush to get out, a woman was knocked to the ground and trampled by the other residents. The woman later sued the man for her injuries.

Which of the following statements is most accurate?

(A) The woman will recover, because the man is responsible for all injuries sustained by the woman.

(B) The woman will recover, because the man is responsible for the foreseeable injuries sustained by the woman.

(C) The woman will not recover, because her injuries were sustained in an unforeseeable manner.

(D) The woman will not recover, because her injuries were sustained by an unforeseeable force.

Essays

Essay Question 1

IE13JUL007

ISSUE SPOTTING EXERCISE

Consider the fact pattern below and then answer the questions that follow:

A woman owned a used bookstore. She was passionate about literature, and spent most of her days behind the counter reading, barely glancing up at customers as they came and went. She had a high employee turnover rate, as her employees usually got frustrated with her lack of management. For this reason, the general upkeep of the shop has suffered substantially. In fact, several cracks have developed in the roof of the shop, and over the past few weeks, rain has leaked in and formed puddles on the floor. The bookstore owner noticed this, but failed to pause her reading in order to clean them.

One rainy day, a customer came into the bookstore hoping to find a first-edition copy of a particular book. The customer, trying to break in a pair of recently purchased five-inch heels that were actually a size too small for her, could barely walk. As she was teetering up and down the aisles browsing the selection, she failed to notice a puddle which had formed as the result of one of the first cracks to appear in the roof. The customer slipped on the wet floor, and broke her ankle as a result.

The customer has now filed a negligence lawsuit against the bookstore owner. Could a jury properly find the bookstore owner liable to the customer for her injuries? Explain.

The call of this question can be broken out into several issues. What issues are being tested in this essay?

Issue 1:

Identify four key facts from the prompt that will help you resolve this issue:

1.

2.

3.

4.

Issue 2:

Identify two key facts from the prompt that will help you resolve this issue:

1.

2.

Issue 3:

Identify two key facts from the prompt that will help you resolve this issue:

1.

2.

Essay Question 1

IE13JUL007

RULE RECOLLECTION EXERCISE

A good rule statement will demonstrate your understanding of the law and provide the foundation for your analysis. This exercise is intended to help you practice: (1) recalling the relevant rules of law; (2) organizing rules of law; and (3) explaining legal concepts completely and concisely.

- PUT AWAY YOUR NOTES for this exercise and practice actively trying to recall the relevant rules.
- In FIFTEEN minutes, write out rule statements for the following issues.
- WRITE THESE RULES OUT IN FULL; do not merely jot down concepts, topics, or fragments.

NEGLIGENCE

***Prima Facie* Case**

Standard of Care

Duty Owed to Business Invitee

DEFENSES

Assumption of Risk

Comparative Negligence

Essay Question 1

IE13JUL007

ANALYSIS EXERCISE

Connect law (rules) to fact, and draft your analysis paragraph for each issue below.

NEGLIGENCE

***Prima Facie* Case**

Standard of Care—Duty Owed to Business Invitee

DEFENSES

Assumption of Risk

Comparative Negligence

Essay Question 2

IE13JUL008

Over time, the post supporting one of the many small lighting fixtures in the parking lot of a hardware store became visibly weakened by age and rust. Several hardware store employees had noticed the problem over the past few months, but none of them reported it, and the manager of the store failed to notice the post's condition.

One day, while shopping for some new tools, a handyman, preoccupied with his rowdy children in the back seat, was not looking where he was going as he was backing his car into a parking space. As a result, he hit the weakened post, which gave way slightly. However, the handyman found that he could push the post back so that it looked as it did before, even though he knew that it might give way at any minute.

One week later, the post fell and struck a shopper's car as she was entering the hardware store's parking lot. It was determined that the post fell due to the combination of its aged, rusty condition and the force of the impact from the handyman's car. Either factor alone would not have been sufficient to cause the post to topple.

The shopper has filed an action for negligence against both the hardware store and the handyman for her damages.

1. *Could a jury properly find the hardware store liable to the shopper for her injuries? Explain.*

2. *Could a jury properly find the handyman liable to the shopper for her injuries? Explain.*

KAPLAN BAR REVIEW

Performance Test

KAPLAN BAR REVIEW

Multistate Performance Test Workshop

I. INTRODUCTION TO THE MPT

Background on the MPT

- Developed by the National Conference of Bar Examiners (NCBE).
- Participating jurisdictions administer the MPT on the Tuesday before the last Wednesday in February and July.
- The NCBE offers two different 90-minute test items per administration; jurisdictions can administer one or both.
- Contact your jurisdiction's board of bar examiners for additional info on how it administers the MPT.

Competencies Tested on the MPT

- The MPT is designed to test an applicant's ability to perform the basic lawyering skills needed to complete common lawyering tasks.
- Six basic lawyering skills are assessed on the MPT:
    - Legal Analysis: The applicant must demonstrate the ability to identify legal issues in the case and apply the legal resources provided to the given assignment, including:
        - Identifying legal issues raised in the **File** and Library;
        - Reading and analyzing the law contained in the source materials provided in the Library;
        - Formulating and/or evaluating legal theories; and
        - Developing and/or criticizing legal arguments.
    - Fact Analysis: The applicant must demonstrate the ability to identify and analyze facts relevant to the given assignment, including:
        - Identifying and evaluating relevant facts among the various source documents contained in the File;
        - Comparing and distinguishing facts in the File from those contained in the legal sources in the Library;
        - Determining the need for further fact development and/or planning such fact development; and
        - Organizing and presenting facts in concise written form.
    - Problem Solving: The applicant must demonstrate the ability to solve problems raised in the assignment, including:
        - Identifying key issues requiring resolution;
        - Formulating and evaluating creative solutions to key issues; and

        - Implementing solutions to key issues through application of relevant facts and law and/or development of a plan of action.
    - Ethical Awareness: The applicant must demonstrate the ability to identify and address ethical issues raised in the case, including:
        - Understanding ethical standards;
        - Recognizing ethical issues raised in the case; and
        - Addressing ethical issues appropriately.
    - Written Communication: The applicant must demonstrate the ability to write effectively, including:
        - Writing the assignment in a clear, concise fashion; and
        - Writing with the appropriate audience in mind.
    - Time Management: The applicant must demonstrate the ability to perform a written legal task under time constraints, including:
        - Planning and organizing the assignment in an efficient manner; and
        - Completing the assignment in the time allotted.

Contents of the MPT

- Applicants must complete a written assignment under timed conditions using materials provided with the test.
    - Applicants have 90 minutes to read the materials provided and draft the assignment.
    - All relevant facts and law are included in the materials.
- Possible assignments include:
    - Memo to supervising attorney;
    - Letter to client;
    - Persuasive memo, brief, or letter;
    - Statement of facts;
    - Contract provision;
    - Will;
    - Counseling plan;
    - Proposal for settlement agreement;
    - Discovery plan;
    - Witness examination plan; or
    - Closing argument.

- The MPT materials consist of three main parts:
  - A Memorandum from the supervising attorney that specifies what the assignment entails;
  - A File that contains various source documents detailing facts of the case; the Memorandum is the first document in the File; and
  - A Library that contains various sources of law relevant to the assignment.
- No outside knowledge of the law is needed to complete the assignment.
- Real-world cases and statutes are sometimes used, but may also be modified from the original, requiring a close reading.
- Standard instructions are included with each MPT, as follows on the next page.

INSTRUCTIONS

1. You will have 90 minutes to complete this session of the examination. This performance test is designed to evaluate your ability to handle a select number of legal authorities in the context of a factual problem involving a client.

2. The problem is set in the fictitious state of Franklin, in the fictitious Fifteenth Circuit of the United States. In Franklin, the trial court of general jurisdiction is the District Court, the intermediate appellate court is the Court of Appeal, and the highest court is the Supreme Court.

3. You will have two kinds of materials with which to work: a File and a Library. The first document in the File is a memorandum containing the instructions for the task you are to complete. The other documents in the File contain factual information about your case and may also include some facts that are not relevant.

4. The Library contains the legal authorities needed to complete the task, and may also include some authorities that are not relevant. Any cases may be real, modified, or written solely for the purpose of this examination. If the cases appear familiar to you, do not assume that they are precisely the same as you have read before. Read them thoroughly, as if all were new to you. You should assume that the cases were decided in the jurisdictions and on the dates shown. In citing cases from the Library, you may use abbreviations and omit page references.

5. Your response must be written in the answer book provided. In answering this performance test, you should concentrate on the materials provided. What you have learned in law school and elsewhere provides the general background for analyzing the problem; the File and Library provide the specific materials with which you must work.

6. Although there are no restrictions on how you apportion your time, you should be sure to allocate ample time (about 45 minutes) to reading and digesting the materials and to organizing your answer before you begin writing it. You may make notes anywhere in the test materials; blank pages are provided at the end of the booklet. You may not tear pages from the question booklet.

7. This performance test will be graded on your responsiveness to instructions regarding the task you are to complete, which are given to you in the first memorandum in the File, and on the content, thoroughness, and organization of your response.

How the MPT Is Scored

- Instructions provided with the MPT say that the test is scored based on your responsiveness to the instructions regarding the assigned task, and on the content, thoroughness, and organization of your response.
- The NCBE provides jurisdictions with a document outlining the points it intended to raise in each test item.
- Jurisdictions are free to score the MPT portion of their bar exam as they see fit. Check with your jurisdiction's board of bar examiners for further information.

II. KAPLAN BAR REVIEW METHOD FOR THE MPT

A Methodological Approach

- Creating a quality piece of written work in the limited amount of time the MPT allows means perfecting a plan before Test Day.
- Mastering a method of approach through practice will ensure that you do not waste any time on Test Day debating what to do next as you draft your response.
- The Kaplan Bar Review method will provide a framework for each successive step on each and every MPT.

Overview of the Kaplan Bar Review 5-Step Method

Step 1. Read the supervising attorney's memo outlining the assignment, and then begin outlining the assignment.

Step 2. Read the **File** documents and update the outline.

Step 3. Read the **Library** documents and update the outline.

Step 4. Complete the outline.

Step 5. Write the requested assignment.

III. USING APPROPRIATE STYLE

Persuasive versus Objective Assignments

Whereas law school trains students to make effective legal arguments, the practice of law often requires practitioners to objectively determine which arguments are winners and which are losers. Similarly, the MPT will sometimes ask you to craft an objective, rather than persuasive, assignment. It is critical to your success on the MPT, and in the practice of law, that you write with this distinction in mind.

Persuasive Assignments:

- Require you to make your best arguments for or against a certain outcome.
  - Use the facts and law available to you to make your best case.
  - Do not ignore law harmful to your position; rather, cite contrary authority and explain or distinguish it.
  - Summarize your arguments in your headings, rather than making bare legal assertions:
    - IMPROPER: "Defendant Did Not Have the Necessary Mens Rea for Larceny."
    - PROPER: "Defendant Did Not Have the Necessary Mens Rea for Larceny Because He Mistook the Hat for His Own."
- Are almost always directed to a particular tribunal in the form of a brief, or less often, to opposing counsel in the form of a letter.

Objective Assignments:

- Require you to accurately and thoroughly analyze one or more legal issues.
  - Address all relevant facts and law.
  - Provide a fair assessment of the outcome of each issue.
    - Although you are not making arguments for or against an outcome, as with a persuasive assignment, you should nonetheless state the likely outcome of each issue.
    - Avoid the temptation to slant arguments in favor of your client; if the facts do not support your client's position on a given issue, say so and explain why.
- Are almost always directed to the supervising attorney in the form of a memo, or less often, to the client in the form of a letter.

Lay versus Legally Trained Audience

Most MPT assignments are directed to attorneys or to a tribunal, meaning that you can safely use legal terminology and sophisticated language in your written draft. However, occasionally you will be asked to draft an assignment to a lay audience, typically the client. In these cases, you should be careful to avoid or explain all legal terminology, and use a written style appropriate to the audience's sophistication.

In re Timothy Popper

INSTRUCTIONS

1. You will have 90 minutes to complete this session of the examination. This performance test is designed to evaluate your ability to handle a number of legal authorities in the context of a factual problem involving a client.

2. The problem is set in the fictitious state of Jefferson, in the fictitious Sixteenth Circuit of the United States. In Jefferson, the trial court of general jurisdiction is the District Court, the intermediate appellate court is the Supreme Court, and the highest court is the Court of Appeals.

3. You will have two kinds of materials with which to work: a File and a Library. The first document in the File is a memorandum containing the instructions for the task you are to complete. The other documents in the File contain factual information about your case. The documents may contain information that is not relevant.

4. The Library contains the legal authorities needed to complete the task. Any cases may be real, modified, or written solely for the purpose of this examination. If the cases appear familiar to you, do not assume that they are precisely the same as you have read before. Read them thoroughly, as if they all were new to you. You should assume that the cases were decided in the jurisdictions and on the dates shown. In citing cases from the Library, you may use abbreviations and omit page references. The cases may contain information that is not relevant.

5. Your response must be written in the answer book provided. In answering this performance test, you should concentrate on the materials provided. What you have learned in law school and elsewhere provides the general background for analyzing the problem; the File and Library provide the specific materials with which you must work.

6. Although there are no restrictions on how you apportion your time, you should be sure to allocate ample time (about 45 minutes) to reading and digesting the materials and to organizing your answer before you begin writing it. You may make notes anywhere in the test materials. You may not tear pages from the question booklet.

7. This performance test will be graded on your responsiveness to the instructions regarding the task you are to complete, which is given to you in the first memorandum in the File, and on the content, thoroughness, and organization of your response.

IN RE TIMOTHY POPPER

FILE

LIBRARY

ANNOTATED FILE

In re Timothy Popper

AN ANNOTATED PERFORMANCE TEST QUESTION: In re Timothy Popper

Bourne & Diaz, LLP
Attorneys at Law
519 Hill Street
Hope City, Jefferson 45111

August 2, 2014

MEMORANDUM[1]

TO: New Associate[2]
FROM: Doug Bourne[3]
RE: In re Timothy Popper (nuisance/defamation)[4]

We represent Timothy Popper,[5] who runs a non-profit animal shelter out of his home in Hope Beach, adjacent to the beach itself. Most of the animals he takes care of are dogs and cats with special health needs, and the business is funded by adoption fees and donations he receives. Six months ago, a for-profit company called XtremeTrain moved into the lot next door and uses both the lot and the public beach for its activities, which primarily consist of conducting group physical fitness training. These activities produce a great deal of noise, which is detrimental to Mr. Popper's enjoyment of his property as well as his ability to conduct his business. Mr. Popper asked Harry Sands, the owner/operator of XtremeTrain to reduce the noise created the business, but to no avail. Mr. Popper then wrote a letter to an editor of the Hope Beach Times expressing his frustrations over the sound, and Mr. Sands responded by threatening to sue Mr. Popper for defamation.

Please draft a memorandum[6] analyzing whether Mr. Popper has any legal recourse regarding XtremeTrain's activities and whether he may liable for defamation. Please answer the following questions:

(i) Can Mr. Popper successfully assert a claim that XtremeTrain's activities constitute a public nuisance?[7]
(ii) Can Mr. Popper successfully assert a claim that XtremeTrain's activities constitute a private nuisance?[8]
(iii) Is Mr. Popper liable for defamation based on his letter to the editor?[9]

In the memorandum, you should incorporate the relevant facts, analyze the applicable legal authority, and explain how the facts and law affect our client's obligations. I expect an answer by the end of the day as I will be meeting with the client again in a few days.

Thanks,

Doug
SEE ENCLOSURES

1 This document will be referred to as "A."

2 Pay close attention to the information provided in this assignment memorandum. You are being asked by your supervising attorney to prepare a memorandum for the firm's client, Timothy Popper.

3 Make sure to use Doug's name in your answer.

4 Note the subject of this assignment.

5 Note the name of the client and be mindful to include his name in your answer.

6 Be sure to draft your response in the form of a memo. Include a section with information on who the memo is being addressed to, who it is from, and what it is regarding.

7 The first issue you will want to discuss in your outline is whether Mr. Popper can successfully assert a claim that XtremeTrain's activities constitute a public nuisance. Use the materials in the File and Library to analyze and thoroughly discuss this point. When a specific piece of information is relevant to your analysis of these issues, we will note it as ISSUE 1.

8 The second issue is whether Mr. Popper can successfully assert a claim for private nuisance. We will note the important information relating to this point as ISSUE 2. Note that there will be numerous facts that relate to both ISSUE 1 and ISSUE 2.

9 The third issue focuses on whether Mr. Popper is potentially liable for defamation based on the letter to the editor he wrote. We will note the important information relating to this point as ISSUE 3.

TRANSCRIPT OF DOUG BOURNE'S CONVERSATION WITH TIMOTHY POPPER [10]

August 1, 2014

BOURNE: Good morning, Mr. Popper. My assistant informed me that you have had some issues with a neighbor. Why don't you explain the problem from the beginning?

POPPER: Okay. I have run a non-profit animal shelter out of my home just off of Hope Beach for ten years. [11] I take in mostly dogs and cats with health problems and do my best to take care of them and find them loving homes. I generally have about twenty to thirty dogs and cats living on my property. People adopt the animals, for which they pay an adoption fee, but 50% of my operating budget is from donations.

BOURNE: What happens if an animal does not get adopted?

POPPER: Then they usually stay with me for the rest of their natural life or until they are too sick to live a happy life, or I find a home to donate the animal to, which means I get no adoption fee.

BOURNE: And so what is the issue with your neighbor?

POPPER: Right. Six months ago, a man named Harry Sands moved into the lot next door to mine and opened an XtremeTrain franchise. [12] Are you familiar with XtremeTrain?

BOURNE: I've heard people mention it, but why don't you tell me?

POPPER: Essentially, XtremeTrain is a gym where members join for a subscription fee, but instead of running on a treadmill, they all work out in large groups in classes that take place all day long. Which, okay, fine, but they make so much noise! They have this attitude that they have to act like they are in a military boot camp with yelling and grunting, but a boot camp that plays extremely loud electronic music at all hours of the day. [13]

BOURNE: Can you be more specific about the noise? What exactly do they do?

POPPER: Starting at six in the morning, Harry brings the members out on the beach adjacent to my lot and they run and do exercises and he yells at them through a bullhorn at full blast [14] all these things like, "Let's get

10 This document will be referred to as "B."

11 Note that the client runs a business out of his home, and has done so for 10 years.

12 Note that the other party also runs a business, and has done so for only six months. This information will be among the factors considered by a court in determining whether his activities constitute a public and/or private nuisance (ISSUES 1 and 2).

13 The client's primary contention with XtremeTrain is that its activities make too much noise, thus any information relating to sound and/or noise will likely be relevant to the court's determination of whether its activities constitute a public and/or private nuisance (ISSUES 1 and 2).

14 Note the time of day, the fact that XtremeTrain is using the beach for its activities, and that it incorporates a bullhorn. This will all be relevant in determining whether XtremeTrain's activities are violative of any applicable statutes (ISSUES 1 and 2).

extreme!" or "I dream of extreme!" or just simply "Extreme, extreme, extreme, extreme!" over and over again. Then he has all these sound effects on the bullhorn that he plays, like the sounds of bombs dropping and explosions, car crashes, gunfire, and one where it's just the sound of babies crying. I think he uses that whenever the members aren't working out as "extreme" as he'd like them to be. On top of that, I hear the members grunting and yelling and generally freaking out all day long. It's hard to tell whether they are happy or upset with how they're doing.

BOURNE: And this is all on the public beach?

POPPER: Both on the beach and on the lot where he runs the actual gym. He keeps the doors open all the time so that people can see and hear the people working out inside. And then when they are at the actual gym, I have to hear their loud, bass-thumping music all day long. For some reason, it's important for them to listen to really annoying music at very high volumes. All day long. (15)

BOURNE: Is there anything else that they do that affects you?

POPPER: Well, the members constantly take pictures of themselves with their phones, usually shirtless and flexing their muscles and making hand signs, and I have to watch that go on all day long. But, no, that's it.

BOURNE: How has this affected you and your animal shelter?

POPPER: It's made the animals very frightened and depressed for one thing. Most of the animals stayed in the outdoor kennels on my lot, but they became jittery from all the noise from the music, the bullhorns, the yelling, and all that. They stopped eating and became scared around people that came to consider adopting them. I've had to move some of them inside, which cost money to outfit my house to accommodate them, but these animals belong outside, and we can still hear the noise inside as well. I've had to pay more for veterinarian and animal specialist bills to deal with this, and I've had fewer adoptions.

BOURNE: Fewer adoptions because of the gym?

15 Note that the noise occurs both on the beach and in the actual gym, where the doors are intentionally left open, and that the noise occurs at high volumes and continues throughout the day, without any apparent utility other than motivating and/or entertaining the members. This will all be relevant in the court's balancing of nuisance-related factors (ISSUES 1 and 2).

POPPER: Well, the animals act more skittish around people now, and the animals don't make as good an impression in my cramped house as they do outside, and then the people that visit us just don't seem as in the mood to adopt a sick pet when they have to listen to a guy yelling "extreme!" through a bullhorn over and over again, and hear loud club music and people yelling and grunting. My donations have also gone down, because the people that donate want to know these animals are in a safe, comfortable environment and so some of them have decided to stop donating because of this. Between my increased expenses and reduced adoption fees and donations, I'm already out $15,000. [16]

BOURNE: What action have you taken thus far to deal with this?

POPPER: I've asked Harry a dozen times to turn down the music, stop using the bullhorn, and generally make less noise [17], but every time he just says, "I'm running a business, man," and then he tells me the only reason people join is because they want an "extreme experience" which means there has to be lots of noise. [18] He also offers me a free week of classes every time, but I always decline.

BOURNE: Have you gone to the police?

POPPER: Yeah, but most of the Hope Beach police department belongs to the gym and they're not really interested in my complaints. I asked the other people who live in the area if they were annoyed and they said they were. None of them run businesses out of their homes like I do which are affected by the noise [19], but I drew up a petition with some general complaints about the gym, and got people to sign it. [20] I gave Harry the petition and delivered it to the city council, but still nothing has changed.

BOURNE: And what is this about a letter to the editor?

POPPER: Right, I finally got so frustrated one night that I wrote up an email expressing all frustrations and anger and sent it off my to friend Priya who runs the Hope Beach Times. I might have been a little meaner than I normally would be,

16 This information indicates that Mr. Popper has suffered specific economic damages in addition to the interference with his peace and enjoyment of the property. This will be relevant to the court in determining whether XtremeTrain's activities constitute a private and/or public nuisance (ISSUES 1 and 2).

17 Note that the other party has been made aware of the effect of his activities. This is relevant in determining whether his activities constitute a public nuisance (ISSUE 1).

18 This information describes the utility of XtremeTrain's conduct in producing the noise and will be a factor considered by the court in determining whether the conduct constitutes a private nuisance (ISSUE 2).

19 The fact that Mr. Popper has suffered a different type of harm than others affected by the noise is relevant to his ability to assert an individual claim for public nuisance (ISSUE 1).

20 The fact that others have signed a petition complaining about the noise is relevant to whether XtremeTrain's activities constitute a public nuisance (ISSUE 1).

but everything I wrote was how I felt. (21) The next thing I know, I get this letter from his lawyer threatening to sue me for defamation. That's when I decided I should come in and see you. I certainly don't have the money to pay damages in a defamation suit, and if I can't get this noise situation resolved I'm going to have close up the shelter and sell my home, although I'm not sure how much I can get for it now, seeing as how it's next to the gym.

BOURNE: I understand. Well, before you do that, let's see if we can get this sorted out.

21 This information regarding Mr. Popper's motivations and the contents of the letter are relevant in determining whether his statements are defamatory and/or whether he was privileged in making the statements (ISSUE 3).

PETITION TO RESTORE SERENITY TO HOPE BEACH [22]

We, the undersigned, petition Harry Sands,[23] owner/operator of XtremeTrain located at 3977 Hope Beach Road, Hope Beach, Jefferson 45113, and the Hope Beach City Council, to take immediate action to curtail the noise emanating from the activities of the XtremeTrain facility and its members at the aforementioned location and on the public beach owned and operated by Hope Beach.

We, the undersigned, are all neighbors living within the vicinity of 3977 Hope Beach Road, and have all suffered the following injuries[24] as a result of the activities of XtremeTrain and its members: 1) our sleep has been repeatedly interrupted by the loud music, bullhorn noise, and yelling from the facility; 2) our quiet enjoyment of our homes and outside lots have been greatly diminished by the same noise;[25] and 3) our view of the normally pristine Hope Beach has been sullied by the more or less constant presence of XtremeTrain members working out, socializing, and posing for pictures on the beach. We request that Sands, XtremeTrain, and its members cease with these activities and that all operations and activities be moved inside the structure at 3977 Hope Beach where they cannot be seen or heard by surrounding residents.[26]

Signed:

Penny Haskell	3961 Hope Beach Road, Hope Beach, Jefferson 45113
Ruthie Haskell	3961 Hope Beach Road, Hope Beach, Jefferson 45113
Ben O'Houlihan	3972 Hope Beach Road, Hope Beach, Jefferson 45113
Rutger Pickens	3993 Hope Beach Road, Hope Beach, Jefferson 45113
Sally Pickens	3993 Hope Beach Road, Hope Beach, Jefferson 45113
Amanda Freehold	4002 Hope Beach Road, Hope Beach, Jefferson 45113
Bo Whitefeld	3945 Hope Beach Road, Hope Beach, Jefferson 45113
Bo Whitefeld Jr.	3945 Hope Beach Road, Hope Beach, Jefferson 45113
Ashley Redwine	4010 Hope Beach Road, Hope Beach, Jefferson 45113
Timothy Popper	3981 Hope Beach Road, Hope Beach, Jefferson 45113

Date: June 21, 2014

22 This document will be referred to as "C."

23 Note that this is additional evidence that Mr. Sands has been made aware of the public's complaints regarding his activities. This is relevant to a public nuisance claim (ISSUE 1).

24 Note that the members of the public who signed this petition have not included within their claims that they have suffered economic losses in the same way Mr. Popper has. This will be important in determining whether Mr. Popper can successfully assert an individual claim for public nuisance (ISSUE 1).

25 This information is evidence that numerous members of the public have indicated that XtremeTrain's activities have interfered with their peace and comfort in their homes (ISSUE 1).

26 This suggests XtremeTrain could continue to conduct its activities in a manner that would not constitute a private and/or public nuisance, and that it is not necessary to create excess noise to do so (ISSUES 1 and 2).

LETTER TO THE EDITOR [27]

Hope Beach Times—July 21, 2014 [28]

I am writing today to inform the residents of Hope Beach of a threat to our way of life here in Hope Beach, a way of life that many of us came here for and have spent decades building and maintaining. [29] For those of you who don't know me, I operate an animal shelter. I take in the dogs and cats that no one else will take and work to find them homes. This job has never been easy, but it has been made all the more difficult over the past six months by the arrival of XtremeTrain next door to my animal shelter.

What is XtremeTrain, you ask? Allow me to explain. It advertises itself as a gym for people seeking intense workouts, but as far as I can tell, [30] it is a gym for lonely narcissists who have absolutely zero meaning in their lives, so they try to fill the yawning chasms of their existences with someone screaming at them [31] through a bullhorn to do a thousand "tummy stingers" (or whatever they call them, it's difficult to discern exact phraseology through the din) whilst being bombarded with a deafening soundtrack of music generally reserved for enjoyment by the disturbed and drug-addled. I guess XtremeTrain owner Harry Sands recognized that there was profit to be found in exploiting our society's twin afflictions of self-hatred and infatuation with body image, but I don't see why he has to feed his members' sadomasochistic tendencies in such a loud, intrusive, and public manner. [32] Whereas 6 AM used to be a time of utter peace and serenity on our beautiful Hope Beach, now 6 AM at Hope Beach means that ten men and women will be grunting up a storm as they attempt to roll enormous tractor tires down the beach, for the sole reason that, I don't know, Daddy didn't love them enough, [33] while Harry screams insults at them through a bullhorn—yes, a bullhorn. Is this the Hope Beach we want? I think not. [34]

The sonic assault generally goes on for the next 12 hours, all day, every day, whether on the beach or in his facility, which seems to lack closeable doors or the ability to play terrible music at anything less than full blast. [35] Harry's neighbors, including myself, have begged him to be more considerate, but his response has been to ridicule and ignore us. Worse, the animals I take care of at the shelter get the worst of it. They don't understand the psychic deficiencies that lead Harry and his clients to make horrendous noise all day long, but still they must suffer the noise pollution. The animals have developed mental and physical ailments as a result of the noise, and, at great expense, I've had to move many of them inside my home rather than outside in the formerly serene air. They are visited by fewer hopeful adopters and donors have reduced their donations to my formerly tranquil reserve. So far, neither the police nor city council have responded to my concerns, which is why I come to you, my fellow residents. If men like Harry Sands are not stopped from polluting the air with their cacophony of execrable music, bullhorns, and psychotic gutturals, then soon Hope Beach will be overrun with a whole army of loud, inconsiderate oafs, and it will not be the Hope Beach that you and I helped build. [36]

Sincerely,

Timothy Popper

27 This document will be referred to as "D."

28 The fact that this letter was published in a local newspaper satisfies the publication requirement for defamation, and it also indicates that Mr. Popper is aware of the public's reaction to his activities (ISSUES 1 and 3).

29 Here, Mr. Popper is explaining why he is writing the letter, which is that he is concerned about preserving the serene way of life in Hope Beach that he believes is threatened by Mr. Sands. This is important in asserting the qualified privilege to make statements in furtherance of a personal or public interest (ISSUE 3).

30 This language indicates that Mr. Popper is asserting an opinion, not a statement of fact, which is important because statements of opinion are not considered defamatory (ISSUE 3).

31 Note that while this statement does not necessarily attack Mr. Sands himself, it does arguably have the intended effect of lowering his and his business's esteem and discouraging people from associating or doing business with him (ISSUE 3).

32 Note again that while such a statement is potentially defamatory, Mr. Popper includes the qualifying phrase "I guess," implying it is an opinion (ISSUE 3).

33 This is another statement that is potentially defamatory, in that it ridicules clients of Mr. Sands, which in turn encourages people to avoid doing business with him, but the inclusion of the statement "I don't know," and the over-the-top statement "Daddy didn't love them enough," indicate that the statements are not meant to be taken as literal fact, such that they would be actionable as defamation (ISSUE 3).

34 Again, Mr. Popper frames his comments about Mr. Sands and his clients within the context of arguing for his personal and public interest regarding Hope Beach, which is relevant to asserting a qualified privilege (ISSUE 3).

35 This is additional evidence relevant to whether XtremeTrain's activities constitute a private and/or public nuisance (ISSUES 1 and 2).

36 While this contains an additional potentially defamatory, albeit indirect, reference to Mr. Sands as an "inconsiderate oaf," the passage places the criticism within the public interest of keeping Hope Beach serene, which, again, is important to asserting a qualified privilege (ISSUE 3).

CEASE AND DESIST LETTER [37]

To: Timothy Popper
3981 Hope Beach Road
Hope Beach, Jefferson 45113

From: Jayne Banks
Banks & Banks, LLP
130 Main Street
Hope City, Jefferson 45115

Dear Mr. Popper:

This law firm represents Harry Sands in his capacity as owner and operator of XtremeTrain, doing business at 3977 Hope Beach Road, Hope Beach, Jefferson 45113. We have reviewed your Letter to the Editor that appeared in the July 21, 2014 edition of Hope Beach Times. [38]

You are hereby directed to cease and desist all defamation of Mr. Sands' character and reputation.

Your letter was a gross mischaracterization of Mr. Sands' unique service to the Hope Beach community. He has suffered injury as a result of your defamatory statements regarding the nature of his business, his clients, and the services he provides his clients. [39] Furthermore, he has not been found to be in violation of any city laws or ordinances. [40] We demand that you retract your statements and issue an apology to Mr. Sands and his clients immediately. We will also be pursuing a defamation claim against you in order to compensate Mr. Sands for his injury.

I recommend that you consult with an attorney regarding this matter. Please contact me or have your attorney, should you retain one, contact me to discuss.

Respectfully,

Jayne Banks
Jayne Banks

37 This document will be referred to as "E."

38 This is definitive evidence that Mr. Sands is aware of the public's concern regarding his business activities, which is important to asserting a public nuisance claim (ISSUE 1).

39 For a claim of defamation, a plaintiff must show an injury. Note here that while the attorney indicates that Mr. Sands has suffered an injury, she does not specify what that injury is, although for the purposes of the memorandum, you should assume that there has been injury and instead focus on whether Mr. Popper is potentially liable (ISSUE 3).

40 Whether a party has violated applicable statutes, ordinances, etc. is relevant to a court's determination regarding public nuisance liability, but note that this is a different factual analysis than whether a party has been "found to be in violation" of such rules (ISSUE 1).

ANNOTATED LIBRARY

In re Timothy Popper

STATUTE A [41]

City of Hope Beach Revised Code [42]

Title IX—Prohibited Activities

Article 31—Amplified Sound and Noise

Section 31.12—Private Residences

The use of any amplified sound audible on the property of an adjacent or nearby private residence outside of the hours of 9 AM to 7 PM is prohibited, [43] unless specifically allowed by temporary permit. [44]

41 This document will be referred to as "F."

42 Note that this statute is binding because it is a Hope Beach-specific law. Be sure to reference this statute in your analysis (ISSUES 1 and 2).

43 This is important because we know that XtremeTrain's activities begin at 6 AM and that amplified noise produced by those activities can be heard on private properties beginning at that time (ISSUES 1 and 2).

44 Note that there was no mention of a permit anywhere in the File, and that the noise occurs daily, suggesting that a temporary permit would not be applicable (ISSUES 1 and 2).

STATUTE B [45]

City of Hope Beach Revised Code [46]

Title IX—Prohibited Activities

Article 31—Amplified Sound and Noise

Section 31.15—Beaches

The use of any amplified sound on the beach audible from a distance of 30 feet is prohibited. [47]

45 This document will be referred to as "G."

46 Note that this statute is binding because it is a Hope Beach-specific law. Be sure to reference this statute in your analysis (ISSUES 1 and 2).

47 This is important because we know that Mr. Sands uses a bullhorn, which qualifies as amplified sound, while on the beach, and that Mr. Popper can hear it in his home (ISSUES 1 and 2).

Najera v. Green Clean, LLC [48] [49]
Jefferson Supreme Court (2002)

Pedro Najera, a Springfield homeowner, here appeals a ruling finding that the activities of Green Clean, LLC, an industrial laundry facility located in the property adjacent to Najera's, did not constitute a private nuisance. [50] Najera is a sculptor whose works populate his backyard and sell for high prices in studios across the region. His sculptures generally consist of spider webs spun by spiders that he owns, and which are painted in various hues and suspended on sticks. Najera presented evidence that exhaust from Green Clean has affected both the spiders and the spider web sculptures on his property, causing the spiders to be unable to produce strong webs and the existing sculptures to become brittle. The trial court found that Green Clean's activities as a laundry facility serving much of Springfield outweighed the utility of Najera's activities, and that, furthermore, Najera's use of his land was unusually sensitive, precluding a private nuisance claim. [51]

In order for a plaintiff to prevail on a claim for private nuisance, he must show that the defendant is engaging in an activity that substantially and unreasonably interferes with the plaintiff's use and enjoyment of his land. [52] A plaintiff may demonstrate unreasonable interference by showing that the gravity of the plaintiff's harm outweighs the utility of the defendant's conduct. [53] Generally, in evaluating the reasonableness of the defendant's conduct we balance several factors: compliance with applicable zoning ordinances; priority of occupation; the frequency and extent of the interference, applied objectively to normal persons; and the utility and social value of the defendant's activity. [54] We have also held that a plaintiff cannot, by devoting his land to an unusually sensitive use, complain of a nuisance based on conduct that would otherwise be relatively harmless. [55]

In evaluating Najera's private nuisance claim, the trial court found that Najera's spider web sculpture creation and maintenance constituted an unusually sensitive use of his property and we agree. While the courts respect the creation of art as being important to our society, we are more likely to find an unusually sensitive use of a property when it is primarily personal and non-essential in nature, whether the use be economically related or otherwise, than when the use contributes in a more fundamental manner to the local or regional society. [56] Furthermore, we agree with the trial court's reasoning in finding that other factors weigh in favor of finding that Green Clean's activities are reasonable. Although Najera was the first party to occupy the area, Green Clean has complied with all zoning ordinances, is providing a necessary service to the Springfield area, and there is no evidence of other parties complaining about the exhaust created by Green Clean's activities. [57]

AFFIRMED.

48 This document will be referred to as "H."

49 Note that this case is binding authority because the case is in Jefferson Supreme Court (the highest court in the state).

50 This case focuses on private nuisance, and will be important for understanding the relevant law for that issue (ISSUE 2).

51 Note that there are similar facts as Mr. Popper's, as the plaintiff was operating a business out of his home that was affected by the activities of another nearby business (ISSUE 2).

52 This provides the general statement of law on what is required to prevail on a claim for private nuisance (ISSUE 2).

53 This provides a more specific statement of what Mr. Popper will need to show to prevail: that the harm done to him by XtremeTrain's conduct is greater than the utility of that conduct (ISSUE 2).

54 This provides further specificity on the four factors that you will want to analyze in the memo to determine whether XtremeTrain's conduct constitutes a public nuisance. Be sure to look for facts that correlate with these factors (ISSUE 2).

55 You will want to discuss whether running an animal shelter such as Mr. Popper's is an unusually sensitive use (ISSUE 2).

56 In our case, we will want to compare and/or distinguish Mr. Popper's use of his land as an animal shelter from Najera's use of his land for his sculptures (ISSUE 2).

57 You should conduct a similar analysis of the facts presented in Mr. Popper's file as they relate to the private nuisance factors (ISSUE 2).

58

Liu v. Artest

59

Jefferson Supreme Court (2013)

Jane Liu, a culture critic for *Jefferson Monthly*, appeals from the trial court ruling finding that she is liable for defamation in connection with an article she wrote regarding Val Artest, a clothing and apparel designer. In her article, Liu described Artest's designs, which are marketed towards teenagers and are notable for their provocative messages and styles, as "born out of Artest's own demented perversity" and "intended to make a quick buck off of the fashion industry's growing hatred for itself and all things modest. 60 Artest, who claims to have suffered a 20% drop in business following publication of the article, brought a defamation suit against Liu, and was awarded $100,000 in damages.

Broadly, a message is considered defamatory if it lowers a plaintiff in the esteem of the community or discourages third persons from associating with him, and is published to at least one other person who understood the message, and that message caused a substantial minority of reasonable third parties to avoid contact with the plaintiff or stop doing business with him. 61 Generally, only statements of facts are considered actionable as defamatory, although expressions of opinion that imply that the speaker knows certain facts to be true, or imply such facts exist, and which a reasonable person would interpret as one of fact, may be found to be defamatory. 62 There are several defenses to a claim of defamation, which include truth and a defendant's qualified privilege to act in his own legitimate interest or in the public interest. With regard to the latter, a defendant must show three factors: 1) that his statements were motivated by a legitimate self-interest or public interest, and not out of malice; 2) the statements at issue did not exceed the scope of that interest; and 3) he believed the truth of those statements. 63

Liu has argued that, as a mother of pre-teen children and fashion critic, her statements were motivated by both a private and public interest in helping to tide what she describes as a "regrettable but not irreversible trend in teen fashion away from the creative and towards the exploitative." We agree that, regardless of the merits of her perspective, this is certainly a legitimate private and public interest. 64 The trial court, however, found that Liu's statements, many of which ascribed exploitative and alarming psychosexual personality traits and motivations to Artest, exceeded the scope of that interest, because such "incendiary statements were not necessary in asserting Liu's stated interests of decrying the popularity and marketing of the fashion products themselves." The court also found that Liu lacked sufficient factual basis for the statements such that she could "believe the truth of the statements." Based on this the court held that Liu could not utilize the defense of qualified privilege and was therefore liable for defamation.

We disagree with the trial court's findings on several grounds. 65 For statements to be within the scope of a legitimate private or public interest, they need not reach the level of "necessary" for asserting that interest, but rather, only reasonably related to asserting that interest. 66 Liu's comments about Artest, while unproven and certainly potentially damaging to him, were reasonably related to her private and public interests, as they described potential motivations for the activity she was attempting to curtail. Also, there is no requirement that a defendant have a factual

58 This document will be referred to as "I."

59 Note that this case is binding authority because the case is in Jefferson Supreme Court (the highest court in the state).

60 Note that Liu uses aggressive language to describe the motivations of her adversary in order to attack his business practices, similar to Mr. Popper in his letter to the editor (ISSUE 3).

61 This language provides the general definition of defamation, which is important to include in your analysis, but make sure to take note of the qualifications that follow (ISSUE 3).

62 The distinction between statements of fact and those that a reasonable person would not interpret as a statement of fact will be important in arguing that Mr. Popper's letter was not defamatory (ISSUE 3).

63 This qualified privilege is an important argument to make in defending Mr. Popper's letter. Apply this three-part test to his statements in your analysis (ISSUE 3).

64 Note that Mr. Popper's interest is in reducing noise in his neighborhood, and argue that his statements were in support of that interest (ISSUE 3).

65 Make sure you are applying the Supreme Court's reasoning, and not the trial court's reasoning that is summarized in the case.

66 Apply this rule of law to Mr. Popper's potentially defamatory statements (ISSUE 3).

basis to support her "belief in the truth of the statements," but rather, all that is required is some evidence that the defendant did in fact hold that belief.[67] Separately, we find that the statements were not defamatory to begin with, because the plaintiff failed to show that the defendant intended them to be received as fact. Although the defendant did not explicitly state that her statements regarding Artest were merely her opinion, the tone of the piece, the nature of the comments (including the fact she never explicitly indicated her comments were meant to be taken as fact), and Liu's role as a critic all suggest the statements were intended as opinions, and the plaintiff has not shown otherwise.[68] Therefore, the statements are not actionable as defamation.

REVERSED.

67 This is a helpful rule of law for Mr. Popper, as he did not necessarily have a factual basis to support all of his statements (ISSUE 3).

68 The position that certain statements made by Mr. Popper should reasonably be interpreted as opinion is another key point to include in your analysis, and you should apply the court's reasoning here to his statements (ISSUE 3).

Ingalls v. Photomoto, Inc.[69]
Jefferson Supreme Court[70] (2004)

This case centers on an ongoing dispute between residents of the town of Hawthorne and Photomoto, Inc., a photo processing plant. Here, Charles Ingalls, a homeowner in Hawthorne, filed suit against Photomoto, claiming that the company's activities constitute a public nuisance because they have caused dangerous chemicals to pollute the water that services his home. Photomoto prevailed on summary judgment at trial, and Ingalls appeals here.

A public nuisance is an unreasonable interference with a right common to the general public. In determining whether activity constitutes a public nuisance, we look to: 1) whether the conduct involves a significant interference with the public health, safety, peace, comfort, or convenience; 2) whether the conduct is proscribed by a statute, ordinance or administrative regulation; and 3) whether the conduct is of a continuing nature or has produced a permanent or long-lasting effect, and, as the actor knows or has reason to know, has a significant effect upon the public right.[71]

While the trial court found that the plaintiff had presented evidence suggesting that Photomoto's chemical disposal constituted a public nuisance, it determined that he was not a proper plaintiff. To maintain a proceeding to enjoin or abate a public nuisance, a plaintiff must: 1) have the right to recover damages; 2) have authority as a public official or public agency to represent the state or a political subdivision in the matter; or 3) have standing to sue as a representative of the general public, as a citizen in a citizen's action, or as a member of a class in a class action.[72]

Ingalls conceded that he was neither a public official nor a representative of the general public, but argued that he was a proper plaintiff because he had a right to recover damages. To recover damages in an individual action for public nuisance, a plaintiff must have suffered harm of a kind different from that suffered by other members of the public. Here, however, Ingalls is only one of hundreds of Hawthorne residents who claim that their drinking water has been polluted as a result of Photomoto's activities, and he has not asserted that he has suffered any other kind of harm.[73] While Ingalls may have other tort remedies available to him, due to his non-unique injuries here, he may not assert an individual action for public nuisance.

REVERSED

69 This document will be referred to as "J."

70 Note that this case is binding authority because the case is in Jefferson Supreme Court (the highest court in the state).

71 This language provides the three factors that a court will look into when analyzing whether activity constitutes a public nuisance. You should analyze XtremeTrain's activities based on these factors (ISSUE 1).

72 This language provides the test to determine who can bring a public nuisance claim. Apply these factors to Mr. Popper (ISSUE 1).

73 Note that Mr. Popper has in fact suffered a different kind of harm from his neighbors. Thus, he could bring a suit for public nuisance (ISSUE 1).

In re Timothy Popper—Sample Answer

TO:[74] Doug Bourne[75]
FROM: New Associate
RE: In re Timothy Popper (nuisance/defamation)[76]

STATEMENT OF FACTS

We represent Timothy Popper[77] ("Mr. Popper"), who runs an animal shelter out of his home just off of Hope Beach. A gym called XtremeTrain, owned and operated by Harry Sands (Mr. Sands), opened next door six months ago, and consistently emanates loud noise, including music, shouting through bullhorns, and yelling, from both its facility and the public beach. The noise has caused significant annoyance to Mr. Popper and his neighbors and has hurt Mr. Popper's business. He wrote a letter to the editor of the local newspaper concerning Mr. Sands, and Mr. Sands has threatened him with a defamation suit.

This memorandum will address the following issues:

I. Whether Mr. Popper can successfully assert a claim that XtremeTrain's activities constitute a public nuisance.

II. Whether Mr. Popper can successfully assert a claim that XtremeTrain's activities constitute a private nuisance.

III. Whether Mr. Popper is liable for defamation based on his letter to the editor.

ANALYSIS

I. **Can Mr. Popper successfully assert a claim that XtremeTrain's activities constitute a public nuisance?**[78]

You have asked me to determine whether Mr. Popper can successfully assert a claim that XtremeTrain's activities constitute a public nuisance.

The Jefferson Supreme Court has held that in determining whether activity constitutes a public nuisance, it would look to: (1) whether the conduct involves a significant interference with the public health, safety, peace, comfort, or convenience; (2) whether the conduct is proscribed by a statute, ordinance or administrative regulation; and (3) whether the conduct is of a continuing nature or has produced a permanent or long-lasting effect, and, as the actor knows or has reason to know, has a significant effect upon the public right.[79] *Ingalls v. Photomoto, Inc.*

An analysis of the above factors does weigh in favor of finding that XtremeTrain's activities, at least to the extent the activities include loud noise which interferes with activities at nearby residences, would constitute a public nuisance. According to the petition put together by Mr. Popper, and alluded to by him in his interview, at least 11 nearby residents have had their sleep and

74 See A, Comment 6.

75 See A, Comment 3.

76 See A, Comment 4.

77 See A, Comment 5.

78 See A, Comment 7.

79 See J, Comment 71.

enjoyment of their homes interrupted by the noise from the gym and its activities, which could be considered a significant interference with public peace and comfort.[80] That said, although both the petition and Mr. Popper complain of having to see various gym members on the beach engaged in various activities, this does not appear to rise to the level of a significant interference with public health, safety, peace, comfort, or convenience. XtremeTrain's activities also appear to be in violation of at least two local statutes. Section 31.12 of Title IX of the City of Hope Beach Revised Code prohibits the use of any amplified sound audible on the property of an adjacent or nearby private residence outside of the hours of 9 AM to 7 PM unless allowed by a temporary permit.[81] Mr. Popper did not specifically indicate that loud music was being played from Mr. Sands' building prior to 9 AM, but he did state that the gym's activities, beginning at 6 AM and lasting throughout the day, included loud music which can be heard on his property and other nearby properties,[82] as evidenced by the signed petition. Section 31.15 of Title IX of the City of Hope Beach Revised Code prohibits any amplified sound on the beach audible from a distance of 30 feet.[83] According to Mr. Popper, Mr. Sands uses a bullhorn, which qualifies as amplified sound, on the beach and is audible within his home,[84] thus Mr. Sands is in violation of this statute. As for the third factor of whether the conduct is of a continuing nature or has produced a permanent or long-lasting effect, and, as the actor knows or has reason to know, has a significant effect upon the public right, Mr. Popper has indicated that this activity has been occurring on a daily basis for a significant amount of time, and Mr. Sands has been made aware of it through repeated requests,[85] the petition,[86] and the letter to the editor,[87] which caused Mr. Sands to send a cease and desist letter.[88]

While the above analysis indicates that XtremeTrain's activities do appear to constitute a public nuisance, Mr. Popper must also demonstrate that he has the ability to individually maintain a public nuisance suit. In Ingalls, the court held that, in order to maintain a proceeding to enjoin or abate a public nuisance, a plaintiff must: (1) have the right to recover damages; (2) have authority as a public official or public agency to represent the state or a political subdivision in the matter; or (3) have standing to sue as a representative of the general public, as a citizen in a citizen's action, or as a member of a class in a class action.[89] In order to recover damages, a plaintiff must have suffered harm of a kind different from that suffered by other members of the public.[90] *Ingalls.*

Because Mr. Popper is neither a public official nor a representative of the general public, the question becomes whether he has the right to recover damages, or, in other words, whether he has suffered harm of a kind different from that suffered by other members of the public. The petition indicates that the other members of the public have suffered the harm of having their peace and comfort in their homes disturbed.[91] Mr. Popper has suffered the additional harm, however, of having his pet adoption business negatively affected, through decreased donations, decreased adoptions, and increased costs of care for the animals, all of which add up to $15,000.[92] Mr. Popper has indicated that no other resident affected by the noise operates a business out of his or her home,[93] thus Mr. Popper has suffered a harm of a kind different from that suffered by other members by other members of the public.

Therefore, it appears likely that Mr. Popper may successfully assert a claim that XtremeTrain's activities constitute a public nuisance.

80 See C, Comment 25.

81 See F, Comments 42–44.

82 See B, Comments 13–15.

83 See G, Comment 47.

84 See B, Comment 14.

85 See B, Comments 17 and 20.

86 See C, Comment 23.

87 See D, Comment 28.

88 See E, Comment 38.

89 See J, Comment 72.

90 See J, Comment 73.

91 See C, Comment 24.

92 See B, Comment 16.

93 See B, Comment 19.

II. **Can Mr. Popper successfully assert a claim that XtremeTrain's activities constitute a private nuisance?** 94

You have asked me to determine whether Mr. Popper can successfully assert a claim that XtremeTrain's activities constitute a private nuisance.

The Jefferson Supreme Court has held that, in order for a plaintiff to prevail on a claim for private nuisance, he must show that the defendant is engaging in an activity that substantially and unreasonably interferes with the plaintiff's use and enjoyment of his land, 95 which is demonstrated by showing that the gravity of the plaintiff's harm outweighs the utility of the defendant's conduct. 96 The court will balance several factors in evaluating the utility of the defendant's conduct, such as: compliance with applicable zoning ordinances; priority of occupation; the frequency and extent of the interference, applied objectively to normal persons; and the utility and social value of the defendant's activity. 97 The court also held that a plaintiff cannot, by devoting his land to an unusually sensitive use, complain of a nuisance based on conduct that would otherwise be relatively harmless, 98 and indicated that it was more likely to find an unusually sensitive use when the use did not contribute in a fundamental manner to the local or regional society. 99 *Najera v. Green Clean, LLC.*

Here, there are good arguments in favor of Mr. Popper's claim that XtremeTrain's activities, to the extent they involve loud noise and music, constitute a private nuisance. As stated above, XtremeTrain's use of loud music and amplified noise appears to place it in violation of Sections 31.12 and 31.15 of Title IX of the City of Hope Beach Revised Code. 100 101 With regard to priority of occupation, Mr. Popper had been running the animal shelter on his property for ten years prior to Mr. Sands opening his business next door six months ago. 102 The frequency and extent of the interference is quite high as Mr. Popper (and his neighbors by way of the petition) 103 indicates that the noise and music occur on a daily basis throughout the day. 104 As for the social utility of XtremeTrain's conduct, there is certainly social utility in promoting physical fitness, but Mr. Popper is specifically taking offense to the noise and music emitted at very high volumes in connection with the physical activity, which a court is likely to find unnecessary and of low social value in and of itself. 105 Furthermore, Mr. Popper indicated that Mr. Sands intentionally leaves the doors open at his facility, thus the sound could be reduced by closing the doors and without losing the benefit of the physical activity. 106 Finally, while Mr. Sands may argue that running an animal shelter for animals with health issues is an unusually sensitive use of the property, per the court's ruling in Najera, Mr. Popper can claim that his activities are not unusually sensitive because taking care of and finding homes for unwanted pets does contribute in a fundamental manner to the local society. 107

Therefore, it appears likely that Mr. Popper may successfully assert a claim for private nuisance against XtremeTrain.

III. **Is Mr. Popper liable for defamation based on his letter to the editor?** 108

You have asked me to determine whether Mr. Popper will be liable for defamation based on his letter to the editor.

A message is considered defamatory if it lowers a plaintiff in the esteem of the community or discourages third persons from associating with him, and is published to at least one other per-

94 See A, Comment 8.

95 See H, Comment 52.

96 See H, Comment 53.

97 See H, Comment 54.

98 See H, Comment 55.

99 See H, Comment 56.

100 See F, Comment 43.

101 See G, Comment 53.

102 See B, Comments 11–12.

103 See C, Comment 25.

104 See B, Comments 13–15.

105 See H, Comment 53.

106 See B, Comment 15.

107 See H, Comment 56.

108 See A, Comment 9.

son who understood the message, and that message caused a substantial minority of reasonable third parties to avoid contact with the plaintiff or stop doing business with him.[109] *Liu v. Artest.* Truth is a defense to defamation. Id. Generally, only statements of facts are considered actionable as defamatory, although expressions of opinion that imply that the speaker knows certain facts to be true, or imply such facts exist, and which a reasonable person would interpret as one of fact, may be found to be defamatory.[110] *Id.* A defendant does not have to have specifically indicated within the message itself that statements were meant as opinions, as opposed to facts, and a court may look to tonal aspects of the message to determine whether the statements were intended as an opinion.[111] Additionally, a defendant has a qualified privilege to make statements in his own legitimate interest or in the public interest. To successfully assert this qualified privilege, a defendant must show three factors: (1) that his statements were motivated by a legitimate self-interest or public interest, and not out of malice; (2) the statements at issue did not exceed the scope of that interest, meaning that they were "reasonably related to asserting that interest;" and (3) he believed the truth of those statements.[112] *Id.*

Mr. Popper's letter to the editor of the local newspaper concerning Mr. Sands certainly includes numerous statements that appear to be intended to lower Mr. Sands' esteem in the community as well as that of his XtremeTrain business. The letter characterizes Mr. Sands as a profiteer and an inconsiderate oaf motivated by "psychic deficiencies" who exploits the shortcomings and preoccupations of his clients (who themselves are referred to as "lonely narcissists" with "zero meaning in their lives")[113] at the expense of the peace and tranquility of the town, and who is unsympathetic to the complaints of citizens like Mr. Popper. It is not clear from the facts presented here whether Mr. Popper's statements, which were published in the town newspaper, had the effect of convincing a minority of reasonable third parties to avoid contact or stop doing business with Mr. Sands or XtremeTrain, but such a result seems to have been part of Mr. Popper's intention in writing the letter.[114]

With regard to whether the statements in the letter are true, Mr. Popper indicated that everything in the letter reflected "how he felt,"[115] and he confirmed elsewhere in the interview that Mr. Sands and his XtremeTrain business have indeed caused noise and been unresponsive to his complaints. The statements regarding Mr. Sands' motivations and his and his clients' mental shortcomings require a more complex analysis, however, as it does not necessarily appear that Mr. Popper had a factual basis for asserting them. However, based on Liu, we can make two arguments: (1) the statements were intended as opinions and not statements of fact, and, furthermore, (2) Mr. Popper had a qualified privilege to make the statements as they were reasonably related to his private and public interest in curtailing Mr. Sands' and XtremeTrain's activities.[116] With regard to the argument that certain statements were intended to be read as opinion, Mr. Popper does soften his more pointed statements about Mr. Sands and the members with language such as "as far as I can tell" and "I guess."[117] Furthermore, he does not suggest that he, as a neighbor, observing these men and women from afar, actually has any factual insight into their psychological motivations,[118] i.e. whether, "Daddy didn't love them enough." Also, there is a humorous, if perhaps overly biting, tone throughout Mr. Popper's letter which suggests that every word and phrase is not meant to be read as a literal statement of fact. Based on the rea-

109 See I, Comment 61.

110 See I, Comment 62.

111 See I, Comment 67.

112 See I, Comment 63.

113 See D, Comment 31.

114 See D, Comment 31.

115 See B, Comment 21.

116 See I, Comments 63–64.

117 See D, Comments 30 and 32.

118 See I, Comment 68.

soning and language in *Liu*, we can make a strong argument that Mr. Popper's more aggressive statements are not meant to be taken as defamatory statements of facts.[119]

As for the second argument that Mr. Popper had a qualified privilege to make the statements as they were reasonably related to his private and public interest in curtailing Mr. Sands' and XtremeTrain's activities, we know that Mr. Popper's statements in the letter were motivated by an interest in reducing the excess noise heard on his property and throughout his neighborhood.[120] This is both a legitimate private and public interest. Although his more vitriolic statements regarding Mr. Sands and his members may not have been necessary in asserting those interests, the statements were all reasonably related to asserting that interest, and are analogous to the statements at issue in *Liu* where a magazine critic "ascribed exploitative and alarming psychosexual personality traits and motivations" to a fashion designer plaintiff in the context of criticizing the popularity and marketing of his designs.[121] *Liu*. Furthermore, Mr. Popper has said that the entire letter reflected how he felt,[122] so we may argue that he believed the statements to be true, even if he did not have factual support for the statements. As held in *Liu*, "there is no requirement that a defendant have factual basis to support her 'belief in the truth of the statements,' but rather all that is required is some evidence that the defendant did in fact hold that belief."[123] In order to make both the opinion and the qualified privilege arguments, we would be in a sense arguing that, with regard to certain statements, Mr. Popper both intended certain statements to be taken as opinion and also that he believed those statements to be true, but there is nothing in the case law indicating Mr. Popper cannot make both arguments.

Therefore, because we can make a strong argument that the evidence indicates that any potentially defamatory statements made by Mr. Popper were intended to be taken as opinion and that, furthermore, Mr. Popper had a qualified privilege to make the statements in service of his legitimate private and public interests, Mr. Popper will likely not be liable for defamation.

CONCLUSION

Based on the above reasoning, it appears that Mr. Popper can successfully assert actions for both public nuisance and private nuisance, and he is not likely to be held liable for defamation.

119 See I, Comments 67–68.

120 See D, Comment 29.

121 See I, Comment 66.

122 See B, Comment 21.

123 See I, Comment 67.

In re Wendy Braun

INSTRUCTIONS

1. You will have 60 minutes to complete this session of the examination. This performance test is designed to evaluate your ability to handle a number of legal authorities in the context of a factual problem involving a client.

2. The problem is set in the fictitious state of Lincoln, in the fictitious Sixteenth Circuit of the United States. In Lincoln, the trial court of general jurisdiction is the District Court, the intermediate appellate court is the Court of Appeals, and the highest court is the Supreme Court.

3. You will have two kinds of materials with which to work: a File and a Library. The first document in the File is a memorandum containing the instructions for the task you are to complete. The other documents in the File contain factual information about your case. The documents may contain information that is not relevant.

4. The Library contains the legal authorities needed to complete the task. Any cases may be real, modified, or written solely for the purpose of this examination. If the cases appear familiar to you, do not assume that they are precisely the same as you have read before. Read them thoroughly, as if they all were new to you. You should assume that the cases were decided in the jurisdictions and on the dates shown. In citing cases from the Library, you may use abbreviations and omit page references. The cases may contain information that is not relevant.

5. Your response must be written in the answer book provided. In answering this performance test, you should concentrate on the materials provided. What you have learned in law school and elsewhere provides the general background for analyzing the problem; the File and Library provide the specific materials with which you must work.

6. Although there are no restrictions on how you apportion your time, you should be sure to allocate ample time (about 30 minutes) to reading and digesting the materials and to organizing your answer before you begin writing it. You may make notes anywhere in the test materials. You may not tear pages from the question booklet.

7. This performance test will be graded on your responsiveness to the instructions regarding the task you are to complete, which is given to you in the first memorandum in the File, and on the content, thoroughness, and organization of your response.

IN RE WENDY BRAUN

FILE

LIBRARY

FILE

In re Wendy Braun

Richards & Sweeney, LLP
Attorneys at Law
716 S. Apple Street
Garden City, Lincoln 97842

April 26, 2013

MEMORANDUM

TO: New Associate
FROM: Barry Richards
RE: In re Wendy Braun

We represent Ms. Wendy Braun, an attorney, in a dispute with Mr. Donald Atkins, a former client of hers. Recently, Mr. Atkins' lawyer sent her a letter threatening to seek an injunction to stop the filming of a television movie based on Ms. Braun's representation of Mr. Atkins in connection with his alleged leaking of internal documents belonging to Lydian Resource Exploration, Inc. ("LRE"), the company that previously employed Mr. Atkins and eventually sued him. Ms. Braun secured Mr. Atkins' life story rights as part of his fee agreement with her, and sold the film rights of the story of her representation of Mr. Atkins to Galaxy Pictures, a production company. Galaxy Pictures is set to begin production next week on the movie, and Mr. Atkins' threatened injunction could endanger the production.

Please draft a memorandum analyzing whether the requirements of Rules 502 and 503 of the Lincoln Rules of Professional Conduct have been met with regard to Ms. Braun's arrangement with Mr. Atkins. Be sure to consider the following:

(i) Is the Life Story Rights Acquisition Agreement between Ms. Braun and Mr. Atkins enforceable?
(ii) Did Ms. Braun violate her duty of confidentiality to Mr. Atkins by providing information to Galaxy Films?
(iii) If the Life Story Rights Acquisition Agreement is deemed unenforceable, what recommendations do you have regarding how Ms. Braun should proceed with the film production?

In the memorandum, you should incorporate the relevant facts, analyze the applicable legal authority, and explain how the facts and law affect our client's obligations. I expect an answer by the end of the day as I will be meeting with the client again in a few days.

Thanks,

Barry
SEE ENCLOSURES

Transcript of Barry Richards's Conversation with Wendy Braun

April 25, 2013

RICHARDS: Good morning, Ms. Braun. I understand you have an issue with a former client of yours?

BRAUN: Yes, I have a letter from a lawyer representing my former client Donald Atkins, threatening to pursue an injunction to stop production on a television movie based on my representation of Mr. Atkins. Here is the letter.

RICHARDS: Please tell me what this is all about.

BRAUN: Sure. I have a practice in Springfield, and I typically take on cases that I find interesting or where I find the client especially sympathetic. Two years ago, I heard about Mr. Atkins's story in the news.

RICHARDS: I remember that. Remind me of what happened with him.

BRAUN: Mr. Atkins was an engineer for Lydian Resource Exploration, Inc. or "LRE" for short. LRE is in the business of natural gas exploration, and its business practice was to go to small, economically depressed towns and persuade the residents of the town to sell mineral exploration rights to LRE.

RICHARDS: And what was Mr. Atkins's role in that?

BRAUN: After landowners in a town would sell their mineral exploration rights to LRE, Mr. Atkins was one of the engineers who would go to the towns and explore and mine for natural gas through a process called hydraulic fracturing.

RICHARDS: That's what's referred to as "fracking," right?

BRAUN: Right. Mr. Atkins was part of the LRE team conducting this work for years, and slowly he came to believe that LRE was keeping these various townspeople in the dark about the potential risks of hydraulic fracturing, which can include water and soil contamination and increased risk of seismic activity. He expressed his concern to his superiors at LRE, but he was not happy with their response. So eventually he decided to make internal copies of LRE documents addressing these issues and he leaked them to an Internet watchdog group and that group published the documents. Because of Mr. Atkins's leak, LRE eventually became the subject of numerous media reports and government inquiries, which are ongoing thanks in part to my work during Mr. Atkins's trial.

RICHARDS: And he was fired and later sued by LRE?

BRAUN: Correct. He was already having financial problems when he was fired, which meant he was stripped of his pension, and then he was sued by LRE for leaking the documents. With his limited finances, he had a difficult time finding counsel that was skilled enough to put on a strong defense to the charges and stand up to LRE.

RICHARDS: And what was the arrangement you and Mr. Atkins agreed on?

BRAUN: I knew that this would be a tough case, but that it would be interesting. My typical fee is $475 an hour, and based on the amount of work this type of case would take, I knew Mr. Atkins's legal bills would quickly go over $100,000. So I offered him an alternative arrangement. I offered him a retainer agreement by which I would represent him without an upfront payment, and when the representation was over, he would have the option of paying the full bill or signing a life story rights agreement with me. He was hesitant about this setup at first, but I told him over the phone he could go seek out another lawyer's opinion on it. I'm not sure if he did, but he did sign the agreement.

RICHARDS: And you ended up winning the case, correct?

BRAUN: I sure did. All of LRE's claims against Mr. Atkins were dismissed, and I was able to bring out so many damaging facts about LRE during discovery that were picked up by the press that the company decided not to pursue any further action against Mr. Atkins.

RICHARDS: And, pursuant to your "alternative arrangement," how did Mr. Atkins choose to pay his legal fees?

BRAUN: When it was all said and done, after the numerous depositions, investigations, hiring of expert witnesses, and the trial and so on, Mr. Atkins owed me over $450,000 in legal bills. So he opted to instead sign a life story rights agreement I drew up for him, which gave me the right to sell the literary and film rights to my representation of him, which essentially waived his right to sue for defamation or invasion of privacy and allowed me to use any information about him and his case that I learned in the course of representing him.

RICHARDS: So he paid you nothing?

BRAUN: Correct.

RICHARDS: Did he speak with an independent lawyer about signing the life story rights agreement?

BRAUN: No, my associate told him over the phone he could, but he chose not to. After he signed it, I then negotiated with various producers and studios and reached an agreement with Galaxy Films where I was paid $200,000 for my story and made a producer of the upcoming television movie to be made about my representation of Mr. Atkins. As a producer, I stand to make more money should the television movie be distributed beyond its initial television airing, whether that be through DVDs, repeat airings, airing on networks in other countries, and so on. But none of that is certain, and, frankly with a threatened injunction, the movie might not be made at all.

RICHARDS: You mentioned the movie has not begun production yet. What subject matter does the movie deal with in its current state of development?

BRAUN: It's mostly about me, and how I almost single-handedly took on a huge corporation over two years without upfront pay, and in the end

I brought LRE to its knees. Obviously Mr. Atkins plays some part in it, and some of the story deals with how I counseled him through some very difficult times during the trial. He even considered suicide at one point when his wife left him on the eve of trial, and I talked him out of it. But it's mostly about me, because that is the real story.

RICHARDS: Why do you think Mr. Atkins's lawyer has contacted you now?

BRAUN: I don't think Mr. Atkins ever thought a movie would actually be made about the trial. He is a private individual who likes to keep to himself, so I am sure he feels distressed about the movie being made, but I'll bet he really just wants to make some money off this now that it's actually going to happen. But he already made his money when he got $450,000 worth of legal services – which were successful I might add – in exchange for signing the life story rights agreement with me.

RICHARDS: I understand.

BRAUN: If his lawyers get an injunction, it could derail the whole production so I'd like to get some answers on how to respond to this very soon.

RICHARDS: OK, I will look into this and get back to you as soon as possible.

Hale and Phillips, LLP
Attorneys at Law
2900 Walters Circle
Lincoln City, Lincoln 97555

April 19, 2013

Re: Donald Atkins—LETTER OF DEMAND

Dear Ms. Braun:

We represent Donald Atkins who you previously represented in his litigation with Lydian Resource Exploration, Inc. ("LRE").

We understand that you, in conjunction with Galaxy Films, are producing a television movie based on the intimate and private details of Mr. Atkins' life and his litigation with LRE. We also understand that the movie includes specific details that you learned in the course of your representation of Mr. Atkins. We further understand you have been paid $200,000 by Galaxy Films for disclosing the confidential aspects of your representation of Mr. Atkins, that you stand to make even more money from Mr. Atkins's life story, and that you have failed to provide any compensation to Mr. Atkins.

Mr. Atkins has provided us with a copy of the "Life Story Rights Acquisition Agreement" that you had him sign as a condition of your representation. A copy is enclosed here. This agreement violates the Lincoln Code of Professional Conduct, and furthermore Mr. Atkins did not give informed consent for you to reveal information related to your representation or Mr. Atkins. Thus the agreement is not enforceable.

We demand that you cease and desist your efforts with the production of the film based on Mr. Atkins's life story immediately, or else we will be forced to seek an injunction and damages.

Very truly yours,

Pamela Hale

Pamela Hale, Esq.

Encl.

RETAINER AGREEMENT

The Law Office of Wendy Braun (Braun) is retained on December 29, 2008, by Donald Atkins to represent him with respect to any claims brought against him by Lydian Resource Exploration, Inc. ("LRE").

Atkins will pay a fee calculated on Braun's hourly charges, which is based on Braun's years of professional experience and level of professional attainment. This fee is $475 per hour, and will remain fixed for the entirety of the representation.

Braun may incur expenses during the course of the representation, including filing fees, overtime expenses, travel expenses, deposition expenses and expert witness expenses. Atkins will reimburse Braun for all expenses.

Atkins will not be required to make payment for any services rendered or expenses incurred by Braun until the completion of the representation. At that time, Atkins will present Braun with a comprehensive bill of services rendered and expenses incurred. Atkins will have the option of paying the bill in full, due immediately, or, alternatively, Atkins may satisfy all obligations pursuant to the comprehensive bill by entering into a "Life Story Rights Acquisition Agreement" with Braun. The terms of such an agreement will be negotiated and finalized at that time, and will include terms giving Braun full rights to depict and portray in any literary or visual medium the events of Atkins's life and specifically Braun's representation of Atkins, and Atkins will waive any claims against Braun in any such production, including claims of defamation, invasion of privacy, or violation of attorney-client confidentiality. Should Atkins and Braun be unable to reach a Life Story Rights Acquisition Agreement that is acceptable to both, Atkins will be responsible for the full and immediate payment of the comprehensive legal bill for services rendered and expenses incurred.

Date: December 29, 2008

The Law Office of Wendy Braun

ACCEPTED AND SIGNED

Wendy Braun

Wendy Braun 12/29/2008

Donald Atkins

Donald Atkins 12/29/2008

MEMORANDUM

TO: Wendy Braun
FROM: Mindy Rockwell
DATE: February 8, 2011

RE: Donald Atkins—Phone Conversation

While you were out of the office, Donald Atkins called back to discuss the final legal bill he had received. He was shocked that the bill was over $450,000 and said there was no way he would ever be able to pay that. I tried to explain to him that I was not sure why he was so surprised as the representation took several years and many hundreds of hours of your time, not to mention the expenses involved in taking on LRE. That seemed to make sense to him.

I reminded him of the alternative fee arrangement option of signing a life story rights acquisition agreement. He asked again whether signing a life story rights acquisition agreement meant that he would not have to pay anything, and I told him that was correct. He had some further questions about what such an agreement entailed, and I told him he we could give him a proposed agreement which he could take to an independent attorney to review. He became very upset at this suggestion and replied that he did not have money to go talk to another attorney. I tried answering more of his questions about the agreement, but he became agitated and finally said he would just come into the office and sign the agreement if it means he is not responsible for paying anything on the bill. I reminded him again he should consider speaking to an independent attorney and that you are open to negotiating the agreement, but he responded that he just "wanted to get this all over with." He will be in the office in the morning to sign the agreement.

LIFE STORY RIGHTS ACQUISITION AGREEMENT

This Life Story Rights Acquisition Agreement (the "Agreement") effective as of February 9, 2011 evidences the acquisition by Wendy Braun ("Grantee") of the life story rights of Donald Atkins ("Grantor").

Whereas Grantee seeks to create an original work, through her own efforts or through collaboration with others, in the form of film, television, and/or other media content, and distributed through various media channels, which recounts actual events and material regarding Grantor's employment and legal dealings with Lydian Resource Exploration, Inc. ("LRE"), Grantee's representation of Grantor, and any and all information communicated by Grantor to Grantee or otherwise observed by Grantee (collectively, "Story Material"), and

Whereas Grantor wishes to grant exclusively to Grantee all rights, title, authority and permission to produce and distribute work based on said Story Material,

Grantor hereby irrevocably grants to Grantee full and exclusive rights in the Story Material, in consideration for full satisfaction of any obligations owed by Grantor to Grantee for legal services performed and expenses incurred pursuant to the Retainer Agreement signed by Grantor and Grantee on December 29, 2008 (the "Retainer Agreement"). The Story Material shall include all elements and episodes of Grantor's life as communicated by Grantor to Grantee or otherwise observed by Grantee, and Grantor hereby waives his right to pursue any legal actions against Grantor for the use and/or disclosure of the Story Material or of his likeness, or to claim that Grantee's use of the Story Material violates any legal or ethical duties of confidentiality related to Grantee's legal representation of Grantor. By entering into this Agreement, Grantor confirms his understanding that use and/or disclosure of the Story Material may be to his disadvantage. Grantor further confirms that Grantee may use any other information relating to Grantee's representation of Grantor, including Grantee's mental impressions, conclusions, opinions, and legal theories relating to the representation of Grantor.

Grantee strongly recommends that Grantor consult an independent attorney to review the contents of this Agreement prior to entering into the Agreement. Grantee asserts that the terms of this Agreement are fair and reasonable, but strongly recommends that Grantor consult independent counsel to independently review the terms of this Agreement to independently determine whether the terms are fair and reasonable. Grantee does not represent Grantor in negotiating or executing this Agreement, and thus cannot provide legal advice or guidance regarding this Agreement. Grantee and Grantor agree that Grantee's representation of Grantor, pursuant to the Retainer Agreement or in any other capacity, ceased as of January 31, 2011. By entering into this Agreement, Grantor confirms that he has received informed consent of his rights regarding this Agreement and that Grantee does not represent him.

Date: February 9, 2011

The Law Office of Wendy Braun

ACCEPTED AND SIGNED

Wendy Braun

Wendy Braun 2/09/2011

Donald Atkins

Donald Atkins 2/09/2011

FILE

In re Wendy Braun

Lincoln Rules of Professional Conduct

RULE 502

(a) A lawyer shall not enter into a business transaction with a client or knowingly acquire an ownership, possessory, security or other pecuniary interest adverse to a client unless:

(1) the transaction and terms on which the lawyer acquires the interest are fair and reasonable to the client and are fully disclosed and transmitted in writing in a manner that can be reasonably understood by the client;

(2) the client is advised in writing of the desirability of seeking and is given a reasonable opportunity to seek the advice of independent legal counsel on the transaction; and

(3) the client gives informed consent, in a writing signed by the client, to the essential terms of the transaction and the lawyer's role in the transaction, including whether the lawyer is representing the client in the transaction.

(b) A lawyer shall not use information relating to representation of a client to the disadvantage of the client unless the client gives informed consent.

(c) Prior to the conclusion of representation of a client, a lawyer shall not make or negotiate an agreement giving the lawyer literary or media rights to a portrayal or account based in substantial part on information relating to the representation.

RULE 503

A lawyer who has formerly represented a client in a matter or whose present or former firm has formerly represented in a client matter shall not thereafter use information relating to the representation to the disadvantage of the former client or reveal information relating to the representation of the former client except where a client has provided informed consent to do so.

Mattingly v. Powers
Lincoln Supreme Court (2006)

This case centers on the application of Rule 502 of the Lincoln Rules of Professional Conduct regarding the propriety of an attorney entering into a business arrangement with a client. Attorney Roger Mattingly of Salinas, LI represented Smoothie Prince, LLP, a small chain of mall-based eateries that had been the subject of several sexual harassment lawsuits. Smoothie Prince eventually became indebted to Mattingly for over $300,000 in legal bills, which it was unable to pay in light of the judgments rendered against it in the various lawsuits. Mattingly offered to accept a 30% ownership stake in Smoothie Prince in order to satisfy the $300,000 plus bill. Smoothie Prince accepted the offer, and Mattingly drew up a contract for the transaction that was then executed. A month later, Mattingly persuaded two other investors to sell their equity stakes in Smoothie Prince to him, giving him a majority stake. Mattingly now intends to effectuate a sale of the company to a large conglomerate, a strategy that the minority stakeholders protest. Those stakeholders now bring this suit, seeking to declare that the initial sale of the 30% stake to Mattingly violated Rule 502 and should thus be voided. The trial court upheld the sale as being in accord with Rule 502, and the minority stakeholders appeal here.

Rule 502 states that a lawyer shall not enter into a business transaction with a client or knowingly acquire an ownership, possessory, security, or other pecuniary interest adverse to a client, unless (1) the transaction and terms on which the lawyer acquires the interest are fair and reasonable to the client and are fully disclosed and transmitted in writing in a manner that can be reasonably understood by the client; (2) the client is advised in writing of the desirability of seeking and is given a reasonable opportunity to seek the advice of independent legal counsel on the transaction; and (3) the client gives informed consent, in a writing signed by the client, to the essential terms of the transaction and the lawyer's role in the transaction, including whether the lawyer is representing the client in the transaction.

The minority stakeholders make two arguments. First, they argue that extinguishing a $300,000 legal bill in exchange for a 30% ownership share was not fair and reasonable, as the Smoothie Prince company had one year earlier, prior to the numerous lawsuits, been valued at $2.2 million through an independent appraisal, and that furthermore it was not reasonable for Mattingly to take advantage of their precarious financial state—a state of which he was intimately familiar through his legal representation – in making his offer. We reject this argument. While this court does not employ a one-size-fits-all rule for what constitutes fair and reasonable business terms for purposes of Rule 502, we will presume that, where there appears to be arms-length dealing among parties, full disclosure of terms, and no evidence of fraud or duress, a deal will be presumed to be fair and reasonable unless specific facts are asserted to the contrary. The fact that the business had been appraised at a higher price a year prior is of no special significance; small businesses, especially those in food services, often change in value rapidly. Furthermore, Mattingly's role as a lawyer, providing him increased insight into the business, does not suggest fraud or duress.

The minority stakeholder's second argument is that they were not properly advised by Mattingly of the desirability of seeking independent counsel, nor of Mattingly's role in the transaction. While they admit that Mattingly did state in writing both of these items and the stakeholders signed the writing, they argue that, because the written statements were included in the agreement itself and not in a separate document, the requirements of Rule 502 have not been met. It is the case that other jurisdictions with similar laws to Rule 502 have required a separate writing, we have held that including these written statements within the agreement laying out the business transaction itself is sufficient for purposes of Rule 502. Thus, we reject the minority stakeholder's second argument and uphold the sale of the 30% stake to Mattingly.

AFFIRMED.

Freeman v. Stevenson
Lincoln Supreme Court (2006)

Attorney Lydia Stevenson here appeals a trial court injunction prohibiting the release of a book she authored entitled *Belly of the Beast*, an account of her representation of Freddy Freeman, who she represented in a murder trial in which Mr. Freeman was acquitted of all charges. Mr. Freeman filed the injunction arguing that Ms. Stevenson's disclosures in the book, irrespective of their veracity, violate Rule 503 of the Lincoln Rules of Professional Conduct.

Ms. Stevenson admits she did not enter into an agreement with Mr. Freeman by which he released her of her duties of confidentiality to him as a former client nor did he provide any other type of informed consent relieving her of such duties. She instead argues that the contents of the book are not within the purview of Rule 503. She claims that the portions of the book relating to her representation of Mr. Freeman do not divulge any confidential facts that she learned in her representation of Mr. Freeman, but instead the book consists of publicly available information regarding Mr. Freeman and his trial as well as her own mental impressions, conclusions, opinions, and legal theories concerning her representation of Mr. Freeman. Ms. Stevenson's argument is essentially that, because she did not "misappropriate" any factual details communicated to her by Mr. Freeman during her representation of him by including such details in her book, then she has not run afoul of Rule 503. We disagree.

Rule 503 states, "A lawyer who has formerly represented a client in a matter or whose present or former firm has formerly represented in a client matter shall not thereafter use information relating to the representation to the disadvantage of the former client or reveal information relating to the representation of the former client except where a client has provided informed consent to do so."

The purpose of Rule 503 is to protect the confidentiality of the attorney-client relationship, and, accordingly, our reading of "information relating to the representation" is far more expansive than Ms. Stevenson's. This "information" is not limited to facts revealed by a client to his or her lawyer in confidence, but rather it means exactly what it says: any information relating to the representation of that client. This certainly includes a lawyer's mental impressions, conclusions, opinions, and legal theories relating to that representation. Furthermore, it also includes information that is otherwise publicly available, so long as it is related to the representation of that client. While it may seem counterintuitive that a lawyer may not disclose publicly available information that any other individual might legally disclose, it is anything but; such is the high standard of confidentiality that is expected when a client enters into a relationship with an attorney. There are, of course, instances when it is appropriate for an attorney to reveal information about a client, namely when, pursuant to Rule 503, the client has provided informed consent to the attorney to do so. No such consent was given here.

AFFIRMED.